W9-AOZ-079

The Politics of Teacher Professional Development

Routledge Research in Education

For a full list of titles in this series, please visit routledge.com

The Politics of Teacher Professional Development

Policy, Research and Practice

Ian Hardy

Routledge
Taylor & Francis Group
NEW YORK   LONDON

First published 2012
by Routledge
711 Third Avenue, New York, NY 10017

Simultaneously published in the UK
by Routledge
2 Park Square, Milton Park, Abingdon, Oxon OX14 4RN

*Routledge is an imprint of the Taylor & Francis Group,
an informa business*

Library of Congress Cataloging-in-Publication Data
Hardy, Ian.
   The politics of teacher professional development : policy, research and
practice / Ian Hardy.
      p. cm. — (Routledge research in education ; 80)
   Includes bibliographical references and index.
   1. Teachers—Training of—Political aspects.   2. Teachers—
Training of—Cross-cultural studies.   3. Education—Social
aspects—Cross-cultural studies.   I. Title.
   LB1707.H365 2012
   371.102—dc23
   2011053391

ISBN13: 978-0-415-89923-9 (hbk)
ISBN13: 978-0-203-11038-6 (ebk)

Typeset in Sabon
by IBT Global.

Printed and bound in the United States of America on sustainably sourced
paper by IBT Global.

To Max and Teresa, my first teachers

Contents

Foreword
On Teachers and Their Learning

We live in strange times. Nowhere is this more plain than in Education, where public money is handed to wealthy private schools, where gender equity is stood on its head, where sensible language teaching is defined as subversion, where universities spend more money on re-branding than on curriculum change. . . .

One of the oddest things on the Education scene is this. We currently have the best educated and most skilled teaching workforce in our schools that the world has ever seen. In the face of this, governments are falling over themselves to impose new controls over teachers, to corral teacher education, to erect new (and expensive) systems to measure the outcomes of teachers' work, and to force teachers' work into narrow channels defined by tests, predetermined curricula and 'best practice' formulae. In short, governments, and the corporate interests they represent, don't trust teachers.

Ian Hardy has a clear understanding of this and rightly sets the current discussion of teachers' professional development in the context of neoliberalism, the market agenda that currently shapes the thinking of all governments in the countries he studies. Neoliberalism has aptly been called not a policy, but a 'meta-policy,' a framework of ideas within which all specific policies are formed. That market choice should be the basis of our collective decisions, on issues from fashion and football to higher education, is no longer debated in our parliaments; it is taken for granted. But it is also assumed that what is market-based is natural, and what is natural is no longer political, no longer a matter for collective deliberation and decision-making.

This book shows that in relation to teachers' professional development, politics really is inherent; it can't be wished away or defined away. Teachers' work—which I think is one of the most complex, difficult and important forms of labor on the planet—is shaped by many institutional pressures and demands, among them those around professional learning. This can be a site of conformity, institutional conservatism, and the reproduction of existing social privileges and hierarchies. But it can be the occasion for creative practice that develops resources for a richer and more open-ended education system.

Building a democratic education system, rather than the privilege-ridden system we have now, will be a long haul. In that process, the self-education of the teaching workforce is important. The capacity to examine and re-shape professional practice has to emerge from inside the profession, if it is to be a profession and not the tool of market-intoxicated governments. The issues that Ian Hardy addresses in this book matter to the future of Education, and getting so much clarity about them is a great contribution.

Raewyn Connell
University Professor
University of Sydney

Preface

During the final stages of preparing the manuscript for this book, I was reading the *Hamlyn Lectures* (2004) delivered at Exeter University and Cardiff Law School, in November 2003, by former Justice of the High Court of Australia, Michael Kirby. This annual lecture series was made possible by the endowment of Emma Warburton Hamlyn of Torquay, England, who died in 1941, and whose father was a solicitor and J. P. By all accounts, Miss Hamlyn was well-travelled, well-read and deeply interested in promoting improved understanding of the common law. The Hamlyn Lectures were her legacy and vehicle for promoting such understanding amongst the people of England and her dominions. Perhaps appropriately, given his long and distinguished commitment to challenging social and civic exclusion, and as a retort to more conservative criticisms at the time, Justice Kirby's Hamlyn lectures were entitled 'Judicial Activism.'

What struck me about Kirby's comments on judicial enactment of the common law was the cogency with which he argued that the law cannot be easily and readily 'applied,' free of interpretation by those entrusted with this responsibility. He contrasted the rigid 'black letter' law approach of, for example, Sir Owen Dixon, Justice of the High Court of Australia from 1929 and Chief Justice from 1952–1961, with the more actively considered, open and honest approach of the likes of the Rt. Hon. Lord Denning, who delivered the first Hamlyn Lecture in 1949, and the much-respected Professor Julius Stone, Kirby's own teacher at the University of Sydney law school. For Kirby, walking in the footsteps of highly accomplished lawyers such as Denning and Stone, problems of the law require a judicial method which openly acknowledges the need to actively interpret the law in light of the conditions in which it is enacted. When exercised in this way, and to its fullest extent, the law becomes a vehicle with the potential to improve the circumstances and conditions of those to whom it is directed, including the most vulnerable members of society. Consequently, the law is less a sacred, incontrovertible text to be applied in a rigid and dogmatic fashion than a product and producer of the social conditions in which it is practised.

What relevance does this have to researching teachers' professional development? I would argue precisely the same principles apply when seeking to make sense of problems of teachers' learning. In the same way that the law is less a stable text than an open act of interpretation, so, too, research into teachers' learning is not so much the revelation of certain 'facts' about teachers' work as the explication of a considered argument in light of the relevant resources at our disposal for making sense of this work under particular social conditions. Research on learning must be actively interpreted in context, and openly acknowledged as such, for it to be of any value for addressing problems of learning.

In this spirit, the approach I have taken in this book is twofold. First, and drawing upon relevant policies, literature and my own empirical research undertaken over a ten-year period, the book seeks to present an overview of the multiple ways in which teacher professional development has been conceptualised, with a particular emphasis upon Anglo-American contexts over the past thirty years. At the same time, the book seeks to present these findings in a way which gives credence to the patently complex, contradictory and contested conditions within which teachers' professional development is researched and enacted. That is, and in a similar way to Kirby's call for a context-responsive, open, honest and productively activist argument in relation to the law, the book seeks to acknowledge the nature and influence of current circumstances and conditions upon research, policy-making and teaching practice, and provides some insights into just how cogently these conditions have played out in practice. The book does not simply provide a descriptive account of teachers' professional development in all its colour and complexity—although it does do this in large measure. Rather, it endeavours to make sense of why and how the conditions in which teachers' learning is enacted and understood influence the ways in which such learning is administered, researched and practised. With the assistance of French sociologist Pierre Bourdieu, I describe what I refer to as the 'field of teacher professional development' as a contemporary and contested space, heavily influenced by competing pressures and demands which, in turn, constitute teacher professional development policy, research and practice.

In this way, I hope the book will serve as a useful resource for educational researchers, policy-makers and practitioners to better understand the nature of their own and one another's work, to realise how each is so necessary to and imbricated in the work of the others, and as a stimulus to challenge those conditions which inhibit more democratic, student-centred learning. The book seeks to encourage open, honest and inclusive discussion, debate and action amongst educators; in short, a robust and genuinely productive 'educational activism.'

Ian Hardy
University of Queensland
Brisbane
January 2012

Acknowledgments

This book would not have been possible without the willingness of the Australian, Canadian and English teachers, principals, state and provincial administrators, policy-makers, academics and other personnel who gave willingly of their time and experiences during the course of various research projects upon which it draws. To these educators, I am very grateful.

The book is a synthesis of research undertaken over a decade, between 2001 and 2011. I would like to acknowledge colleagues from Charles Sturt University and the University of Queensland with whom I have been fortunate to work during this period, and whose intellect and insights have assisted in its gestation, and the development of its principal arguments. Thank you to Bob Lingard and Jane Mitchell for their support throughout this time. I would like to acknowledge the work and encouragement of Stephen Kemmis and the Pedagogy, Education and Praxis international consortium, including Karin Rönnerman, University of Gothenburg, and Wilfred Carr, University of Sheffield, for their engagement with many of the issues concerning teachers' learning over several decades, and for their hospitality and generosity of spirit over the time we have had the opportunity to work together. Institutionally, I would like to thank Allan Luke for facilitating a culture and climate in which academic excellence and rigor are the norm at the University of Queensland, and Bob Meyenn for creating the space early in my working career at Charles Sturt University to help realise initial academic ambitions. Thank you also to Peter Renshaw, current head of the School of Education, University of Queensland, for further fostering necessary institutional support. Richard Niesche provided very useful insights on a full version of the manuscript. Space precludes acknowledgment of the many colleagues deserving of individual and collective recognition.

Finally, for the support of family and friends whose unwavering encouragement over many years have been crucial to producing this book, and the ideas it seeks to convey, I am very appreciative.

1 Introduction
Professional Development in Context, and as Contest

> We do not say that a man [sic] who shows no interest in politics is
> a man who minds his own business; we say that he has no business
> here at all.
>
> (Pericles' funeral oration, in Thucydides,
The Peloponnesian War, p. 147)

INTRODUCTION

Teacher professional development ('PD') is increasingly seen as vital for
renewing and reforming national education systems in a global context
of pressure for improved educational outcomes. National governments
throughout the world promote professional development as a way of fostering quality teaching, student learning and enhanced learning outcomes.
However, despite more directed attention to and interest in professional
development, the influence of the broader conditions in which decisions
about professional development are made remains insufficiently recognised
and understood. For this reason, teacher professional development needs to
be thought anew.

PD is not simply a program of activities, lectures or workshops undertaken by teachers at the beginning of a new school semester, or at other
specific times during the school year. PD is not just an abstract, individualistic undertaking—something which happens inside teachers' heads—in
response to a variety of departmental, bureaucratic, school or teacher-instigated initiatives. Rather, PD is a multi-faceted, reflexive social practice
involving the active decision-making by individuals and groups under the
specific social settings in which they live and work. This book argues that
teacher professional development (PD) (sometimes described as 'continuing
professional development' (CPD)) is a situated, socio-political practice. As
a result, teacher professional development practices, and support for such
practices, are inherently political.

The book conceptualises teacher professional development in new
ways—theoretically, empirically and practically. It applies Pierre Bourdieu's
theory of the social world as comprising identifiable 'social fields,' comprising contestation between the practices considered of most value, to reveal
how teacher professional development exists not as a single, decontextualised entity, but as the product of competing policy, research and work

practices. Specifically, the book provides fresh insights into how broader neoliberal and managerial pressures exist in tension with more profession-oriented and democratic impulses, and how these competing influences help constitute PD as policy, as a research product and process (both in schools and beyond), and as part of teachers' work. The book draws upon existing literature in each of these domains, and empirical research from international cases of professional development undertaken in England, Canada and Australia, to theorise how these tensions play out in practice. This international case data reveals the complexity and specificity of professional development practices, *in practice*, and also how broad competing pressures have influenced the PD considered of most value.

Importantly, this book reveals not only how these neoliberal and managerial influences have exerted influence, but also how they have been challenged by educators seeking to sustain a focus upon more educational practices, even as they experience significant pressure to conform to such demands. Policy-makers, researchers and practitioners have not simply sat idly by and passively accepted the changes which have characterised their work. Rather, they have sought to challenge and critique narrowly focused conceptions of their work, striving to enact and facilitate alternative practices under sometimes trying conditions. Consequently, while this volume provides insights into how educators have been treated as instruments of economic and bureaucratic fiat, it also reveals how they have simultaneously sought to foreground the intrinsically educational qualities of their work, and the needs of the students whom they serve. While the conditions under which educators work influence the relations between individuals and groups and the broader circumstances in which they act, these conditions are also a product of the actions and influences of these same individuals and groups. These conditions are amenable to change, alteration and improvement. It is the relationship between individual/groups of educators, and their conditions, which is responsible for the teacher learning which arises.

Consequently, PD is not conceptualised as something simply 'done' to teachers—such as a series of one-off days at the start of a school term—which seek to 'produce' teachers who will enact and manage particular state-sanctioned initiatives and programs. PD is not a unified, formulaic process which is applied in all instances and designed to ensure homogeneity of practice. Nor is it understood as an individual or group activity, or activities, which are somehow practised beyond the contexts and conditions within which they are undertaken; teachers are not simply the architects of their own learning, even when it may seem as if they are learning 'alone,' and to be making active decisions about the nature of the learning in which they will engage. Rather, it is the relationship between educators and the conditions under which they work which serves as the primary unit of analysis.

In exploring the complexity of this relationship, the book firstly reveals teacher PD as policy and policy-making, as a research process and product, and as an important part of teachers' work. It then draws upon empirical research undertaken in England, Canada and Australia to reveal how these conceptions of PD play out within and across different national contexts in relation to specific PD practices. Awareness of professional development as a multi-faceted and complex social practice is a necessary precursor to cultivating the conditions and dispositions likely to lead to improved teacher learning for student learning. In this way, this book is a positive intervention in the work of promoting productive teacher learning.

In brief, this book argues that:

- PD is a social and political practice. PD is intimately influenced by the circumstances under which PD is undertaken, and the individuals and groups engaged in, supporting and creating PD. The relationship between these conditions and individuals/groups is responsible for the PD which arises.
- PD can be understood as policy, as research, and as a part of teachers' work.
- PD practices reflect competing socio-political tensions within and between PD as policy, as research and as part of teachers' work, and the individuals and groups who participate in policy, research and practice.

UNDERSTANDING CURRENT CONDITIONS: PD AS COMPLEX AND CONTESTED

This book is written on the assumption that teachers are learners, and that teachers can learn. The book challenges those conceptions of teachers as already pre-formed, 'constructed'—as born, not made—as a finished canvas, rather than works in progress. In this regard, it seems counterintuitive to the ways in which teachers' work and learning are often, perhaps typically, framed. At the same time, this learning does not occur in isolation from the multi-faceted conditions under which it occurs, and which seek to influence teachers' learning. The conditions under which teacher learning occurs, and the conditions which seek to influence teachers' learning, matter. However, teachers, and those who support and endorse teacher PD, are able to influence these conditions. They are able to exert influence upon the teaching and learning practices in which they engage; they are not simply 'fleas in a cage' (Connell, Ashenden, Kessler and Dowsett, 1982, p. 78) powerless to make decisions about their own or others' actions, or the settings in which they work and learn.

While possibilities and options for change are always open to teachers and school-based administrators, they are not open-ended, but are instead influenced by the broad circumstances under which educators work and learn. These circumstances do influence teachers' dispositions, capacities and proclivities to learn, and the ways in which such learning is manifest. In very broad terms, the circumstances in which teachers engage with professional development may inspire teachers to engage fully with their learning needs, or may actively inhibit or quash the desire to learn, or, perhaps more likely, encourage an approach to learning somewhere along a spectrum between these poles. These conditions may stimulate creative, imaginative educational experiences or act as an enervating influence—leading to apathetic approaches to teachers' learning. They may encourage teachers to engage passively with information delivered to them by an external 'expert' at the start of a school term, or to construe PD activities as something to be endured. These conditions may lead to involvement in a series of related short-term courses and workshops within or away from school sites, foster ongoing classroom and school-based enquiries, promote participation in institutionalised modes of study—such as Masters-level work through a university or professional association—or involvement in a plethora of other self-directed modes of learning. PD is construed as multi-faceted, and intricately connected to the specific and broader social settings and circumstances in which it is undertaken—circumstances which are not uniform, and always subject to change. From a normative position, this book argues that everything possible should be done to ensure that these conditions are conducive to improved teacher learning for student learning oriented to a more socially, politically, economically and environmentally sustainable world, and that there are opportunities for wider participation of educators in decision-making about PD, and that barriers to engaged, ongoing, student-centred teacher learning are dismantled. To fail to do so is to condemn teachers and students to circumstances which militate against their active engagement in making the most of life opportunities, and contributing as productive social, political and economic citizens.

This book construes the current contexts and conditions within which PD is enacted as multi-faceted, and productive of competing demands. Understanding the relationship between educators and the conditions in which professional development is undertaken means acknowledging the multiple and competing standpoints of those who seek to influence professional development practices in schooling settings. That is, there is a need to recognise and appreciate the tensions which invariably characterise teachers' learning. The positions these individuals occupy, and the dispositions they display, influence how individuals and groups of teachers respond to their learning needs. Providing insights into the competing approaches which characterise professional development practices—including those most likely to lead to beneficial change, and those which seem to be detrimental to such change—is an important goal of this volume.

In recent times, these conditions have been influenced by broad sets of processes which encourage a focus upon the individual within society, the economy, and the management of resources. While these processes, in and of themselves are not problematic—who could argue against our recognition

as individuals, that a strong economy is important for a stable and functioning society, and that resources should be managed appropriately?—the
way in which they have become reified within society over recent decades,
influencing all aspects of our lives, relationships and work, makes them
worthy of further scrutiny and critique.

Setting the Scene: Neoliberalism, Economism and Globalization

The logic of neoliberalism has had a significant influence upon all sectors
of the public service, including education. Harvey (2005) defines neoliberalism as a theory of political economy which advocates the safeguard-
ing of private property rights, free markets and free trade as the principal
means of addressing the needs of all in society. Sometimes described as
'economic rationalism,' (after Pusey (1991)), neoliberalism is seen as syn-
onymous with free market economics, structural adjustment and supply-
side economic reform. Such approaches frame the economy as paramount,
and government's role as ensuring circumstances for the establishment of
market mechanisms throughout both the public and private sectors. This
necessitates a strong state only insofar as governments are able to support
institutions in the interests of private accumulation. The role of the state
should not include involving itself in markets any more than is absolutely
necessary. However, and paradoxically, the state does have a role in establishing markets in areas which have not previously been subject to market mechanisms. In this way, neoliberalism differs from more laissez-faire
approaches in that it actively involves the state in the creation of the 'free-
doms' associated with free enterprise by 'creating' markets (Rose, 1999).
Neoliberal logics frame governments as actively promoting more economically oriented practices and principles.

In terms of traditional public sector service provision, this has resulted
in a redefinition of the role of the state into one of promoting market
mechanisms, leading to reconceptualising the polity in new and unfamiliar
ways. Peters and McDonagh (2007) argue neoliberalism redefines citizens
as consumers, or what Clarke, Newman, Smith, Vidler and Westmarland
(2007) refer to as 'citizen-consumers.' Traditionally provided public services then become just another commodity to be consumed in the market.
In educational contexts, such commodification is exemplified by the way in
which curricula are rearticulated into packages of materials to be applied
by teachers in classrooms. Luke (2004) describes teachers dominated by
such commodification of education and educational resources as 'commodity fetishists.'

This emphasis upon the commodification of everything, including public
services, has been achieved by promoting a general ethos of 'economism,'
beyond the economic field. Economism advantages the economic above
other realms of socio-political endeavour: 'The politics of economism is
a strategy of defining certain institutions as "economic" and using the

doctrine of economic neutrality to produce a boundary between the "economic" and "political" sphere' (Teivainen, 2002, p. 1). Teivainen (2002) argues that economism exerts influence through various mechanisms including the privatisation of formerly public institutions, and the application of practices typically associated with private industry to the public sector. The rise of neoliberalism has meant that economistic emphases are dominant in all areas of public endeavour, including education. So pervasive are these principles that anything which hampers the economising of all areas of human endeavour is construed as problematic (Cobb, 1999; Collier and Esteban, 1998).

In their efforts and struggles to respond to the economic challenges presented by an increasingly neoliberal ethos on a global front, governments have typically responded by adopting neoliberal principles in a wholesale manner; such responses are evidence of the deliberate linking of notions of neoliberalism with globalization (Colas, 2005), even though the latter is manifest in a myriad of cultural and political, as well as economic ways. Pusey (2003) points out how economic globalization and interests have dominated over other interests, resulting in the naturalization of economistic, neoliberal iterations of globalization. That is, more economistic, neoliberal logics of practice become dominant within fields beyond the broader political (and economic) fields in which they are perhaps more obviously evident.

However, this reconstruction of public policy and the polity have not gone unchallenged. Wright (2003) calls into question the ethics surrounding neoliberalism, and its effects. Neoliberalism is not seen as the solution to providing for the needs of the citizenry because some services are simply not practically amenable to provision via markets. Wright (2003) uses examples such as footpaths and lighthouses which serve important public functions which cannot be sufficiently regulated to determine who benefits from them, and how they should pay for this benefit. Pusey (1991; 2003) is particularly critical of what he sees as government policies which do not take into account the needs of all within society. Writing from what he describes as a 'middle-of-the-road social democratic position,' Pusey (2003, p. 12) argues that moderate positions such as his are often construed as irrational oppositions to beneficial public policy. Finally, the effects of neoliberalism as a global orthodoxy are recognised as being far from uniform. In spite of the influence of the movement, in local contexts, there is evidence of resistance, accommodation and active engagement with globalized, neoliberal principles and practices (Appadurai, 2001; Muppidi, 2004; Ozga and Lingard, 2007; Rizvi and Lingard, 2010).

Managerialism

Education, as with all other social arena, has also been influenced by the rise of managerialism. Since the mid-1980s, there has been an increasingly centralised focus upon the provision of public services within the public sectors of western countries. As part of this process, finance ministries have exerted increasing influence, leading to an emphasis upon public service provision as a cost. Private sector practices and principles have been adopted and adapted to the public sector, with a view to minimising 'waste'—thereby seeking to increase efficiency—and more carefully scrutinising the effects of public expenditure—thereby seeking to increase effectiveness. The push for efficiencies resonates with the cost-cutting measures associated with the 'New Public Management' in the UK, and 'economic rationalism' in Australia (Pusey, 1991). Managerialism has resulted in increased scrutiny of the effects of the expenditure of public funds, increased control on the part of managers to achieve greater efficiencies within their departments, and the development of mechanisms to account for this expenditure.

Since the 1990s, and in conjunction with neoliberal principles, there has been a further shift towards a more entrepreneurial model of service provision which has seen the construction of a more marketised approach to the provision of public services. This construes managers as managing various 'providers' of public services competing against one another for the provision of services. In this way, the logics of regulation have given way to market-mechanisms as the means of ensuring improved service provision. Such an approach, with its emphasis upon economic rationalism, contrasts with what Yeatman (1997) refers to as the 'post-bureaucratic' model of public management which she describes as a more consultative and trust-oriented approach.

As these more managerial logics have become increasingly pervasive, there has been an increased push for accountability within the public sector, including amongst educators, resulting in the accumulation of data as evidence of the attainment of various levels of achievement deemed beneficial by the state. This has included a strong focus upon quantitative measures of student attainment, particularly standardised tests (Hursh, 2008; Lingard, 2010; Stobart, 2008). In part, such an approach may be seen as a natural extension of Lyotard's concept of performativity (Lyotard, 1984), with its emphasis upon satisfying the demands of the particular language games which constitute the current high modern/postmodern world:

> The decision makers . . . attempt to manage these clouds of sociality according to input/output matrices, following a logic which implies that their elements are commensurable and that the whole is determinable. They allocate our lives for the growth of power. In matters of social justice and scientific truth alike, the legitimation of that power is based on its optimizing the system's performance—efficiency. The application of this criterion to all of our games necessarily entails a certain level of terror, whether soft or hard: be operational (that is, commensurable) or disappear. (Lyotard, 1984, p. xxiv)

The fear of elimination contributes to this pressure to perform; being responsive to managerial imperatives is necessary for survival, such are their effects.

Impact on PD Policy, Research and Practice

This volume provides insights into how these broader social influences have had effects upon teachers' professional development. Specifically, the book outlines how these influences have affected PD policy, PD research and PD practice. As policy, PD is understood as the product of particular values—what Prunty (1985) describes as the 'authoritative allocation of values' (p. 136)—and therefore as inherently contested. PD policy is also understood as more than text on the page; policy is the enactment of particular processes and practices. After Ball (1994), policy is understood as 'both text and action, words and deeds, it is what is enacted as well as what is intended. Policies are always incomplete insofar as they relate to or map on to the "wild profusion" of local practice' (Ball, 1994, p. 10). This volume adopts this expansive definition of policy to explore PD as policy, revealing how such policies are the product of broader neoliberal and managerial processes, as well as more local responses to these broader conditions.

As research, professional development is considered as both a product and process, and as with PD as policy, there is a lack of agreement about the relationship between teachers and research. On the one hand, teachers have been encouraged to take an active role in their own learning—to be researchers of their own practice. The action research, teacher research and teacher-as-researcher movements have been emblematic in this regard. However, and at the same time, more recent pushes to centralise and regulate educational practices by governments of all persuasions in western settings have resulted in the promulgation of a more passive relationship between teachers and the research process. Rather than being active researchers in their own right—'research productive'—teachers are framed as recipients of research undertaken by others—'research responsive.' Under these circumstances, the professional development research which is valued is limited to more traditional research undertaken in the academy, and often under the auspices of reductionist, 'what works,' 'evidence-based research' (Biesta, 2007).

As with PD as policy and PD as research, professional development as teachers' work, and as practice more generally, is similarly influenced by the conditions in which it is undertaken and contested. In schooling settings, there has been a resurgence of professional development as a process of information dissemination at the start of a school year or term, focused on specified content areas considered significant within school systems or states/provinces/local governments/authorities. However, there is also evidence of a myriad of other initiatives, often on a smaller scale, and involving teachers inquiring into aspects of their own practices, specific subject disciplines, pedagogical and educational practices more generally, either individually or collectively, in-school and beyond. These more active approaches contrast with the more passive information dissemination approaches often associated with teachers' professional development.

It is the contested nature of professional development, as policy, research and teachers' work, within current, broadly conceived neoliberal and managerial conditions, which is the primary focus of attention in this volume. That is, the book foregrounds teacher PD as political, and it is the politics surrounding PD provision which is considered crucial for understanding how and why teacher professional development practices exist as they do.

WHAT THIS BOOK IS NOT . . .

Many books on teacher professional development seek to *prescribe* particular traits, approaches or characteristics, which, if followed, will result in successful teacher learning, and subsequent student learning. The very titles of recent, well-received PD volumes attest to the dominance of the prescriptive approach: *Professional Development: What Works* (Zepeda, 2008); *Professional development for language teachers: Strategies for teacher learning* (Richards and Farrell, 2005); *Schools as professional learning communities: Collaborative activities and strategies for professional development* (Roberts and Pruitt, 2009). While acknowledging the potential value of such books, and the important role they can play in stimulating teachers' learning (and that some are informed by research), instead of adding to the voluminous literature of 'how-to' books, this volume seeks to reveal the complexity of *actual* professional development practices, how they are conceptualised differently in policy, research and as part of teachers' work, and practice more generally—and from this evidence, to gesture towards how they could be practised differently. By drawing extensively upon research into specific cases in different national settings, the book also seeks to provide substantive evidence of how this politics of professional development plays out in practice. To this end, the book seeks to draw upon this empirical research to inject what Connell et al. (1982) described as 'a good dose of awkward facts' (p. 29) into existing literature, drawing upon actual PD practices to inform the typically decontextualised, prescriptive literature on teachers' learning—thereby helping teachers, school-based administrators and affiliated educators to understand why and how their efforts have transpired in sometimes peculiar and unpredictable ways. In this way, the book is focused upon professional development practice *in practice*—that is, how professional development plays out or unfolds in real time, as a product of particular histories, and the specific desires and circumstances of those involved.

To this end, this book also does not pretend to be able to 'get inside' educators' heads. That is, it is not underpinned by *psychologising* tendencies, which pervade dominant conceptions of professional development practice, and western knowledge traditions more generally, and which are often evident in more prescriptive, atheoretical texts. Teacher professional development is not simply construed from an internal, psychological perspective. Such approaches treat teachers as disembodied minds, without due regard for the influence of the circumstances under which teachers' professional development is undertaken. The book also eschews formulaic, technicist approaches to teachers' professional development which frame teacher PD as the enactment of a generic set of procedures which have cogency regardless of context.

Overwhelmingly, these more technicist, psychologistic and prescriptive approaches treat teachers as *individuals*, and teacher professional development as an *individualistic* undertaking. As a result, the intrinsically social nature of such practices is ignored or downplayed. From within these traditions, professional development can be reduced to a disparate array of options, possibilities or encumbrances, depending upon teachers' prior experiences, and individual teacher proclivities. Professional development becomes a narrow set of individualistic approaches, traits or 'recipes for what works,' which do not reflect the nature and diversity of the circumstances within which teachers' learning transpires. Rarely are such practices seen in relation to the broader contexts in which they are enacted, and of which they are an integral part. That is, the conditions for professional development are rarely taken into account as teachers try to understand these activities and their responses to them. Such a response is part of a broader condition within society which tends to emphasise individualism and individuality—what Charles Taylor (1993, p. 49) refers to as the 'reification of the disengaged first-person-singular self,' which, again, has its origins in the enlightenment tradition. This book seeks to foreground the 'invisibility' of the social, arguing that the intrinsically social nature of teachers' professional development has a significant influence upon the PD which transpires, and that PD cannot be understood as either an individualistic activity, or as an activity able to be directed solely by the individual. Instead, the relationship between the practitioner and society is understood in this volume as one of mutual co-construction in which the practitioner and their circumstances are always subject to change, a change which is always mediated by this mutually constitutive relationship. In this way, this book is an alternative, an 'antidote,' to those more *de-contextualised* articulations of professional development which frame PD as the prerogative of individual minds, sometimes involving collaboration with others, but always acting from a position of isolation from the context within which learning is supposedly undertaken.

The book also serves as a challenge to purely *rationalistic* theories of action which construe professional development as the product of 'knowing' agents who understand what is required in any given situation, and simply apply this understanding, resulting in predicted and predictable outcomes. It argues that social practices are already pre-shaped, and therefore influenced by particular ways of doing things, including sanctioned approaches to PD. By foregrounding the messy reality of competing approaches to PD, and the co-relationship between policy, research and work practices, the book critiques those conceptions of professional development which argue for a simple, linear relationship between intentions and outcomes, or which focus on one or other element of the policy-research-practice nexus.

At the same time, the book rejects those conceptions of professional development understood in terms of a simple binary which problematises employer-provided PD and eulogises profession-driven approaches *per se*, or vice versa. Such ascriptions fail to take into account the situated complexity and tensions inherent within different approaches, and the way in which the conditions under which they are enacted can promote or inhibit beneficial professional development content or approaches to teachers' learning. While a normative argument is presented in the concluding chapter which endorses the value of more active engagement on the part of teachers in their own learning, this is built out of the argument presented in the forgoing chapters of considerable evidence of the effects of policy and professional conditions which have contributed to the deprofessionalisation of teachers. Such advocacy must occur at the same time as attention is simultaneously focused upon how the conditions within which teachers' learning occurs influence the PD which transpires in practice, which is endorsed in policy, and which influences how PD is researched and practised.

DEFINING AND DELINEATING PROFESSIONAL DEVELOPMENT

Professional development is a contested concept, and has been conceptualised in varied ways. Drawing upon earlier work by Friedman, Durkin, Phillips and Davis (2000), Friedman and Phillips (2004) draw upon promotional literature from UK professional associations to reveal the complexity of, and competing claims about, professional development:

- Lifelong learning for professionals;
- A means of personal development;
- A means for individual professionals to ensure a measure of control and security in the often precarious modern workplace;
- A means of assuring a wary public that professionals are indeed up-to-date, given the rapid pace of technological advancement;
- A means whereby professional associations can verify that the standards of their professionals are being upheld; and
- A means for employers to garner a competent, adaptable workforce (p. 362).

Bolam and McMahon (2004) reveal how teacher PD, or what they describe as 'continuing professional development' is described by different authors as in-service education and training (INSET), teacher development, continuing education and lifelong learning, staff development, career development, and that these terms are defined differently by different authors. Day and Sachs (2004) construe professional development as: 'all the activities in which teachers engage during the course of a career which are designed to enhance their work' (p. 3). Kelchterman's (2004) understanding of continuing professional development is more explicit about the significance of the conditions/context in which learning occurs; continuing professional development is a: '*learning process* resulting from *meaningful interactions* with the context (both in time and space) and eventually leading to *changes in teachers' professional practice* (actions) and in their *thinking about that practice*' (p. 220; emphasis original). Muijs, Day, Harris and Lindsay's (2004) understanding of continuing professional development involves more than in-service training or on-the-job learning, which are seen as narrowly focused upon specific workplaces, and the much broader term 'lifelong learning,' which is seen as encompassing a variety of learning approaches and settings throughout one's lifetime.

From the perspective of a professional development 'provider,' Zepeda (1999) argues 'staff development' as she refers to PD, is multifaceted, difficult to define, and tends to be determined by the specific purposes at hand:

> Staff development, in-service education, and training are terms that are often used interchangeably in educational arenas. Are these words synonymous with one another? That depends! . . . Staff development is the chameleon of public education; it can adapt itself in shape or size to fit the need it is asked to address. (Zepeda, 1999, p. 1)

Such a perspective also exemplifies the nebulousness and often atheoretical nature of the concept of professional development. More 'pragmatic' understandings of PD tend to hide an underlying psychologistic emphasis, and a relative lack of concern about or for the conditions under which PD is undertaken.

Some authors attempt to draw across both the social and the psychological paradigms in their understandings of PD. Drawing upon authors such as Cobb (1994) and Driver, Asoko, Leach, Mortimer and Scott (1994), Borko (2004) applies what she describes as a 'situative perspective' to teacher professional development, which construes learning as both individual and sociocultural in nature. Both the individual and the social are considered important for understanding teachers' learning:

> For teachers, learning occurs in many different aspects of practice, including their classrooms, their school communities, and professional development courses or workshops. It can occur in a brief hallway conversation with a colleague, or after school when counselling a troubled child. To understand teacher learning, we must study it within these

multiple contexts, taking into account both the individual teacher-learners and the social systems in which they are participants. (Borko, 2004, p. 4)

Similarly, but from a different vantage point, Opfer and Pedder (2011) adopt a complexity theory approach to understand professional development practices, how these practices arise, and how they change teachers' knowledge and classroom practices. Hoban (2002) also draws upon the principles of complexity theory to contrast a 'professional development program' with a 'professional learning system.' The former is described primarily as an individual, one-off workshop experience, while the latter entails greater cognisance of the interrelationships and more 'systemic' nature of PD practices:

> A professional development program, therefore, is usually a one-off workshop or an isolated professional development day based on limited conditions for teacher learning—the presentation of new *content* over a relatively short *time*. In contrast, the design of a professional learning system is long-term and encapsulates multiple conditions for teacher learning that interrelate as a system. (p. 68; emphasis original)

Hoban (2002) argues against the linear, mechanistic approach to learning which typically characterises school, pre-service and in-service teacher education programs. Instead, he advocates a 'systems thinking approach' to education in general, and teachers' learning, in particular. This systems thinking approach is sympathetic to understanding the conditions within which teachers' work and learn, and:

> acknowledges that some cognition does occur 'in the head,' but it does not claim that 'the head' is an exclusive site, as there are other influences that contribute to an individual's learning, and vice versa. The transfer of learning from one context to another, therefore, can occur because some of the learning is carried 'in the head,' although it may not represent all the interactions that have occurred. (Hoban, 2002, p. 59)

From a different epistemological position, Fraser, Kennedy, Reid and McKinney (2007) exemplify those scholars who draw a distinction within the literature between professional development and professional learning. These authors characterise professional development as a broader process of change influencing the profession as a whole, while professional learning is construed as a more specific undertaking focused on the particular learnings of individuals and groups:

> . . . teachers' professional learning can be taken to represent the processes that, whether intuitive or deliberate, individual or social, result in

specific changes in the professional knowledge, skills, attitudes, beliefs or actions of teachers. Teachers' professional development, on the other hand, is taken to refer to the broader changes that may take place over a longer period of time resulting in qualitative shifts in aspects of teachers' professionalism. (p. 157)

Drawing upon an extensive literature review across multiple professions, including teaching, social work and engineering, Webster-Wright (2009, p. 705) endeavours to move beyond such binaries between professional development and professional learning through what she describes as 'continuing professional learning.' She focuses upon the learning which may (or may not) occur within more traditional CPD (continuing professional development), PD (professional development) and CE (continuing education) activities, rather than narrower conceptions of PD which focus on particular, standardised modes of delivery and content. Webster-Wright (2009) advocates PD be reconceptualised to recognise more holistic rather than atomistic approaches to professionals' learning, and a focus on participants' actual learning, rather than generic conceptions of development. More interpretive approaches, such as ethnographic and phenomenological approaches are privileged as means of distilling the nature of this learning.

Like Webster-Wright (2009), this volume also takes an ecumenical approach to the term teacher professional development, but actively chooses to retain the term professional development, and seeks to rearticulate it so that it encompasses a broad conception of teachers' learning, rather than construing it as specific, often state-mandated, workshops, programs or like activities.

There is also an increasing body of literature under the rubric of teacher professional learning communities (and its variants—'professional learning communities;' 'learning communities') which seek to foreground various ongoing, collaborative, typically (although not always) site-specific initiatives which involve teachers working and thinking together to improve elements of their practice (Stoll, Bolam, McMahon, Wallace and Thomas, 2006). Drawing upon Lave and Wenger's (1991) 'communities of practice' learning theory with its focus upon 'legitimate peripheral participation,' Kimble, Hildreth and Bourdon (2008) focus upon creating learning communities for educators through various communities of practice. Stoll and Louis (2007) and McLaughlin and Talbert's (2006) support for professional learning communities are further examples of this focus on professional learning communities. Importantly, McLaughlin and Talbert (2006) do construe PD practices as influenced by the socio-political conditions within which they arise. And some authors are explicit about the power relations inherent within professional learning communities: Hargreaves (2003) reveals collaborative arrangements of teacher networks may be contrived; Grossman Wineburg and Woolworth (2001) show how such communities may be very difficult to establish; Lipman's work (1998) reveals how they may entrench already established racial prejudices; McLaughlin and Talbert (2001) indicate how they may foster dominant beliefs that some students simply can't learn—typically those from marginalised socio-economic backgrounds. However, much of the professional learning communities literature, is also either relatively thinly theorised, or gives inadequate attention to the socio-political. There appear to be few books explicitly focused upon PD as a social practice, and which substantively theorise the power relations attendant upon PD practices in and across policy, research and work contexts.

CAPTURING CONTESTATION: A BOURDIEUIAN APPROACH

To reveal the socio-political nature of PD practices, this book draws upon French sociologist Pierre Bourdieu's concept of social space as comprising multiple, identifiable 'fields,' each characterised by tensions between competing practices.

For Bourdieu, dominant ways of being, or 'dispositions,' are a product of ongoing contestation between competing social practices. Any given social practice does not make sense in and of itself, but only 'in relation' to other possible ways or modes of being within identifiable 'fields' of practice. Professional development for accountability purposes, for example, stands in tension, and contrasts with, professional development for student social and academic learning. These different possibilities cannot exist somehow outside of the broader social conditions which ascribe meaning to them. They only make sense, as do all practices, 'in relation' to other possible practices, possibilities which involve a process of 'choice-making' and 'choice-taking.' Bourdieu (1998) makes this point about difference when describing the title of his substantive ethnography of France in the 1960s, *Distinction: A Social Critique of the Judgement of Taste*:

> The very title *Distinction* serves as a reminder that what is commonly called distinction, that is, a certain quality of bearing and manners, most often considered innate (one speaks of *distinction naturelle*, 'natural refinement'), is nothing other than *difference*, a gap, a distinctive feature, in short, a *relational* property existing only in and through its relation with other properties. (Bourdieu, 1998, p. 6)

Consequently, PD practice may be best understood as the interplay between the individual and the social, and as a site of possibility amongst a myriad of possibilities. It is this capacity to 'choose,' and be 'chosen' by the circumstances in which individuals and groups find themselves which validates the theoretical, methodological and political cache of a Bourdieuian approach. For these reasons, the conditions for PD matter, as they contribute to the PD practices which transpire, and are influenced by those engaged in all aspects of PD. The effects of professional development practices are not simply individualistic responses in isolation from the broader circumstances in which they are enacted. Furthermore, these circumstances contain evidence of different possibilities, and of enabling practices in relation to teachers' professional development.

Bourdieu argued that to investigate any given field, it is necessary to engage in three related steps. The first is to understand the field in relation to the broader power structures which influence the specific field in question (in this case, the field of teacher professional development), to understand the relations between key players within the field, and to investigate the particular dispositions, or 'habitus' of those involved:

> First, one must analyse the position of the field vis-à-vis the field of power ... Second, one must map out the objective structure of the relations between the positions occupied by the agents or institutions who compete for the legitimate form of specific authority of which this field is the site. And, third, one must analyse the habitus of agents, the different systems of dispositions they have acquired in internalizing a determinate type of social and economic condition, and which find in a definite trajectory with the field under consideration a more or less favourable opportunity to become actualized. (Bourdieu and Wacquant, 1992, p. 104–105)

This book seeks to understand the nature or 'logic of practice' (Bourdieu, 1990b) which characterises the 'field of teachers' professional development' by engaging in this three-step process. Furthermore, conceptualising teacher PD as policy, research and practice within the current broader social and political context, enables a critique of what is understood as the PD field in relation to the broader field of power. The second analytical move entails determining how the various educational players are positioned within and across the PD field in the context of increased individualism, economism and accountability. Finally, analyses of the habitus of various members of the field make it possible to identify the dominant logics of practice in relation to policy, research and teachers' work, and how these seek to influence those positioned differently within the field.

BUT HOW IS CHANGE POSSIBLE?

A focus upon how the broader social circumstances influence practice sometimes attracts the criticism that simply understanding practice is insufficient for changing practice; as Marx argued in the Eleventh Brumaire of Louis Napoleon, 'the point is not to understand the world, but to change it.' However, this book argues, and provides evidence, that understanding is imperative to the change process, and that, as a consequence of understanding, change does occur, even under conditions which make it difficult to effect positive and proactive change. Social actors are capable of strategising within the constraints under which they work and learn, and are able to exert influence in perhaps unforseen ways. Such strategising is made possible by a reflexive disposition of actors, who, through a process of close scrutiny of their circumstances—'socio-analysis,' in Bourdieu's terms—are able to better understand their actions in light of the immediate and more distant history/ies acting on them, and which they enact. Evidence of change is more powerful than exhortations to change.

It is this notion of strategising which enables us to move beyond understandings of professional development practices as understood from 'outside' these practices, and as a means of responding to the oft-put claims that Bourdieu's epistemological approach is essentially structuralist, 'exterior' to practice, and overemphasises the reproductive at the expense of the agentic. In relation to teachers' PD, this is expressed in the way PD is sometimes described, for example, as simply the product of large, unresponsive education 'systems,' and typically construed as a series of activities orchestrated for broad economic purposes over which teachers and other educators have little influence. However, for Bourdieu, people are not simply passive beings beholden to the circumstances within which they find themselves. Instead, they are capable of actively working to alter their circumstances, albeit always within pre-existing conditions which influence decision-making. Strategising does not imply individuals have 'perfect knowledge' of their circumstances, and are somehow able to overcome various socially inscribed practices and approaches. It does not mean that actors are agents who act beyond constraint. Rather, people are able to exert influence, but always within the context of their own peculiar circumstances, experiences and histories.

For Bourdieu, the capacity for socio-analysis is the result of a two-stage process. From the perspective of the researcher-of-practice seeking to understand practice, this firstly involves objectifying the experiences of social actors. This is followed by a second stage in which recognition of this process of objectification occurs, and which necessitates responding to the fallacies involved in such accounts—specifically the initial lack of recognition of the constructedness of such accounts on the part of both the researcher and the subject. To fail to do so results in the observer importing his/her own biases and prejudices, without recognising them as such. This is particularly the case in relation to efforts to understand the practice of others (as this book seeks to do):

> Social science must not only, as objectivism would have it, break with native experience and the native representation of that experience, but also, by a second break, call into question the presuppositions inherent in the position of the 'objective' observer who, seeking to interpret practices, tends to bring into the object the principles of his relation to

> the object, as is shown for example by the privileged status he gives to communicative and epistemic functions, which inclines him to reduce exchanges to pure symbolic exchanges. (Bourdieu, 1990a, p. 27)

It is the recognition of this two-fold process which makes it possible to recognise and reinscribe the agentic possibilities within a social world which also simultaneously imposes constraints. That is, the 'subject' of inquiry, who is neither entirely rule-governed nor capable of absolute knowledge about any given circumstance, is recognised as having the same reflexive capacity as the 'observer.'

With this in mind, educators' professional development practices, and approaches to professional development, can be understood as the product of the interplay between possibilities and constraints, rather than being seen as simply the passive responses of those dominated by circumstances over which they have no influence, or accounts of action from all-knowing agents free of all social and political limitations. These possibilities are evident when educators begin to analyse their practices as influenced by circumstances beyond their own control, but at the same time, in the knowledge that they are capable of exerting influence. It is this level of reflexivity—socio-analysis—which acts as the engine-room for change. Under these circumstances, actors' actions can then become recognised as practical strategies, rather than evidence of alignment with particular sets of prescribed rules or laws, or the result of some state of omnipotence.

Bourdieu achieved these theoretical and methodological insights via an analysis of his own circumstances. By recognising his own actions as those of a knowing individual within a particular set of circumstances, he was able, as Jenkins (2002, p. 51) puts it, to objectify 'the position of the social scientist as a competent actor in his/her own social world(s).' By doing so, it was a small step to similarly characterise research subjects in a similar way, to ascribe agency to these individuals, recognising their capacity to strategise.

This makes it possible to recognise social actors as able to exert influence within their particular circumstances, and as knowing agents within these circumstances. In seeking to reinscribe agency into understandings of social action, Bourdieu (1990b) was unequivocal about what he believed was required. This is evident in the way he described how he made the shift from conceiving of matrimonial practices as a rule-bound practice to one which was much more strategic in intent:

> I wanted, so to speak, to reintroduce agents that Levi-Strauss and the structuralists, among others Althusser, tended to abolish, making them into simple epiphenomena of structure. And I mean agents, not subjects. Action is not the mere carrying out of a rule, or obedience to a rule. Social agents, in archaic societies as well as in ours, are not automata regulated like clocks, in accordance with laws which they do not understand. In the most complex games, matrimonial exchange

for instance, or ritual practices, they put into action the incorporated principles of a generative habitus . . . I am talking about dispositions *acquired through experience*, thus variable from place to place and time to time. This 'feel for the game,' as we call it, is what enables an infinite number of 'moves' to be made, adapted to the infinite number of possible situations which no rule, however, complex can foresee. And so, I replaced rules of kinship with matrimonial strategies. (Bourdieu, 1990b, p. 9; emphasis original)

At all times, these agentic possibilities are recognised as occurring within and influenced by a broader set of social structures and influences necessarily beyond the full control of agents, 'knowing' or otherwise. To better understand the recursivity between actors' circumstances and capacities, to draw together actors' agentic position-taking within these broader social circumstances which influenced their actions, Bourdieu developed the concepts of 'habitus,' 'capital' and 'field.'

For Bourdieu, society consists of numerous quasi-autonomous social spaces, or 'fields,' each of which possesses its own peculiar characteristics, or 'logic,' and all of which are overarched and influenced by a broader field of power, and a field of gender relations (Bourdieu, 2000). Fields are social sites characterised by interacting groups and individuals, all of whom are seeking to dominate these circumstances. Fields both influence and are influenced by those who comprise them; that is, there is a recursive relationship between the individuals and groups and their broader social contexts.

It is the interplay between these individuals and groups, and the social spaces which they occupy, which is responsible for the particular practices which come to dominate. This interaction is the product of the particular proclivities or disposition of those within particular social fields. Bourdieu described these dispositions as the 'habitus' of these individuals and groups. The habitus is both a social product and 'producer' of the social circumstances in which people find themselves. Change is effected by the habitus' capacity for socio-analysis on the part of those associated with any given field.

The habitus is itself the product of the particular traits, resources, capacities people have at their disposal. These 'capitals' are manifest in social, cultural, economic, political, symbolic (Bourdieu, 1986) and national forms. These capitals are accumulated in an ongoing manner and confer a degree of distinction upon those who possess valued capitals (Bourdieu, 1984). While particular capitals dispose people to particular proclivities and capacities which enable them in some situations, in different circumstances, such capitals may result in a habitus which is constrained, which appears 'out of place' amongst those whose experiences have predisposed them to very different social circumstances and proclivities.

From a normative position, the book draws upon this notion of a strategising habitus to argue that those approaches to professional development which frame teachers as active, collaborative student-centred participants should be foregrounded. In a context of increased technicisation of teachers' work and learning, standardisation of curricula and pedagogical instruction, testing and managerial approaches to orchestrating education and teachers' work more generally—what Groundwater-Smith and Mockler (2009) refer to as 'an age of compliance'—it is important to flag the possibilities and opportunities fashioned by educators seeking to foster teacher learning aimed at improving students' outcomes across a range of social and academic arena. Such approaches encourage teachers to work collectively and strategically, rather than individually, thereby challenging the individualism, conservatism and presentism identified by Lortie (1975) in his sociology of school teaching over a quarter of a century ago, and the individualism, managerialism and economism which currently constitutes the public sphere. These approaches contain within them the capacity to challenge isolated PD activities which teachers experience as an intermittent part of their working lives—part of the rhythms of schooling—but which do not necessarily contribute a great deal beyond this. Measures of the success of these alternative approaches include teachers' participation in more active inquiry approaches, and their ability to articulate the nature of these approaches. As well as shedding light on the complexity and tensions which characterise teacher PD, this book also seeks to provide evidence of teachers and associated educators' more strategising capacities.

LAYOUT OF THE BOOK

The layout of the book is informed by three principal domains within which teacher professional development is conceptualised and enacted—policy, research and work/practice. In a two-part process, the book reveals PD practices as the product of tensions within and between competing policy, research and work pressures within what is broadly conceived as the 'field of PD practices.' To understand this complex politics of PD, in Part I, the book firstly describes how PD may be understood as policy, and as research, and the inherent tensions within each of these conceptions. Specifically, tensions are revealed between PD policy for more educational reasons, and PD policy to serve broader economic, administrative and accountability purposes. Similarly, tensions are revealed between support for teachers as researchers of their own practice, and as the passive recipients of research generated by others.

   In Part II, the book then seeks to indicate how this complex politics plays out in practice by drawing upon a broad range of literature associated with teachers' work, as well as data from several cases of teachers' professional development at the level of schools and school systems collected during the previous decade. The teachers' work literature provides insights into tensions between advocacy for more traditional PD approaches, such as workshops, and support for more long-term, work-place based approaches which encourage active learning on the part of teachers. The former are revealed as increasingly common within a broader context of pressure to comply with demands for teachers to engage in PD related to specific disciplinary areas deemed more closely associated with economic growth, and pressures upon educators to manage, and to be seen to manage, resources for maximum economic effect.

The case-based data are drawn from three Anglo countries—England, Canada and Australia—and, together with the literature on teachers' work more generally, reveal the complex, convoluted, sometimes contradictory, competing conceptions of teachers' professional development in practice. Importantly, the three cases reveal how competing and contested policy, research and work practices play out in specific settings, across national contexts, as well as within national contexts. While the range of national contexts is limited, the specific cases themselves are quite diverse, revealing the complexity of PD practices in varied schools and school systems. That themes can be drawn across case studies from three different national settings, in the Anglo world—Australia, Canada and England—also reveals important commonalities in relation to teachers' learning, including how broader neoliberal and managerial pressures exert influence beyond national boundaries. However, and at the same time, evidence is provided of the specificity and peculiarity of PD within national boundaries. The cases draw upon the PD experiences of teachers and school-based administrators' responding to a raft of federal and state policies focused on educational reform in Queensland, Australia; principals, senior Ministry officials and academics' conceptions of PD during a period of significant reform in Ontario, Canada; and teachers' experiences of PD in a secondary school in an inner city comprehensive school in the British Midlands, England.

Like the explorations of PD as policy and research, and in spite of their obvious diversity, the cases all serve to highlight the contested and political nature of actual PD practices. Individually and collectively, the cases reveal that professional development practices are not isolated activities which arise in individual schools, or in response to individuals' desires and proclivities. Nor are they solely the product of dominant policy prescriptions, research outputs or approaches, or dominant work practices which influence and seek to influence teachers' work and learning. Rather, they are the product of the interplay between educators and the broader sociopolitical circumstances within which PD practices transpire. Teachers, school-based and system administrators, policy makers and academics are revealed as simultaneously influenced by, and influencing, the complex and contested conditions under which they work, and this recursive relationship is reflected in the teacher professional development content and processes which they support and enact. In this way, the book reveals the political nature of teacher professional development, thereby helping to make sense of why and how professional development plays out in complex and sometimes peculiar ways in schooling settings.

In the final chapter, the book draws conclusions from the previous chapters, and takes a more overtly normative position on the nature of PD policy, research and work practices which could or should inform teachers' learning. Drawing upon Bourdieu's notion of socio-analysis, Chapter 6 argues for a reflexive stance on the part of educators who can and should serve as the principal arbiters of the teacher professional development in which they engage. The chapter argues for the concept of a 'learning disposition' on the part of researchers, policy-makers and teachers as part of a productive politics of possibility.

CONCLUSION

This book argues that teacher professional development is heavily influenced by the broader social and political conditions within which educators work and learn. These conditions are currently characterised by pressures for increased economic competitiveness, a tendency towards increased individualism, and pressures to ensure accountability for the use of scarce resources. Under these conditions, some PD content and forms of learning are considered more valuable than others, and so dominate over possible alternative approaches. However, even when specific approaches seem to exert influence seemingly unconditionally, the inherently social and political nature of PD practices means that alternative, perhaps more productive approaches, are always evident or possible. The way in which this contestation plays out within interrelated policy, research and teachers' work settings is construed as responsible for the PD practices supported and enacted within schooling settings.

By seeking to explore the contested conditions which characterise teachers' professional development, this book endeavours to make a contribution to debates about what PD looks like at the current moment in time, why particular modes and foci are so prevalent, and why the effects of PD cannot be easily predicted. Also, by revealing educators' responses to the contexts in which they administer, teach, research or otherwise seek to influence teacher and student learning, the book reveals how PD is not simply something 'done' to educators, but something which they actively create through their participation and involvement in such practices. In this way, *The Politics of Teacher Professional Development: Policy, Research and Practice* seeks to shed new light on the nature of professional development practices in an effort to stimulate educators to think beyond current conceptions of PD, and, where necessary, to encourage them to respond more positively, proactively and productively to PD provision. This is not a how-to book, but instead a call for much greater attention to who is involved in making decisions about the PD considered of most value, how this decision-making is undertaken, and the circumstances under which such decisions are made.

Part I

Professional Development as Policy and Research

2 Educational Policy, Politics and Professional Development

[S]tate capacity to make policy and to manage economic, political and social life within national boundaries is considerably affected by globalization . . . However we want to avoid over-privileging globalization, or regarding it as a black box. Instead, we want to attend to context, to capture the possibilities of simultaneously 'local' and global development, and reflect the influence of historically embedded assumptions and beliefs on the mediation and translation of global policy pressures. (Ozga and Lingard, 2007, p. 66)

INTRODUCTION

An analysis of key educational policies and associated politics from a range of national settings reveals the influence of broad global neoliberal, managerial and economistic logics of practice within the field of professional development (PD) practices. However, these influences are not unchecked, but are simultaneously challenged by continued and more fundamentally educational practices within the field, at national and sub-national levels. The tensions between these alternative approaches to PD inevitably influence how educational policy more generally, and professional development policy in particular, are framed. This chapter draws upon key educational and PD policies, and the broader politics within which they are produced in specific national contexts, to reveal how and why PD policy-making is so contested. These policy texts, associated documents and commentary are treated as the residues of a much broader process of policy production involving specific contexts, texts and consequences (Taylor, Rizvi, Lingard and Henry, 1997).

At present, policy-making is significantly influenced by broader global processes, particularly those associated with neoliberalism, economism and managerialism. Rather than advocating for active participation on the part of teachers in their own learning, and a variety of outcomes including social outcomes, and the needs of specific students/schools/teachers in local schooling settings, there has been increasing pressure over the past two decades to treat learners as discrete individuals, to focus more exclusively upon education as part of a broader economic enterprise, to account for the way in which resources are utilised, and to ensure that the outcomes of student and teacher learning are quantifiable. In short, educational policy has been heavily influenced by the global spread of more neoliberal, economistic and bureaucratic logics of practice.

However, even as learning focused upon economic development is emphasised, individualistic approaches to teachers' needs are endorsed, and teacher and student learning are reduced to quantifiable measures, there is also evidence of advocacy for teacher learning beyond narrow economically focused areas of the curriculum (particularly literacy and numeracy), support for teacher participation in addressing their own learning needs, and a desire to promote a broader conception of educational outcomes beyond standardised measures, or bureaucratised standards of teacher performance. Such endorsement and advocacy are evident in formal policy texts and associated documents, statements and commentary, both in the recent past (two decades) and at present. Collectively, these texts constitute ongoing historical 'traces' of PD policy-making and associated educational policy production practices.

This chapter gestures towards the logics of practice which characterise these policy production processes, and explores the consequences of these logics within the broader policy and political contexts in which they develop. By drawing upon current and recent PD policies, and associated policies and politics in selected Anglo settings—Australia, England and Ontario, Canada—the chapter seeks to reveal how teacher professional development as policy is intrinsically complex, and that these policies cannot be easily understood as advocating a particular, homogeneous conception of teachers' learning. Rather, the chapter reveals that as policy, teacher PD is deeply contested, reflecting the similarly contested conditions within which policy-making is undertaken.

THE EDUCATIONAL POLICY CONTEXT

Educational policy practices have not arisen in isolation, but instead reflect the broader field of power and power relations, characterised by specific global patterns and processes. As outlined in Chapter 1, this volume, the logics of neoliberalism, economism, globalization and managerialism have had a significant influence upon all sectors of the public service, including education. Such approaches focus strongly upon individualism, economic growth and development, employ a reified economic conception of global processes to describe an extraordinarily complex phenomenon (manifest culturally, socially, politically as well as economically), and emphasise resource expenditure as a cost rather than a benefit. The neoliberal, economistic and managerial logics have converged to create a complex, and frequently contradictory assemblage of influences which have come to increasingly typify educational policies in general, and professional development policies in particular.

Not surprisingly, these broad influences have affected educational policy and practice, resulting in increased central control of educators' work and roles, and the development of quasi-markets in education, characterised by choice and competition:

> Under the influence of neoliberal ideologies and associated new mana-
> gerial technologies—with their privileging of cost-containment, effi-
> ciency and productivity goals—this period has seen an increase in the
> central regulation of the work of teachers and an increased role for
> quasi-markets centred on the ideas of choice and competition. (Gewirtz,
> Mahony, Hextall and Cribb, 2009, p. 5)

In educational policy contexts, broader competitive and accountability
pressures have led to an increased focus upon performance measurement,
where measurement implies the quantification of educational outcomes.
Specifically, there is strong pressure to determine whether and how local
educational outcomes 'match up' against broader national, and especially international, measures. The increased focus upon data collection
and quantification of educational outcomes in policy reflect national
governments' concerns about how to respond to globalization. Drawing
upon Rose (1999), Ozga and Lingard (2007) refer to this process as a
form of governance characterised by 'policy as numbers;' the educational
capitals most valued are those which can be counted. Within an emerg-
ing globalized education policy field (Ozga and Lingard, 2007), these
measures are increasingly international in origin with political structures
beyond nation states framing what is construed as possible actions on
the part of national governments. Various international bodies—government and non-government—are both product and advocate of these
managerial and neoliberal global processes and practices. The United
Nations; United Nations Educational, Scientific and Cultural Organisation (UNESCO); World Bank; Organisation for Economic Cooperation and Development (OECD) and International Monetary Fund (IMF),
all influence one another, and nation states, and may be construed as
examples of a nascent global policy community (Henry, Lingard, Taylor
and Rizvi, 2001), or global field of educational policy (Lingard, Rawolle
and Taylor, 2005). Through a process of 'policy-borrowing,' neoliberal
practices and principles endorsed in the policies of these cross-national
bodies are taken up within nation states, which are affected by global
flows of information (Henry et al., 2001). The work of this global policy
elite results in, and is founded upon, an epistemological consensus which
foregrounds the value and validity of numerical measurement. This is
exemplified in the European context, for example, in the way in which
national 'policy brokers' are described as mediating calls from the European Commission for particular policy agenda within individual member
states (Grek, Lawn, Lingard, Ozga, Rinne, Segerholm and Simola, 2009).
This emphasis upon quantitative measures, and the tendency to compare
such outcomes internationally has a profound influence upon particular countries (especially those which are net beneficiaries of resources
provided by international bodies such as the EU and OECD) (Lingard,
Rawolle and Taylor, 2005).

These numbers and data collection processes are recognised as powerful modes of governance for distributed systems which devolve responsibility for educational provision at the same time as they seek to maintain control over the outcomes of such provision. Such indicators serve as capitals productive of and responsive to educational markets, evident, for example, in how parent and student consumers choose schools on the basis of published league tables. This process is encouraged by the increased tendency of nation-states to compare their results against international indicators of performance, such as the iconic OECD Program for International Student Assessment (PISA) tests of literacy, numeracy and scientific literacy, and the International Association for the Evaluation of Educational Achievement (IAEA) Trends in International Mathematics and Science Study (TIMSS) tests of mathematics and science capability. Within such governance structures, teachers are framed as active subjects engaged in both producing and responding to such data. A focus upon 'evidence-based' practice within policy-making becomes translated into decontextualised, data-driven goals. The educational capitals most valued are quantifiable student performance measures on standardised tests designed to enable international comparisons.

However, and at the same time, the more homogenised logics encouraged by global processes, and reflected in subsequent practices, are always only part of the picture. Education policy is a contested space in which quantitative indicators of performance are always mediated by local contexts (Ozga and Lingard, 2007; Rizvi and Lingard, 2010). Those affected by these processes, including governments, are not simply passive recipients of such materials but are able to exercise agency (Ozga and Lingard, 2007; Lingard, Rawolle and Taylor, 2005). Educational restructuring is the result of economic globalization, but it is also the product of how specific nation-states and governments responsible for education respond to this push for globalization. Appadurai (2001) refers to more agentic responses as instances of globalization 'from below.' Lingard (2000) captures this complexity in his application of the vernacular 'it is and it isn't' to describe this complex politics of engagement with global processes. Ball's (1998) 'big policies in a small world'—the trend towards homogenisation of global policies as a result of policy borrowing across national contexts—are also understood as mediated by the peculiar conditions and circumstances in which they are understood in state and local educational contexts. Under such conditions, Evetts (2009) distinguishes between what she describes as 'organizational professionalism,' dominated by concerns about standardization of work practices, managerial control, and external evaluation (such as via target-setting and performance review), and 'occupational professionalism,' with its emphasis upon greater autonomy, collegial authority and accountability to professional ethics determined and enacted by professional bodies and associations. Rather than there being a shift from organizational to occupational professionalism, there is evidence of both

co-existing (Evetts, 2009). The result is a heterodoxy of practices, best indicated via close scrutiny of nation-states' efforts to frame PD policy, and the
conditions under which they try to do so.

PD POLICY PRACTICES WITHIN ANGLO NATION-STATES

Increasing neoliberalism, economism and accountability pressures within
the broader global educational policy field have influenced policies associated with teachers' professional development in Anglo settings. However,
the ways in which nation-states have responded to these broader pressures
and processes also reveals evidence of contestation over the professional
development practices most valued within the field, and of more occupational, professional logics of practice beyond those associated with narrow
conceptions of globalization, and managerialism. While increased pressures of accountability in recent times have contributed to a general 'quest
for certainty' in relation to professional development practices (Webster-
Wright, 2009, p. 717), these pressures have not gone unchallenged. Such
contestation is evident in relevant policies in selected regions of specific
Anglo nation-states—Australia, England and Canada—drawn upon in the
remainder of this chapter as exemplars of these broader processes.

To understand current contested logics, it is necessary to situate PD
practices within the specific, recent histories of each national setting, which
necessarily influence how professional development policies and politics are
construed, implemented and responded to by those involved in their development and implementation. It is important to recognise the specificity of
education/PD policy-making within each nation-state, and how this par-
ticularity influences responses to broader homogenising, global processes,
as well as evidence of commonality across these contexts. The remainder of
this chapter provides insights into the key logics of practice influencing PD
policy in Australia, England, and the Canadian province of Ontario. Some
key similarities in relation to these contested practices across the three
national contexts are flagged briefly in the conclusion to the chapter.

Australia

While education is the constitutional responsibility of the individual states
in Australia, the federal/national government has taken a particular interest in PD-related issues over the past two decades. The field of PD as policy
reveals professional development policies in Australia have focused upon
encouraging individual and collective PD associated with state-centric concerns about economic development, as well as PD inclusive of more localised, democratic contingencies. While individualistic, economistic logics
have become increasingly influential, more collective, broadly focused, progressive logics have also had impact.

During the 1970s and 1980s, the *Disadvantaged Schools Program*, a national program designed to address educational equity issues, encouraged collegial forms of inquiry, including via action research initiatives. These were designed to redress educational inequality as a result of ethnicity, indigeneity and/or poverty. To access funding, schools were required to develop school-based rather than individual projects, and to evaluate their collective efforts, thereby invoking a more collaborative inquiry approach (Groundwater-Smith and Dadds, 2004).

More collective, school-based logics of inquiry were also evident during the 1990s. The *National Schools Project*, supported by the federal government of the time, addressed the provision of teacher learning in a much more systematic manner than had many previous programs. The *National Schools Project* was designed to align teachers' learning with a research program concerned with how best to promote beneficial organisational restructuring and change (Ladwig and White, 1996). The program was premised upon much more substantive relationships between teachers and researchers, which enabled teachers to take a more active stance in relation to their own learning needs, and it highlighted the need to take local context into account. The *National Schools Project* resulted in the development of the *National Schools Network* (NSN) and the *Innovative Links between Universities and Schools for Teacher Professional Development' (Innovative Links)* projects. These initiatives, developed from the 1993 Education Accord between the teacher unions and the federal Labor government, were designed to contribute towards systematic and systemic education reform (Angus, 1996). They also ascribed a professional focus to the teacher unions. This was a significant development because it institutionalized the involvement of the teacher unions in the change process, together with (state) employing authorities and the Commonwealth government, reflecting (and promoting) a much more educationally oriented rather than industrially based habitus.

The logics of collaboration and participation dominated the provision of teacher learning associated with the *National Schools Project*. The *National Schools Network* was coordinated by a centralised authority consisting of members from state employing authorities, teachers' professional associations, government and non-government teacher unions, academics from teacher education faculties and members of the wider community. The *Network* sought to include all major groups in the educational change agenda. Both the *National Schools Network* and the *Innovative Links* projects were designed to improve students' learning by encouraging teachers to research and reconsider their daily classroom practices (Sachs, 2003). For those schools involved, state supported, collaborative teacher inquiry became the dominant practice of teacher learning under these programs (Sachs, 2003). The *National Schools Network* was designed to better understand the link between the organisation of teachers' work and student learning, as a precursor to assisting teachers to improve their teaching

(Sachs, 2003). Reflecting a more democratic disposition on the part of policy-makers, the emphasis was upon teachers being involved in collaborative action research projects to determine factors inhibiting schools from engaging in renewal. The *Innovative Links* project focused upon schools' specific issues, and forged connections between schools and teacher education faculties in universities as a means of fostering teacher learning for renewing teacher professionalism (Sachs and Groundwater-Smith, 1999). Part of the *Innovative Links* program was to promote whole-school reform by advocating learning communities which embraced students, teachers and academics as learners (Yeatman and Sachs, 1995).

More recently, neoliberal pressures reflect, and have resulted in, the promotion of an increasingly individualistic and competitive habitus in relation to professional development policy-making. In Australia, this is evident in the way in which dedicated federal Australian government policies associated with teacher professional development have been framed within a competitive paradigm which encourages schools to compete against one another for funds for purposes of professional development. The *Australian Government Quality Teacher Programme* (Commonwealth of Australia, 2005) and its predecessor policies, *Commonwealth Government Quality Teacher Programme* (Commonwealth of Australia, 2003) and *Quality Teacher Programme* (Commonwealth of Australia, 2000) required prospective participants to submit applications outlining the nature of the professional development initiatives in which they wished to be involved, as part of a competitive tendering process for federal funding. Such an approach is in keeping with the general trend towards the development of quasi-markets (Whitty, Halpin and Power, 1998) in education in Australia, and part of a broader process of contestation between competing logics of practice which has been ongoing since the mid-1980s. As more neoliberal and economistic logics have exerted influence, this process has resulted in educational institutions being reframed as service-providers to student-consumers, who are themselves framed within broader human capital terms as particular types of 'products' designed to address the needs of industry (Marginson, 1997).

In keeping with the influence of more economistic logics, the earlier instantiations of the *Quality Teacher Programme* policy ensemble led to support within the field of professional development for those subject areas deemed most likely to result in economic improvement. The initial policy, the *Quality Teacher Programme*, emphasised professional development in the curriculum areas of literacy, numeracy, science and information and communications technology (ICT) (Commonwealth of Australia, 2000). Such emphases were perceived as most likely to result in economic benefits. Also, the two earlier instantiations of this policy—*Commonwealth Government Quality Teacher Programme* (Commonwealth of Australia, 2003) and *Australian Government Quality Teacher Programme* (Commonwealth of Australia, 2005)—described those teachers working in rural and remote areas, and teachers of Aboriginal and Torres Strait Islander students, and other disadvantaged urban students as 'secondary target groups' (Commonwealth of Australia, 2000; 2003). Such groups were 'secondary' in both name and in the way they were framed as foci for government intervention. More inclusive PD logics for the development of a literate and informed citizenship appeared less evident than those associated with economic individualism.

Nevertheless, it is important to recognise that the various iterations of the *Quality Teacher Programme* also revealed evidence of more social democratic and inclusive logics of practice within the field of PD practices. In keeping with professional development policy as contested in Australia (Hardy, 2008), the 2000 and 2003 versions of the program focused at least some attention upon the needs of students from rural and remote areas, Indigenous students and students from disadvantaged urban communities (Commonwealth of Australia, 2000; 2003). Also, the latest version of the program included as priority areas students with disabilities, and Indigenous students (Commonwealth, 2005). There was at least some evidence of PD logics for the development of a literate and informed citizenship to sustain social democratic practices and processes.

The original *Quality Teacher Programme* policy also reflected a more progressive habitus amongst policy-makers in the way the various guidelines promoted more active teacher learning, rather than simply responding solely to neoliberal and economistic pressures (Commonwealth of Australia, 2000). The policy referred to the value of professional development which had clearly defined outcomes and goals, was grounded in the needs of specific teachers and schools, and took into account whole-of-school approaches and networks already existing in regions (Commonwealth of Australia, 2000). Furthermore, mention was made of the importance of involving multiple stakeholders in PD initiatives, and addressing both curriculum and pedagogical foci. Finally, this policy document suggested a field of PD practices which also valued the development of resources by teachers themselves, rather than simply construing teachers as the recipients of information delivered by others. Explicit mention was made of the need to avoid what were described as 'one-off events' (p. 4) as much as possible, and to ensure that PD encompassed a variety of activities in which participants may engage.

Such foci were similarly reflected in the 2005 policy guidelines, which included an extensive list of approaches deemed of value for teachers' PD in schooling settings. A strong focus upon student-centred, school-based, ongoing, classroom-relevant, collaborative, problem-focused, teacher-involved approaches again reflected a more context-responsive policy-making habitus which challenged more general economistic practices:

Will the planned professional learning:

- Contain content that focuses on what students are to learn and how to address the different problems students may have in learning the material?

- Be based on analyses of the difference between actual student performance and goals and standards for student learning?
- Involve teachers in the identification of what they need to learn and in the development of the learning experiences they will be involved in?
- Be primarily school-based and built into the day-to-day work of teaching?
- Engage teachers in concrete teaching tasks, based on teachers' experiences with students?
- Be organised around collaborative problem solving?
- Be continuous and ongoing, involving follow-up and support for further learning—including support from sources external to the school that can provide necessary resources and new perspectives?
- Incorporate evaluation of multiple sources of information on learning outcomes for students and the instruction and other processes that are involved in implementing the lessons learned through professional learning?
- Provide opportunities to gain an understanding of the theory underlying the knowledge and skills being learned?
- Provide learning opportunities that are meaningful and professionally empowering?
- Be connected to a comprehensive change process focused on improving student learning? (Commonwealth of Australia, 2005, p. 14–15)

As with the 2000 guidelines, the 2005 guidelines were overt in their support of PD practices focused on localised student, teacher and school needs. Such learning was also described as needing to be inquiry-oriented, whole-school focused, collaborative, reflective and capable of drawing upon various online technologies to promote interaction between teachers:

At an operational level, *AGQTP* funded activities should:

- Show teachers how to connect their work to specific standards for student performance;
- Be based on teacher and school needs;
- Address student learning needs;
- Have clearly defined goals and outcomes;
- Have practical relevance to teachers;
- Provide a balance of curriculum and pedagogical issues;
- Use techniques which model inquiry forms of teaching;
- Encourage a whole-school focus on student learning;
- Involve stakeholder partnerships;
- Consider whole school approaches and regional network activities;
- Connect to other aspects of school changes focused on improving student learning;
- Provide opportunities for reflection and sharing with peers;

- Consider approaches that demonstrate the innovative use of ICT to support teaching and learning and whole-school reform;
- Where appropriate, utilise online networking tools (e.g., discussion groups, extranets, etc.) to support collaborative activities, particularly for rural/remote teachers. (Commonwealth of Australia, 2005, p. 15–16)

More recently, and in contrast with many of the more progressive logics evident in such earlier guidelines, more economistic and neoliberal logics have become more evident. This is apparent in the way in which issues of teaching and teacher learning are addressed in the policies of groups not traditionally overtly concerned with educational issues, and in how these have been taken up by government. In a paper commissioned by the Business Council of Australia (BCA), for example, teaching and teacher learning are framed as valuable for their contribution to Australia's economic survival in an increasingly uncertain, global economy (Business Council of Australia, 2008). Within such a paradigm, there is considerable emphasis upon attracting and retaining excellent teachers within the profession. One way in which this is to be achieved is through stratifying the teaching profession and increasing salaries of the best teachers (up to $AUD130, 000). Such an approach is seen as a way of valuing teachers and teaching, and encouraging those students who may be concerned about the relatively low pay and poor working conditions to consider a career in teaching. Such emphases clearly reflect the influence of the broader neoliberal and economistic cultural arbitraries which currently frame education.

In the context of these more neoliberal logics, the Business Council of Australia favours connecting increased salaries to particular types of professional development construed as leading to high teaching standards and student learning:

> Newly conceived career paths are needed for the teaching profession to ensure that teachers have strong incentives to engage in the type of professional learning that leads to high teaching standards and improves student learning outcomes. Salary structures for teachers need to be more effective as instruments for promoting widespread use of successful teaching practices. (Business Council of Australia, 2008, p. 8)

The intimation of a more reductionist approach to the link between PD, standards and student outcomes within such a statement reveals how the field of PD practices is potentially narrowed under more economistic pressures.

Reflecting the pervasiveness of neoliberal logics, this report is also endorsed by the current federal Labor Government in Australia, as evident in a speech to the Australian Labor Party by the then Deputy Prime Minister and Minister for Education, Employment and Workplace Relations, Julia Gillard:

> I welcome this week's report from the Business Council of Australia on teacher pay and career structures. It is time for a far-reaching debate, not just on how we reward teaching properly, but how we ensure that all teachers everywhere achieve a quality of work that meets our 21st century expectations. (Gillard, 2008a)

Such an approach is also in keeping with the Australian Federal Labor Party's earlier policy position while in opposition, entitled *Teaching Standards: Recognising and Rewarding Quality Teaching in Public Schools* (Macklin, 2006). This policy supported a more differentiated salary scale to reflect high quality teaching, and encouraged teachers engaging in professional learning to maintain registration, as well as registration for a set period of time of five years.

However, while neoliberal and accountability logics have exerted significant influence upon teachers' learning policies, other more local pressures and genuine concerns about providing sustainable education for Australian students have also been evident within the field of teacher PD. The retention of teachers, and concerns to ensure exemplary teachers are able to forge careers in the classroom are other areas of ongoing concern. Again, this is reflected in comments by Julia Gillard:

> When teachers are in classrooms, we want to encourage, provide incentives and rewards for people to be doing the best they can and staying up-to-date with the best of professional learning. We want to make sure that for those people who are trained as teachers, they're retained in the system and not going off to other jobs. We also want to make sure there are career paths that keep the best in front of the classroom, rather than necessarily having to go elsewhere in the system. (Gillard, 2008b)

Albeit in a very broad sense, such advocacy seems more inclusive and broad-based than purely neoliberal, economistic or accountability-dominated conceptions of teacher learning within the field.

Since 2009, tensions between more economistic and social-democratic logics are also evident in federal government efforts to increase partnerships between the federal government and the individual states as part of the *Smarter Schools National Partnerships* program. Within this program, explicit mention is made of PD in the context of teacher and principal professional development. Fifty million dollars is earmarked to support principal development, with a further $56 million to support joint federal/state initiatives (Department of Education, Employment and Workplace Relations, 2010). The latter include a focus upon improving students' learning in low socio-economic status schools, as well as in improving literacy and numeracy outcomes. Support is also provided to assist schools to collaborate more effectively to improve learning outcomes. Such stances exemplify a policy position which reflects a more socially aware habitus on the part of policy-makers. However, more neoliberal logics continue to exert strong influence as evident in the focus upon literacy and numeracy, often in relation to narrow measures of student attainment on standardised national tests. As with earlier policies and programs, in their entirety, later policies and associated programs are influenced by more localised logics of practice, at the same time as broader neoliberal, managerial and economistic logics exert influence. In this way, the field of PD practices, as expressed in the Australian policy context, is revealed as deeply contested.

England

Since the passing of the 1988 *Education Reform Act* in England, there has been a strong shift towards increased public accountability for educational outcomes, evidenced in national testing associated with the introduction of a compulsory traditional academic national curriculum, and the introduction of national teaching standards. At the same time, more neoliberal and economistic logics are evident in the development of school markets, assisted by a bureaucratic system of accountability involving the public 'naming and shaming' of schools deemed to have produced unsatisfactory outcomes. These trends have been accompanied by greater devolution to schools, and a subsequent weakening of Local Authorities (previously known as 'Local Education Authorities'). Collectively, these practices constitute a new orthodoxy, encouraging the quasi-marketisation of educational provision, the development of 'beacon' schools specialising in particular aspects of the curriculum, and the opening up of restrictive enrolment policies to encourage greater competition between schools for students (Mahony and Hextall, 2000). A combination of centralisation of decision-making, together with devolution of responsibility, has had effects upon all aspects of educational practice, including those related to teacher PD. However, as well as being influenced by these more neoliberal, bureaucratic and managerial logics, the field of PD practices as expressed in English educational settings is also characterised by efforts amongst policy-makers and stakeholders to promote more sustained and sustainable localised approaches to teachers' professional development.

The links between more neoliberal, managerial and accountability-oriented logics in England were established via market-based conceptions of 'choice' in earlier policies. Pring (2002) reveals how the trend towards neoliberalism from the late 1970s/early 1980s led to increased faith in market forces: 'The emphasis lay in "consumer choice," in contrast with professional expertise' (p. 18). This process, in tandem with the implementation of national testing, eventually led to the widespread publication of school results of national tests to enable parents to exercise their newly found 'choice' within the educational market. Since 1993, the Office for Standards in Education (Ofsted) has been instrumental in the development of such data, and has become recognised as a powerful vehicle influencing the work and learning of teachers throughout the country. This is particularly the case given concerns about the public naming of 'failing' schools or what have more recently been euphemistically referred to as schools requiring 'special measures' (Day, Sammons, Stobart, Kington and Gu, 2007, p. 5). In this context, the development of national performance tables as ranked 'league tables' by newspapers has served as a vehicle for the potential marketisation of schooling. Under these circumstances, Troman, Jeffrey and Raggl (2007) refer to English primary schools being increasingly subjected to policies oriented towards 'cultures of performativity' (p. 549). This occurs not only through the use of school league tables developed from students' standardised test scores, but also via Ofsted inspections, the use of performance pay for teachers, and performance management of teachers. All of these measures are designed to ensure improvements in student performance on standardised tests, which are themselves valued capitals construed as a proxy for future economic competitiveness in an increasingly competitive international climate.

Pring (2002) argues that while the market-oriented provision of education has proved less successful than intended, the continuation of administrative arrangements which contribute to this approach constitutes part of this new orthodoxy which enables governments to account for, and influence, how public monies are spent in education. The 1998 *School Standards and Framework Act*, for example, served as an extension of the accountability-oriented logics informing previous legislation and policy-making, and how such foci would continue to influence educational practices in general, and the field of PD practices in particular. The strong language of accountability employed by central administrative branches of government has reduced the capacity of professional bodies to exert influence upon educational practices (Pring, 2002). In the English context, such bodies have included the peak educational authority, *Her Majesty's Inspectorate*, which is emblematic of how the profession is at arm's length from government. The perception is that the profession is respected as possessing valuable, specialist knowledge which is not readily available from other sources. Traditionally, the Ministry of Education was able to call upon such knowledge as necessary to ensure that the administrative decisions being made were in keeping with the best professional judgement about what was required to maintain a viable educational system. Pring (2002) makes this point by citing Dr Marjorie Reeves' response in 1947 to the then Permanent Secretary, John Maude, when asked about the responsibilities of the *Central Advisory Committee for Education* (England) to which she had just been appointed: 'to be prepared to die at the first ditch as soon as politicians try to get their hands on education' (p. 16). The more prescriptive nature of the reforms arising from the *Education Reform Act* has curtailed the influence of professional educators in relation to educational decision-making. This change in direction is symbolised by the Chief Inspector having become a political appointment. It is also evident in the contradictory way in which local management of schools has given greater control over staffing and resources to those in schools, but tightened control over the curriculum and testing procedures (Barker, 2008).

In this context, teacher professional development has been construed symbolically as a management tool to respond to centralised pressures for reform. Often, this is directly related to curriculum issues. The focus on the *National Curriculum*, since the 1988 *Education Reform Act*, has resulted in considerable attention and allocation of resources to the areas of literacy, numeracy and science. The professional development supported nationally, and subsequently, within Local Authorities/Local Education Authorities, reflects these foci—foci which, as in the Australian setting, place considerable emphasis upon those discipline areas deemed most likely to contribute to broader economic development. Teacher assessment practices and procedures have been added to these initial foci (Day et al., 2007). A more narrowly focused policy-making disposition amongst policy-makers was evident in the introduction of the *National Literacy Strategy* (NLS) implemented in 1998, and the *National Numeracy Strategy* in 1999, and with the implementation of the Key Stage 3 strategy designed to improve student attainment in English, Mathematics, Science and ICT amongst students aged 11 to 14 (Day, et al., 2007).

At the same time, market logics were and are evident in the way in which education policy has supported and continues to support the provision of educational services by different 'providers,' who compete with one another in the marketplace. Continuing professional development constitutes part of a broader policy process of what Ball (2009) describes as 'organisational recalibration.' This involves the privatisation of educational programs, including the marketing and 'selling' of PD programs to those in schools. Relevant educational policies construe PD as a 'commodity'—something to be bought and sold. Schools are able to 'purchase' models of school improvement which can be used to create new school and schooling identities through various 'turnaround services.' Educational businesses are also able to offer services to institutions to assist those in schools to interpret policies: 'In effect, on behalf of the state, they disseminate the discourses of reform, of improvement and of competition through 'improvement' packages, CPD or consultancy work' (Ball, 2009, p. 85). Consequently, the orthodoxy of business models informs both the form and content of PD provision.

Market logics have also been apparent in the push to connect teachers' pay, performance and professional development. By increasing teachers' pay according to performance, teachers have been construed as having greater incentive to improve their performance, which is no longer tied to a set ceiling, beyond which teachers' income cannot be raised, regardless of the increased efforts they may employ in their work. This emphasis upon linking pay and performance has implications for teachers' PD. Odden and Kelley (1997) argue that linking pay and performance makes sense if teachers are provided with the opportunity to improve upon their performance through professional development. However, such a model is premised on the assumption that PD should simply respond to already prescribed ends set by governments rather than being a vehicle for establishing alternative educational agenda. Pring (2002) argues the conception of professional development which is valued under these circumstances is based upon a notion of effective teaching informed by state-commissioned research. While such research may represent a valued educational capital beyond its symbolic value as a mechanism to endorse particular approaches and content deemed important by governments, the way in which these principles are articulated in relation to prescribed national standards and/or other foci determined by government, typically reflects an accountability-oriented habitus on the part of policy makers, and leads to a narrowing of what is considered valid and valuable PD. The foci for PD have already been established, rather than being open to deliberation amongst educators themselves.

Such restrictions are evident even as there is also evidence of more progressive logics of practice at play, and a broadening of the PD considered of most value. In a significant PD policy document released in 2001, *Learning and Teaching: A Strategy for Professional Development,* teachers were encouraged to participate in a broad-based conception of professional development. This strategy construed PD as ' . . . any activity that increases the skills, knowledge or understanding of teachers, and their effectiveness in schools' (Department for Education and Employment, 2001, p. 3). The document expressed a desire to:

> . . . support the aspirations of the overwhelming majority of teachers; build on the excellent practice already in place in many schools; underpin, integrate and reinforce the many other existing initiatives to raise teachers' skills and spread good practice; maximise the potential of performance management; and increase the quality and impact of teaching.' (p. 3)

While considerable effort was made to promote a more expansive conception of PD, including acknowledging good practice in local settings, there was also significant interest in a technical conception of PD which could be 'administered' to other settings. There was also a strong focus upon the place of performance management in fostering teachers' PD. More progressive logics of PD practice were less evident within a field heavily influenced by more managerial and prescriptive approaches to teachers' learning.

These tensions were similarly reflected in a later key professional development policy aimed at secondary schools, *Leading and Coordinating CPD in Secondary Schools* (Department for Education and Employment, 2005). The emphasis in this policy was upon increasing teachers' skills and knowledge, and of doing so as quickly as possible. Pickering (2007) argues that these specific professional development policy initiatives primarily focused on more technicist approaches, rather than promoting deeper learning:

> This highly technicist view of teacher development suggests that an increase is best achieved by a standardised approach to CPD, in which knowledge, skills and understanding are 'delivered' to teachers, and thereby transferred, by a combination of top-down experts and examples of best practice. (p. 193)

The influence of more technical logics was also evident in efforts to establish national standards, as in other countries, against which the teaching profession could be held accountable, and against which decisions could be made about the nature of the teaching and teacher learning which should constitute teachers' work. In relation to cultivating teachers' learning, such standards have been construed as both useful (Mayer, Mitchell, Macdonald and Bell, 2005) and problematic (Mahony and Hextall, 2000; White and Hay, 2004). Part of the concern about teaching standards has been that within a context of increased scrutiny over how resources are used within a globalized, neoliberal world, the application of such standards has been seen as an effective means of simply managing this resource allocation, rather than focusing upon the challenges of effecting improvements for teachers of all students. It is the purported potential to measure or calculate performance which makes educational standards so attractive, in spite of the conceptual fuzziness which attends the concept (Mahony and Hextall, 2000).

These more accountability-oriented logics of practice have been evident since *National Professional Standards* were first established by the Teacher Training Agency (TTA) in England during the 1990s. The TTA was established to foster improved teaching practices to enhance student learning, and to determine how to fund school-based teacher education which had been promulgated as the way to improve teaching practices (Mahony and Hextall, 2000). Such changes occurred within a political context of considerable hostility towards higher education institutions engaged in teacher education, which were seen as self-serving, and promulgating teaching approaches which had little validity in the field or in relation to the perceived needs of the country—particularly economic needs. The Teacher Training Agency was also responsible for a host of other initiatives associated with teaching including developing a framework for ongoing professional development. The successor to the TTA, the Training and Development Agency for Schools (TDA) (2007; 2009a; 2009b), continues to advocate for national standards, and actively promotes professional development associated with such standards. However, with the establishment of the General Teaching Council for England (GTCE), the development of standards themselves and teacher accreditation and registration, have been shifted from the TDA to the GTCE.

At present, within the TDA, more accountability-oriented logics are evident in the way strong links are forged between teacher development and performance management. Such logics are also apparent in the links to individual school improvement plans, and professional teaching standards more generally. Teaching standards, performance management, school improvement and professional development are intimately intertwined:

> Performance management is the process for assessing the overall perfor-
> mance of a teacher or head teacher, in the context of the individual's job
> description and the provisions of the School Teachers' Pay and Conditions
> Document (STPCD), and making plans for the individual's future devel-
> opment in the context of the school's improvement plan. Professional
> standards provide the backdrop to the discussions about performance
> and future development. The standards define the professional attri-
> butes, knowledge, understanding and skills for teachers at each career
> stage. (Training and Development Agency for Schools, 2009a, p.1)

Indeed, within the TDA's policy *Professional Standards for Teachers: Why Sit Still in Your Career?* (Training and Development Agency for Schools, 2007), performance management is construed as pivotal to decision-mak-ing about PD:

> performance management is the key process. Performance manage-
> ment provides the context for regular discussions about teachers' career
> aspirations and their future development . . . The relevant standards
> should be looked at as a whole in order to help teachers identify areas
> of strength and areas for further professional development. (Training
> and Development Agency for Schools, 2007, p. 3)

In this way, dominant logics of practice are reflected in the increased influ-ence of technical accountability mechanisms to effect improvement, such as performance management. The conflation of standards for regulatory and developmental purposes assists in the misrecognition necessary for such mechanisms to be taken up in policy.

More instrumental logics are also evident in how teaching standards are currently explicitly construed as a vehicle for identifying PD necessary to secure career advancement, and in relation to teachers' stages in their careers:

> The standards will support teachers in identifying their professional
> development needs. Where teachers wish to progress to the next career
> stage, the next level of the framework provides a reference point for all
> teachers when considering future development. Whilst not all teachers
> will necessarily want to move to the next career stage, the standards
> will also support teachers in identifying ways to broaden and deepen
> their expertise within their current career stages. (Training and Devel-
> opment Agency for Schools, 2007, p. 3)

While acknowledging the potential value of standards for teachers' learn-ing, such policy approaches to PD reflect a broader culture of human resource management and training designed to effect improved individual motivation within a context of organisational capacity-building (Barker, 2008). The strong connection between PD and career stage within the *Professional Standards for Teachers: Why Sit Still in Your Career?* (Training and Development Agency, 2007) policy, together with a relative lack of attention to issues explicitly related to student learning, and the lack of endorsement of a broader conception of PD, suggest a policy-making habitus heavily influenced by structural parameters and external motivators to effect improved teaching and learning.

These policies also reflect PD as something 'done to' teachers, rather than being an active process involving teachers in interrogating their own practices. Hodkinson (2009) argues that, typically, English educational policies have focused upon learning as 'acquisition,' rather than a process of more active engagement and involvement by teachers. While the establishment of the General Teaching Council in 2000, and subsequent development of a dedicated professional development policy *Learning and Teaching: A Strategy for Professional Development* held the hope of ensuring adequate resourcing for high quality, career-long professional development (Department for Education and Employment, 2001), considerable controversy surrounds professional development policy and politics in England:

> Teachers' continuing professional development (CPD) in England is a controversial area, and there is arguably little evidence of a 'coherent' framework around which consistently high-quality CPD has been developed, provided and accessed despite the establishment of the General Teaching Council in 2000, the publication of the CPD strategy in 2001 by the Department for Education and Employment, and the extension of the Training and Development Agency for Schools' remit to include CPD in 2005. (Passay and Waite, 2008, p. 311)

'CPD' (continuing professional development), as it is often described in the English context, is seen as lacking coherence because of disputation over how it should be conceptualised—whether as training, focused upon improved and efficient delivery of pre-determined outcomes, or as an educational process involving active and critical inquiry into the nature of teaching practices. While there is some capacity for teachers to define the nature of their inquiries, in a climate in which educational policy is increasingly prescribed and dominated by governments, with teachers and educational researchers treated as functionaries of the state rather than members of an intrinsically inquiry-based profession, there is strong pressure to ensure that such inquiries are also in alignment with national educational priorities (Groundwater-Smith and Dadds, 2004). These priorities are often couched in terms of national testing regimes to the extent that what is tested becomes the dominant driving force for PD:

the unswerving central emphasis on CPD as the means of improving standards (i.e., pupil performance) inevitably means that episodes of professional learning tend to be gauged by their potential for impact on pupil achievement. In practice, achievement refers to pupil performance on national tests and, therefore, the emphasis is ever more limited. (Pickering, 2007, p. 197)

Nevertheless, and at the same time, more engaged, proactive and active logics of practice are evident in various educational policies associated with teachers' professional development. The TDA is explicit about the more intrinsic value of professional development activities, including more reflective approaches:

Continuing professional development (CPD) consists of reflective activity designed to improve an individual's attributes, knowledge, understanding and skills. It supports individual needs and improves professional practice. (Training and Development Agency for Schools, 2009b)

Such an articulation of PD moves beyond construing teachers' PD as simply a managerial prerogative, or as a vehicle to address performance management or broader concerns of the state.

Furthermore, the TDA website elaborates the multitude of sources of continuing professional development:

There are many possible sources of CPD . . . Some forms of CPD may encompass elements from more than one of these sources: within school, e.g., induction, coaching and mentoring, lesson observation and feedback, collaborative planning and teaching, shadowing, sharing good practice, whole school development events; school-networks, e.g., cross-school and virtual networks; and other external expertise, e.g., external courses or further study or advice offered by local authorities, FE (Further Education) colleges, universities, subject associations and private providers. (Training and Development Agency for Schools, 2009b)

This variety of potential sources of learning opportunities reflects a more holistic conception of professional development than the generic array of government-sanctioned short-courses typical of the field of PD practices, and reflects a more context-sensitive habitus than that evident in support for more generic approaches to PD.

Similarly, within the GTCE, professional development is construed as an important component of the work of this body, which is responsible for improving such learning: 'We work to . . . improve the quality of teachers' initial training and their access to continuing professional learning and development opportunities' (General Teaching Council for England, 2008). One of the four subheadings which characterises the 'professionalism of teachers in practice' within the *GTCE Statement of Professional Values and Practice* makes explicit mention of teachers' learning and development. More active logics of practice are evident in support for teachers as engaged individuals responsible for their professional development: 'Initial education has prepared them to be effective teachers, and they take responsibility for their continuing professional development' (General Teaching Council for England, 2006, p. 4). While such an approach to PD is in keeping with more neoliberal logics of individualising teachers' work and learning, the proactive way in which teachers are positioned also reflects respect for their agentic potential and capacities. This is also apparent in the way in which teachers are encouraged to improve their work through reflection on their practice: 'They reflect on their own practice, develop their skills, knowledge and expertise, and adapt their teaching appropriately to take account of evidence about effective practice and new technology' (General Teaching Council for England, 2006, p. 4). Simultaneously, teachers are actively framed as collaborative learners seeking to learn from colleagues within and beyond their specific school contexts:

> Teachers make use of opportunities to take part in mentoring and coaching, to evaluate and adapt their own and institutional practice, and to learn with and from colleagues in the wider children's and school workforce. (General Teaching Council for England, 2006, p. 4)

In this way, more collaborative, interactive inquiry logics are evident.

Various 'creativity' policies also provide evidence of alternatives to broad, neoliberal, performative policy logics. These creativity policies were originally designed to increase engagement amongst both students and teachers in a context in which performativity pressures were construed as adversely affecting motivation. These efforts at increasing creativity were first in evidence in the National Advisory Committee on Creative and Cultural Education (1999) policy *All Our Futures: Creativity, Culture and Education*. Subsequent policies and related materials included an Ofsted (Office for Standards in Education, 2003) report, *Expecting the Unexpected: Developing Creativity in Primary and Secondary Schools*, which provided information about good practice related to cultivating creativity in schools, and a joint Department for Education and Skills and Department of Culture, Media and Sport report, *Nurturing Creativity in Young People* (Roberts, 2006), which advocated creativity for its own sake, for economic development, and for improved student learning outcomes. While the emphasis upon identifiable, measurable (quantifiable) targets has led to a challenging of the more intangible 'creative' aspects of teaching—which are so necessary for educational success (Jeffrey and Woods, 2003)—these policies and associated documents do reveal the field of PD practices as influenced by more than just the logics of performativity.

The influence of more progressive logics is also evident in analyses of the *Creative Partnerships* program designed to enhance creativity and enjoyment in education. This program encourages creative teaching approaches across the curriculum, particularly in the most deprived schools, and promotes collaboration between teachers and partners from outside agencies engaged in all aspects of creative education. This initiative does not conform to more top-down policy approaches, but instead focuses upon local needs: '*CP (Creative Partnership)* activities are in many practical senses initiated, managed and interpreted through regional offices, in response to what are presented as contextualised local needs rather than detailed national specifications' (Jones and Thomson, 2008, p. 716). While not a specific, individual PD policy, many of the initiatives and programs associated with *Creative Partnerships* serve as a mechanism for the professional development of the teachers involved. Such is the extent of change encouraged by the *Creative Partnerships* program that Jones and Thomson (2008) have argued that as a result of the initiative, dominant managerial approaches to educational provision occupy 'an increasingly insecure place' (Jones and Thomson, 2008, p. 718).

Such initiatives build out of earlier curriculum and pedagogical related policies, such as *Excellence and Enjoyment: A Strategy for the Primary Years* (Department for Education and Skills, 2003), which were designed to foster creativity amongst teachers and students. A related policy, *Excellence and Enjoyment: Learning and Teaching in the Primary Years* (Department for Education and Skills, 2004), focused specifically on teachers' professional development needs, and was supported by a set of books and videos to be utilised by schools in the context of their specific needs, to encourage both improved student learning outcomes, and the more intrinsic joy of learning. *Excellence and Enjoyment* has been described as both a 'bonus' and 'onus' for schools (Passay and Waite, 2008), with teachers expressing concerns about broader accountability pressures associated with Ofsted inspections, school rankings on league tables developed from the Standard Assessment Tasks (SATs) at ages 7 and 11, limited time to engage in new approaches and the large number of different initiatives to which schools are expected to respond, all of which are seen as quashing innovation. However, more progressive logics are apparent in an evaluation of the program which found the initiative provided a focus on specific teaching and learning problems relevant to teachers' needs, opportunities for teachers to draw upon and inquire into their own experiences and experiment with new ideas, opportunities to determine how to incorporate relevant approaches into teaching practices, and a long-term focus on professional practice (Passay and Waite, 2008).

While remaining critical of the way in which PD is construed in policy, Pickering (2007) also makes the point that much of the PD associated with the GTCE (and National College for School Leadership (NCSL), with its remit to foster enhanced school leadership practices) also: 'appears to try to move away from the delivery, top-down model of the national strategies, and locates CPD in local teacher networks' (p. 196). Again, there is at least some evidence of attempts to engage with alternatives to the information dissemination approaches which influence PD policy and practice.

Recent changes within the newly formed Department for Education, following the 2010 election of the new conservative-led coalition government includes a renewed focus upon teacher learning. Teacher professional development is part of a broader reform agenda aimed at promoting the importance of teaching. Also, there is considerable emphasis upon professional development with arguments that the best school systems provide the conditions to enable teachers' professional development throughout their careers, including opportunities to observe and work with other teachers. However, this process also entails structural changes and what Michael Gove, the Secretary of State for Education describes in the recently released white paper *The Importance of Teaching* as 'rigorous attention to standards' (Department for Education, 2010, p. 7). Furthermore, the push to ensure that teachers 'receive effective professional development throughout their career' (p. 9) also construes this PD as something provided to teachers—essentially a continuation of more passive approaches to teachers' learning. A new national network of Teaching Schools, based on the Teaching Hospitals model will ensure adoption of 'best practice.' The introduction of competitive national scholarship schemes to support PD in teachers' subject knowledge reflect both neoliberal and more economistic logics. What is described as 'the proliferation of teacher standards' is to be reviewed to better 'steer' professional development (p. 25).

Given such mixed messages, and the significant budgetary constraints within which this government's work is framed, it is not unreasonable to expect that teacher PD will continue to characterised by significant tensions between competing logics, that it may be allied even more tightly to pressure to improve economic performance, and/or that it may become marginalised as a 'frill' in difficult times, deemed insufficiently significant to attract funding.

Nevertheless, and in their entirety, these varied conceptions of teacher PD as policy provide evidence of not only more neoliberal, managerial and economistic logics of practice, but also of a more progressive habitus on the part of policy-makers, resulting in advocacy for teachers to take a more active, collaborative role in relation to their learning at their school sites. As in Australia, the field of teacher PD as expressed at the level of policy in England is heavily contested with significant tensions between competing approaches.

Ontario, Canada

As in Australia and England, to understand the competing pressures which characterise the way in which professional development is construed as policy in Canada, it is necessary to locate these practices in context. This peculiar policy history reveals how support for professional development reflects the times in which polices are implemented, and how these have changed over time. However, while national PD policies have been important in Australia and England, provincial policies and policy contexts arguably play a more significant role in PD provision in Canada (Wotherspoon, 2004). Consequently, this section draws upon the way in which professional development has been construed as policy in Ontario, the most populous province with 40 percent of the national population of Canada.

The past two decades have witnessed several phases and shifts in emphasis, and have revealed that the field of PD, as expressed in policy in Ontario, is characterised by considerable tension. These concerns reflect, in large measure, the influence of neoliberal and managerial logics within the province. However, and at the same time, there is also evidence of support for more educational and progressive professional development practices, and education in general. Consequently, the current policy moment contains evidence of tensions between more neoliberal and economistic state-centric logics, and more progressive educational logics.

As in Australia and England, current emphases and interests in education in general, and PD in particular, have emerged out of and been influenced by earlier policy moments. The late 1980s and early 1990s were a period of relative stability for educators in Ontario, and throughout the provinces more generally. School boards were more numerous than at present, and were responsible for much of the professional development which occurred. A more collaborative logic prevailed, as evident in curriculum specialists liaising with teachers in schools to improve teachers' capacity to interpret curriculum documents effectively, and assist teachers in developing beneficial learning experiences for students. Professional development was also typically undertaken by individual teachers attending 'AQ' (Additional Qualifications) courses— province-sanctioned short courses aimed at improving teachers' understandings of a myriad of education-related focus areas. These included courses related to curriculum, management (including behaviour management) and the law. At the same time, individual school boards undertook various short-term PD initiatives over the course of the school year, which were typically allied with particular school board or Ministry objectives (although the latter were relatively scant in comparison with the former).

However, an economic downturn in the mid-1990s within the province (and Canada more generally) led to a significant reduction in public expenditure, including in education. A more economistic logic was evident in the significant reduction of school boards (from 172 to 106 in Ontario alone (Wotherspoon, 2004)) and the drastic cutting of subject consultancy teams which operated at the individual board levels. The profile of professional development in the boards was subsequently reduced within the educational bureaucracy, and the activities of board-based 'curriculum services' branches, within which professional development had previously featured prominently, were severely curtailed.

Just prior to these cuts, in May 1993, the New Democratic Party government (elected in 1990) instigated a Royal Commission into the nature and status of learning in Ontario. Drawing upon 1400 submissions, the royal commission produced a 550-page document, *For the Love of Learning*, to serve as a blueprint for the development of Ontario's educational future (Bégin, Caplan, Bharti, Glaze, DiCecco and Murphy, 1994). The report made a total of 167 recommendations which related to four broad categories of intervention to reform Ontario's elementary and secondary education systems: shared vision to guide the development of Ontario's education system; the nature of the learning experiences or school program which should characterise education in Ontario; accountability of students and teachers; and educational governance issues which need to be addressed to attain this shared vision (Bégin et al., 1994). Amongst other things, the commission argued in favour of improving the quality and status of the teaching profession in Ontario. This included a recommendation to establish a statutory body, at arm's length from the Ministry of Education, which was to serve as a regulatory body responsible for admission to the profession, and for overseeing all elements of practice within the profession. This included responsibility for maintaining a record of teachers' qualifications and ongoing professional development activities.

Reflecting a more educational disposition amongst policy makers, this body would signify the maturity of the profession, as it sought to regulate itself. *For the Love of Learning* also recommended the development of an *Office of Learning Assessment and Accountability* to monitor students' learning outcomes. Mention was made of the need for literacy tests, initially at Years 3 and 11 (Bégin et al., 1994). As a result, the field of PD practices, as expressed in policy, reflected more educational logics of practice, as well as a more accountability-oriented disposition amongst policy-makers.

By the late1990s, however, both the political and economic landscape had changed significantly, with dramatic effects on the nascent education reform agenda at the province level. The election of a new conservative government, the Progressive Conservative Party, led by Michael Harris in 1997, heralded further and substantial reforms. Reflecting an economistic orthodoxy, at the beginning of its mandate, the conservative government passed an omnibus bill, *Bill 160*, which, amongst other things, resulted in the capacity to tax and fund education being shifted from the school board district level to the province level. This was construed by the government as a way to ensure greater accountability over public expenditure, and to minimise administrative costs by centralising revenue raising and expenditure processes (Gidney, 1999). However, at the district level, it was frequently perceived as a mechanism to reduce the autonomy of the individual districts, and had a significant impact upon the specific local programs and initiatives, including those related to PD, which had developed within the individual districts over time. More administrative and accountability logics exerted influence within the field of PD practices, severely curtailing more educational practices.

Economistic logics were also reflected in cuts to the public education budget, resulting in a decrease in teacher preparation time, an increase in classroom contact time, expanded use of non-certified instructors in difficult-to-staff specialty areas, and the amalgamation of school boards. A raft of new, detailed and highly prescriptive curriculum documents was implemented, a 'Teacher Qualifying Test' was legislated for new teachers, and a province-wide performance appraisal system was established. Organisational changes were made at the school level with the introduction of school councils, and principals and vice principals were required to withdraw from the teachers' federations. These changes revealed the dominance of more administrative over more educational logics, with a concomitant 'crisis of habitus[1]' (Zipin and Brennan, 2003, p. 353) amongst the educators affected.

The Harris government adopted many of the reforms suggested by the earlier Royal Commission on learning but within a much more stringent regime of resource accountability, and a climate of distrust between the government and the teaching profession (Gidney, 1999). The recommendation to establish a self-managing college of teachers was one of these initiatives. However, the final Ontario College of Teachers, which initially held out the promise of a self-regulating authority to enhance the status of the profession, including through fostering and facilitating teacher learning, transformed into a more authoritarian body, dominated by government appointees, and became a vehicle for the provincial government to scrutinise and criticise teachers and teaching practices. Again, bureaucratic logics of practice dominated. The currency of accountability was the capital of most value within a field within which more educational practices were under threat from more administrative foci. The result was considerable antipathy towards the new government, distrust of the newly formed College of Teachers, and a sense amongst teachers of being under siege within this new political climate (Bedard and Lawton, 2000). In 1998, the Education Quality and Accountability Office was established—a product of the Royal Commission's recommendations to establish an Office of Learning Assessments and Accountability, but with a much more authoritarian ethos than advocated in *For the Love of Learning*.

More recent government policy statements reveal that it was the way in which the Ontario College of Teachers was implemented, rather than the principles underpinning the initiative, which stymied its potential benefits:

> On paper, the mandate of the College provides for self-regulation. Even though a significant organization has developed around this purpose, several key weaknesses have now become apparent. The College of Teachers can be seen as one of the education reforms of the last several years where a useful goal was harmed by poor implementation. (Ministry of Education, 2004, p. 1)

Within a climate of increased scrutiny of teachers and teaching, the College was perceived as an adversarial institution which was more focused upon sanctions rather than the enhancement of the teaching profession. More bureaucratic logics were reflected in concerns about teacher compliance and conduct, and dominated over the intrinsically educational practices which should have characterised such a body. This situation has since altered, as a majority of positions on the Board have recently been allocated to teachers, and as a new government has sought to rearticulate the role of the College away from one informed by a more regulatory logic towards one of advocacy for the profession.

As in other western settings, PD has also been influenced by the push for a more tightly regulated and prescribed curriculum within Ontario. This has been part of a broader trend towards increased centralisation in response to concerns about national and regional global positioning over the past two decades, and reflective of policy steering for accountability purposes in education provision in Canada more generally (Ben Jaafar and Anderson, 2007). In the Ontario context, pressure to reform the curriculum was in part a reactive response to what was perceived as an inadequate emphasis upon specific content, particularly literacy and numeracy—foci indicative of the continued influence of more accountability-oriented and economistic logics. Such a focus was firstly manifest in literacy and numeracy testing in Ontario at Year Three, and subsequently at Year Six. This testing has since been extended to Year Nine.

Such testing, undertaken through the Education Quality and Accountability Office, has been construed cautiously by individual schools and school boards, and there are concerns about the nature and value of such data, including 'teaching to the test' (Volante, 2004). There are also concerns about how such material has been made publicly available, and used to criticise schools, particularly when results fall below board or provincial averages—a problematic situation given that, by definition, half the schools within any given board or province will fall below this arbitrary bar. The EQAO office itself cautions against extrapolating from EQAO results to classroom and school-related learning more generally:

> Of course, EQAO data are but one factor in determining strategies that can be used to support students' success. Ongoing classroom evaluation is the richest source of information about students' progress. (Jackson, 2009)

> Schools should not be judged on the EQAO data alone. The EQAO results provide a 'snapshot' of how students are achieving at one point in time and do not fully represent the richness and depth of multifaceted schools and their students. (Education Quality and Accountability Office, 2005)

Nevertheless, such results have been utilised as a way of responding to cen- tralised pressures for increased teacher accountability. These accountability logics are expressed in the way in which many school websites highlight the nature of their results in comparison with board or provincial averages, even as the same websites warn against the use of such data alone. Such responses treat these results as valued capitals in and of themselves, feeding into current discourses around the individualisation, privatisation and com- modification of education, and are reflective of how the field of education more broadly has become increasingly influenced by market-oriented pres- sures (Ozga and Lingard, 2007). These figures also serve as a wedge within the schooling community, and typically encourage increased competitiveness between and within schools, a situation which is particularly problematic for those schools which are least able to compete on an uneven playing field. This in turn influences the nature of the PD which becomes possible, and limits the potential collaboration recognised as benefiting teachers' learning (Cochran-Smith and Lytle, 1999; Sachs, 2003; Wilson and Berne, 1999). Those schools whose results fall significantly below provincial benchmarks are subject to increased support and scrutiny in an effort to 'turn-around' these results. Such foci inevitably influence the nature of the PD practices which come to characterise the field, providing evidence of tensions between more profession-oriented and systemic PD practices, and revealing the influ- ence of accountability logics within Canadian educational policy contexts more generally (Ben Jaafar and Anderson, 2007).

Another accountability mechanism explicitly related to issues of pro- fessional development is the *Professional Learning Program*, first imple- mented in 2001. This initiative originally required all teachers to undertake 14 compulsory courses every five years to maintain registration with the Ontario College of Teachers. Seven categories of professional learning were specified in the relevant legislation: curriculum; student assessment; special education; teaching strategies; classroom management and leadership; use of technology; communication with parents and students (Canadian Legal Information Institute, 2009). Managerial logics of practice were evident in the way in which continued registration was tied explicitly to engagement with the compulsory courses. Subsequent managerial practices clashed against teachers' participation in PD, and valuing of PD, for more intrinsic education-oriented purposes, rather than as a means to satisfy registration requirements. The compulsory nature of this initiative caused consternation amongst teachers, and the teachers' federations, who objected to the explicit linking of professional development with registration requirements.

The election of the Liberal government led by Dalton McGuinty in 2003 resulted in a softening of many of the more authoritarian aspects of the previous government's education agenda. Indeed, rather than cultivating a more reactive and at times adversarial position, reflecting the established bureaucratic-managerial habitus of politicians at the time, the McGuinty government sought to promote a more proactive position in relation to educational issues, and more positive relations with the teaching profession. This took the form of substantial funding allocated to education from the beginning of this government's term. More educational logics were evident in the way the McGuinty government provided additional funds to decrease class sizes, and dramatic increases in funding to enhance students' literacy and numeracy outcomes. This emphasis upon literacy and numeracy was evident in the establishment of a separate body—the Literacy and Numeracy Secretariat—within the Ministry of Education, answerable directly to the Deputy Minister. Additional resources were also provided to assist schools which consistently performed well below state-endorsed benchmarks, and significant resources and additional staff were made available to these schools to assist them in improving students' learning outcomes (Fullan, 2007).

For the self-styled 'Education Premier,' these goals and aims have particular resonance, and are reflected in a desire to allocate resources to education above other areas in the provincial budget (cf. the 1997 British Labor government's mantra of 'education, education, education'). Indeed, McGuinty is attributed as claiming that 'if given the choice of spending my next dollar on health or on education, I will choose education every time' (cited in Fullan, 2007, p. 255). Consequently, the attainment of these goals has significant political cache, representing valued political capital within the broader educational field as expressed in Ontario at the moment.

However, there have also been criticisms that the allocation of resources has been too selective, and that the government's target of achieving 75 percent of students at 'level 3' or above (the benchmark defined as indicative of a satisfactory level of achievement for any given curriculum outcome), has driven the way in which resources are allocated in education in the province. That is, even as more educational dispositions appear to have influenced administrative decision-making, more bureaucratic and managerial logics continue to exert influence, and are constitutive of a more administrative habitus, even if not always recognised (explicitly/publicly) as such. The Literacy and Numeracy Secretariat itself may be understood as the product of tensions between both educational and more managerial dispositions of politicians, educators and bureaucrats involved in its development. Hargreaves and Fink (2006) argue that externally imposed targets, such as the 75 percent figure flagged in Ontario, result in superficial compliance rather than deep engagement on the part of educators. For these educators, more managerial logics are seen as dominating over more educational dispositions and proclivities, including in relation to teachers' PD. However, for Michael Fullan (2007), who has been intimately involved in educational policy development in Ontario through his appointment as special education advisor to the Premier during this period, buy-in occurs for educators in the way they negotiate how they will improve upon existing literacy and numeracy outcomes. These tensions reveal that more educational dispositions are seen as influencing, (and having the potential to influence), the field of PD practices even as more managerial logics simultaneously have an impact.

. An overview of the Ontario Literacy and Numeracy Strategy provides some insights into the nature of potential teacher learning opportunities. In broad terms, Fullan (2007) describes the Ontario Literacy and Numeracy Strategy as involving eight components:

1. Establishing a guiding coalition [of stakeholders] to be constantly in communication;
2. Developing peace and stability with labor unions and addressing other 'distractors' [to ensure a sustained focus on improving student learning rather than industrial issues, etc.];
3. Creating a Literacy and Numeracy Secretariat;
4. Negotiating aspirational targets [involving educators setting ongoing targets to reach a province-wide benchmark of 75 percent of 12-year-olds attaining province-set standards];
5. Building capacity in relation to the targets;
6. Growing the financial investment [through investing substantially in education, and using previous successes to justify further increases in expenditure];
7. Evolving positive pressure [involving providing additional resources and assistance as a vehicle to effect improvements];
8. Connecting the dots with key complementary components [involving addressing issues of literacy and numeracy in elementary schools, but also high school reform, leadership, teacher education and intervention in the early childhood years]. (adapted from p. 247–248)

Of these different components, the issue of capacity building relates most overtly to teacher PD. This entails the provision of ongoing PD associated with how different districts and schools within districts have engaged with the reform agenda, learning from specific case studies of districts which have effective change strategies, and which are achieving improved results, and focusing on assessment literacy (Fullan, 2007, p. 252–253). While there is also a focus upon and support for PD during summers and evenings—shorter term initiatives which seem to imply the need to 'cover' valued information or knowledge (in this case, in relation to provincial conceptions of literacy and numeracy)—there is also an emphasis upon supporting teachers to collaborate with one another in teams, and to consider how the learning they experience relates to their specific school settings. In this way, more progressive educational and managerial logics seem to be evident concurrently, reflecting the intrinsically contested nature of PD practices.

Other evidence of the influence of more educational PD logics include a renewed focus upon new members to the profession, with the development of the *New Teacher Induction Program* policy within the province. This initiative is specifically designed to assist teachers within the first two years of employment within school boards (Ministry of Education, 2009a). There is also interest in the post-schooling outcomes for secondary students. The *Student Success/Learning to 18* strategy focuses upon reforming secondary schooling with a view to increasing retention rates in secondary schools, and ensuring that schools are more responsive to the particular needs of their students, rather than simply focusing upon implementation of the academic curriculum (Ministry of Education, 2009b).

Such policies and programs have emerged from earlier efforts by the McGuinty government to broaden conceptions of teacher PD beyond typical workshop approaches through overtly supporting teachers in taking their local contexts into account, and orchestrating their own professional development. This was evident in the Ontario Ministry of Education's (2004) *Teacher Excellence—Unlocking Student Potential through Continuing Professional Development* discussion paper. This paper was the fifth in a series of discussion papers designed to encourage educators' participation in the decision-making surrounding education in the province more generally. It overtly rejected the former government's prescriptive *Professional Learning Program*, which was seen as narrowing the PD deemed legitimate. Instead, it supported more context specific professional development practices which also took teachers' needs into account:

> Our outlook is for policies that will see as many teachers as possible engaged in professional development, appropriate to their daily challenges and the stage of their career, by streamlining and making better sense of existing processes. (Ministry of Education, 2004, p.2)

Schools and school boards/districts were required to record the nature and amount of professional development undertaken by teachers in schools, and teachers encouraged to maintain a portfolio outlining their learning achievements. A site specific disposition amongst policy-makers was evident in the emphasis upon teachers' actual teaching practices: 'We would like to see existing teacher development programs, like annual learning plans, professional development days and additional qualifications, harmonized and made relevant to the challenges that teachers face at the schools where they work' (Ministry of Education, 2004, p. 4). Furthermore, concerns were expressed about existing accountability mechanisms as being too draconian, and there was a perception that teachers needed to be provided with the opportunity to improve, rather than simply being sanctioned through unrealisable timelines:

> The current system is so structured in timelines, requiring improvements in 60 school days, as to almost preclude real development for teachers who need to address problems. While it is important to have some means of dealing with the small number who cannot reach

standards, the first priority should be on helping teachers meet standards and succeed. (Ministry of Education, 2004, p. 5)

In this way, more managerial logics of practice seemed to have been challenged by a policy-making disposition informed by more progressive educational logics. This was further evident in the way informal learning opportunities were openly acknowledged as valuable in terms of students' learning:

A great deal of valuable professional development is gained from informal activities such as: improving personal technology skills; academic programs; participating in subject associations and curriculum development; federation seminars and workshops; applied research; collaborating with other teachers; collaborating with outside organizations; and extracurricular activities. (Ministry of Education, 2004, p. 6)

The policy-making disposition at play was not one dominated by concerns to ensure teachers were engaged primarily in state-sanctioned learning initiatives but was instead influenced by broader logics which construed teachers' learning as an always unfolding activity which cannot be readily limited or measured. Concerns about students-at-risk in secondary schooling contexts in this policy also reflected concerns beyond simply economistic foci.

At the same time, however, and reflecting the broader neoliberal and economistic context in which it was located, the *Teacher Excellence—Unlocking Student Potential through Continuing Professional Development* discussion paper also construed PD simultaneously as a mechanism for skill development and as something to be provided to teachers. More economistic logics were belied by the way in which the provincial government referred to the teaching 'workforce,' and that it was responsible for ensuring adequate skill levels amongst this workforce: 'The McGuinty government accepts the responsibility to ensure that Ontario has a highly skilled and highly motivated workforce in our schools' (Ministry of Education, 2004, p.1). More technicist PD logics were also evident in the way in which PD was described in relation to an increase in the number of 'lead teachers' in elementary/primary literacy and numeracy from 8,000 to 16,000 teachers. The professional learning of these lead teachers was framed within dominant logics of PD practice as something provided to teachers, rather than something to be cultivated through their own practice: 'These teachers will be exposed to the best practices and most effective techniques' (Ministry of Education, 2004, p. 2). Relatedly, concerns about high attrition rates amongst new teachers were not only construed as problematic in terms of lost potential, but also in relation to the economic costs to governments:

The 20 to 30 percent of new teachers exiting the profession with less than three years represent not only a very significant lost potential, but also a financial cost to government of $21 million for every year that was spent on faculty subsidies, and another $14 million annually from wasted recruitment and hiring costs. (Ministry of Education, 2004, p. 3)

The embodied capitals accrued as a result of the learning of these teachers were no longer available within the field, and could not be converted to economic capital beyond the field (i.e., the economic field/field of work). Similarly, the decision to increase the number of professional development/activity days was also construed in economic, as well as educational, terms: 'each PD day represents $41 million in cost to the system and, of course, inconvenience to students and parents' (Ministry of Education, 2004, p. 6). In this way, more economistic logics were readily evident, and encouraged practices which competed alongside more intrinsically educational practices.

An updated *Professional Learning Framework* for the teaching profession, issued in 2006, reflects similar tensions between more progressive and accountability-oriented logics. The *Framework* is outlined in the current *Foundations of Professional Practice* policy document released by the OCT, which also describes the ethical standards and standards of practice for the teaching profession (Ontario College of Teachers, 2006). Contestation between more prescriptive and other approaches to PD is outlined in the initial sections of the *Framework* which differentiates between 'accredited' and 'other' PD options:

> This framework identifies accredited pre-service and in-service programs of professional teacher education designed to reflect the ethical standards and standards of practice as well as a wide range of other opportunities for professional growth and development. (Ontario College of Teachers, 2006, p. 5)

More bureaucratic and potentially restrictive administrative logics are partially evident in the way ongoing professional learning is seen as an important vehicle for realising the ethical standards and standards of practice for teaching prescribed by the OCT:

> The ethical standards, the standards of practice and the professional learning framework are interconnected. Their overarching purpose is to guide College members in their practice so they can more readily enhance student learning. (Ontario College of Teachers, 2006, p. 27)

More administrative logics are at least partially evident in how explicit mention is made of the courses and programs which teachers can undertake and which are formally recognised by the College to satisfy these standards, as outlined in Regulation 184/97, Teachers Qualifications, under the *Ontario College of Teachers Act* (Ontario College of Teachers, 2006, p.

22). Only those programs which are supportive of the standards of practice and ethical standards attract formal accreditation by the College.

However, importantly, the standards are described as not being designed for the performance appraisal of individual teachers, which is the responsibility of employing authorities (Ontario College of Teachers, 2006, p. 5). Also, information about the standards is indicative of a progressive policy-making disposition supportive of teachers engaging in learning communities, being involved in ongoing self-directed professional learning, critiquing their own experiences, collaborating with colleagues and researchers (Ontario College of Teachers, 2006, p. 13). Explicit mention is also made of the need for teachers to be involved in a process of continuous inquiry, reflection and discussion with colleagues (Ontario College of Teachers, 2006, p. 13). Such foci represent a challenge to more economistic and bureaucratic logics which make it difficult to foster more active learning on the part of teachers, and which encourage reductionist and regulatory approaches to standards.

Evidence of the influence of more expansive educational logics is apparent in how the updated *Framework* is also supportive of learning initiated and reviewed by teachers on an ongoing basis, and of teachers taking both individual and collective responsibility for their teaching practices. Individuals' careers and personal growth are recognised as needing to be taken into account, and activities promoted which are 'varied, flexible and accessible to members of the College' (Ontario College of Teachers, 2006, p. 23). The *Framework* outlines a variety of opportunities for professional growth and development which include involvement in formal academic programs, research activities, professional networks, professional conferences, workshops, publications, mentoring and networking, maintaining professional portfolios, reading educational books and journals, learning through practice (such as developing and implementing curriculum materials, engaging in school-based inquiry or piloting new initiatives) and engaging in technology-related learning initiatives. As well as supporting a diverse array of possible modes and content of professional development, the way in which the Framework does not foreclose other possibilities reflects a policy-making disposition inclusive of as wide a variety of initiatives as possible. Professional development is valued in its many and varied manifestations, and active endorsement of this plethora of options indicates how more educative logics have influenced the field of teacher PD.

Finally, conflicting logics of practice in relation to PD as policy are also evident in how the Ontario College of Teachers' five standards of professional practice are represented, as indicated in its recently released policy *The Standards of Practice for the Teaching Profession*. The last of these standards relates specifically to teachers' learning:

1. Commitment to students and student learning
2. Professional knowledge
3. Professional practice

4. Leadership in learning communities
5. Ongoing professional learning

(Ontario College of Teachers, 2009)

The final standard encourages teachers to reflect upon their own experiences, to engage in research into their practice and other forms of research, to construct knowledge relevant to their own experiences, and to collaborate with colleagues and others in relation to their practice. Unlike previous prescriptive approaches to PD, such as the original *Professional Learning Program*, there is no formal schedule of professional development activities which teachers must complete to maintain registration. In these ways, this articulation of professional learning reflects a more progressive, educationally oriented disposition amongst policy-makers. At the same time, the strong emphasis upon an extensive array of short-term AQ (Additional Qualification) courses—which range across a plethora of topics associated with schools and schooling—challenges more long-term and sustained approaches on the part of teachers, at specific schooling sites. These short courses are typically undertaken during summer or other holiday breaks, and are considered beneficial for promotion purposes. While such courses may indeed be beneficial, a strong history and ongoing advocacy for such courses in Ontario may also make it difficult for alternative, more context-specific approaches to gain sufficient traction within the field to disrupt more orthodox approaches.

Consequently, PD practices supported in policy in Ontario reflect tensions between broader accountability, neoliberal and economistic logics of practice, and more progressive, localised logics. On the one hand, significant additional resources have been distributed throughout the system, with some emphasis upon more progressive and inclusive educational practices, indicative of the influence of a more genuinely educational habitus amongst policy-makers and decision-makers in Ontario. On the other hand, the strong focus upon ensuring that this resourcing will result in tangible, typically quantifiable educational outcomes simultaneously reflects the influence of more managerial and bureaucratic logics.

CONCLUSION: THE COMPLEXITY OF PD POLICY PRACTICES IN AND ACROSS NATIONAL CONTEXTS

There are clear resonances across the Australian, English and Ontario policy and political contexts, as manifest in teachers' professional development. Neoliberal, managerial and economistic pressures have exerted influence, and, in many ways, have had a homogenising effect upon PD content and processes advocated at the policy level in each of these countries. This has occurred both incrementally, over the past two decades, as well as more disjunctively, in response to significant, individual policies and policy ensembles. The prescriptive policy positions of the English Teacher Training Authority, the Ontario College of Teachers and the Australian Government through the *Quality Teacher Programme*, for example, all reflect a degree of convergence around issues of PD content deemed of most value, and considerable advocacy for traditional modes of delivery which construe teachers as being in deficit. Similarly, advocacy for more reductionist conceptions of teaching standards across national settings also have the effect of homogenising PD practices considered acceptable. Much of the PD which is supported in each national setting is seen as aligned with relatively narrow conceptions of economic development.

However, at the same time, there is also evidence of how more progressive, educational logics of practice are able to exist alongside and perhaps challenge these more managerial and economistic logics. As a result, relevant national and provincial policies also serve as vernacular responses—a form of 'grassroots globalization' (Appadurai, 2001)—to homogenised iterations of economic globalization and managerialism in educational policy settings (Ball, 1998; Ozga and Lingard, 2007). This occurs differently in different contexts, but there are also important resonances across national contexts in relation to how these more educative logics play out within the field of teacher professional development. While some policies reflect a compliant disposition on the part of policy-makers who seem to acquiesce to dominant neoliberal and economistic paradigms, and resist more activist approaches on behalf of teachers (Sachs, 2003), the tensions within and between policy documents infer a somewhat conflicted habitus on the part of those involved in their production. Indeed, individual policies may be described as simultaneously conservative, progressive, student-focused, teacher-focused, inquiry-based as well as supportive of more deficit-oriented approaches to teachers' learning.

The *Quality Teacher Programme* policy ensemble certainly reflects an emphasis upon specific modes of PD practice, and content deemed most valuable within a broader neoliberal national and international context. Similarly, the Ontario *Professional Learning Framework*, for example, seems to be influenced by a desire to foster teacher learning focused on a conservative desire to provide various Additional Qualifications through short-term, summer courses and workshops at other times throughout the school year. The policy position of the English Training and Development Agency for Schools is similarly influenced by conservative logics of practice. The very name of the body, melding both 'training' and 'development,' intimates a somewhat hybridised habitus on the part of those associated with it. The focus upon teacher learning as training serves as a default position in relation to teachers' learning, and is in tension with the more ongoing continuous learning implied by the notion of development. These similarities across national contexts also confirm how nation-states are affected by global flows of information (Henry et al., 2001). More individualistic logics of practice (Harvey, 2005) are evident in the way teachers are treated as individuals within broader accountability regimes, and are expected to respond proactively within a context heavily influenced by standardised testing regimes, the development of league tables (whether formally or informally), and an emphasis upon economistic conceptions of PD.

This, however, is clearly not the full story. At the same time, there is also policy support for more intrinsically valuable PD approaches focused upon improving educators' teaching practices in the contexts of their everyday schooling practices, and evidence of more progressive logics in general. The earlier Australian *National Schools Network* and *Innovative Links* projects indicate the influence of collaborative logics. The *Quality Teacher Programme* policy ensemble continued this work by supporting active, collaborative teacher involvement, and the current *Smarter Schools National Partnerships* program holds out the hope of continuing this legacy. Later iterations of the *QTP* encouraged more systemic teacher learning across a much more diverse range of discipline areas—beyond a focus upon literacy and numeracy. The logics of practice of PD as policy are also reflected in policy-makers' support for context-specific learning. Consequently, teachers are not simply treated as consuming citizens (Peters and McDonagh, 2007) or citizen-consumers (Clarke et al., 2007) as occurs when teachers' roles are limited to receiving and responding to external prescriptions. The later iteration of the Ontario *Professional Learning Framework* (Ontario College of Teachers, 2006), while operating within a broader context strongly focused on PD related specifically to literacy and numeracy, is similarly simultaneously supportive of learning focused on other subject areas, teachers' specific needs, and school-wide foci. This policy is much more progressive and represents a significant disjuncture with the earlier *Professional Learning Framework* issued during the Harris administration. Endorsement of reflective activity within the TDA's description of continuing professional development complements the General Teaching Council for England's advocacy of PD which is collaborative, site-based and ongoing. Across these programs and policies, there is evidence of collaborative PD logics in the form of inter and intra-school learning communities, as well as broader networks and associations. In these ways, a process of vernacular globalization of educational policy-making (Lingard, 2000) is evident as educators seek to make sense of broader global processes *in situ*.

Finally, even as there is clearly significant evidence of broad patterns of similarities between different national contexts, it is important not to ignore or downplay the differences which must necessarily exist in relation to how policy-makers appear to have responded to broader neoliberal, managerial and economistic logics in different national settings. While there are significant similarities between the approaches adopted to generate and collect nation/province-wide standardised data on students' literacy and numeracy in England and Ontario, for example, as Fullan (2007) argues there are also important differences between the approaches adopted in the two settings. The English seem, perhaps, to be more 'fixated on targets' (Fullan,

2007, p. 247) to a greater extent than is the case in Ontario. Also, the English Office for Standards in Education seems to have taken a more punitive approach by publicly 'naming and shaming' failing schools, and moving to immediately instigate intervention measures (although this situation has ameliorated considerably since Ofsted inspections first began); such measures invariably influence what is considered possible or desirable PD by policy-makers. Finally, teaching practices seem to be specified much more overtly in the English setting, which also has a much more prescriptive curriculum than is the case in Ontario. More conservative logics do appear to have been disrupted quite abruptly since the Harris administration, resulting in advocacy for a wider range of PD content and processes. Arguably, the approach to teacher professional development in Australia lies somewhere between what appears to be a more regimented English educational system, and a relatively resource-rich approach to PD in Ontario which, while clearly influenced by broader neoliberal, managerial and economistic logics, seems to have responded to these pressures more flexibly, and progressively. However, the Ontario example also reveals why history matters in specific national/sub-national settings; arguably, the more progressive PD logics currently reflected in relevant Ontario policies are a correction to hyper-neoliberal and managerial logics which led to PD being treated as little more than an individual responsibility of teachers, and a cost to the state, under the Harris administration.

While all aspects of education are broadly influenced by neoliberal, managerial and economistic logics, an investigation of actual PD policies, and the associated politics surrounding their development in specific contexts, suggests a much more convoluted, complex, sometimes complementary, sometimes contradictory set of associations between broader, global processes and local settings. The multifaceted foci and modes of learning in policy reveal the influence of, and support for, more genuinely educative, localised and progressive practices, alongside more reductionist, economically focused conceptions of globalization. Simultaneous support for these sometimes contradictory practices gestures towards the multiple logics which inform PD policy production within the wider field of teacher PD. This complex politics of contestation between competing logics of practice helps to make sense of why PD as policy is so complex, and why it is characterised by significant and ongoing tensions.

3 Professional Development as Research
From Process to Product?

The gap between aspiration and practice is a real and frustrating one. The gap can be closed only by adopting a research and development approach to one's own teaching, whether alone or in a group of co-operating teachers. (Stenhouse, 1975, p. 3)

When we create binaries where one body engages in the design of professional development and another is developed, where one group has power and agency and the other is positioned as merely a functionary; where one group is seen as engaging in intellectual labour and the other practical activity, then contributing to authentic professional learning is unlikely at best, and strongly resisted at worst. (Groundwater-Smith and Campbell, 2010, p. 201)

INTRODUCTION

Teacher professional development is sometimes characterised by teachers researching their own practice. The 'teacher-as-researcher,' action research and teacher-research movements all construe teachers as not simply passive 'consumers' but also active 'creators' of knowledge about their own work and learning. The logics of practice which characterise support for such approaches reveal a more democratic conception of, and relationship to, the research process. This more democratic disposition is reflected in support for teachers as interested and engaged participants in learning about their own practice, and involved in sharing insights about practice within and beyond their local sites. Within such conceptions, research is not only *about* professional development; research *is* professional development. Under these circumstances, a research orientation to learning becomes an embodied capital valued for its capacity to improve classroom practice. Such site-based research may result in changed classroom and schooling practices. This research may be reported in the form of local reports and journals on teachers' practice, as articles in teaching journals, or in the form of more traditional academic referred journals and monographs.

However, recently, there has been a stronger focus upon more traditional conceptions of research—as a product to inform practice, rather than as a process constitutive of part of teachers' practice. Debates around 'evidence-based practice' are the most significant manifestation of this push to encourage teachers to inform their practice by reviewing relevant research undertaken by others. Furthermore, the outsourcing of educational research—part of what Ball (2009, p. 89) refers to as 'the export of "statework" to private providers and "agencies"' as part of a broader privatisation process of educational policy and education more generally—limits the capacity of other forms of research, such as teacher research, to be accepted as legitimate. Alongside these processes, the immediacy of schooling settings, the limitations of resources for teachers' professional development and the entrenchment of more passive, dissemination-oriented PD practices also ensure the dominance of more conventional approaches to PD. These more traditional approaches are typically aligned with conceptions of educational research as something done by 'experts' in the academy, and 'delivered' to teachers in schools. That is, at times, the logics of practice of teacher PD are not characterised by research by teachers as a legitimate part of the field of teachers' professional development. (Chapter 4 of this volume explores these issues in more detail in relation to PD as part of teachers' work.) Rather, teacher PD practices are construed as involving learning *about* research. This leads to considerable tensions between advocates of research as a product, and research as a process.

This chapter draws upon literature on research *into*, and research *as*, teacher professional development to reveal the tensions between these conflicting perspectives. That is, the chapter reveals how teacher professional development is both a product of research, as well as a research process designed to inform teachers' practices. Much of the literature on research into PD practices is prescriptive, often outlining how academic or consulting researchers believe professional development should be undertaken by those constructed as its objects/subjects. In contrast, the literature pertaining to research as PD is often more descriptive of the nature of teachers' efforts to improve their teaching by inquiring into some aspect of their work in specific settings, and reflective of a more democratic disposition on the part of its proponents. This chapter seeks to reveal the complexity and tensions between these two broad approaches to PD. The chapter also provides some glimpses into how recent trends in the university sector have led to an increased focus upon the provision of professional development to teachers, rather than encouraging teachers to be researchers of their own practice. In its entirety, the chapter provides insights into the logics of practice which characterise professional development as educational research, and reveals the contestation which attends varying research practices.

TEACHER PD AS A RESEARCH PROCESS

While different practices have been emphasised at different moments, many researchers of teacher professional development argue in favour of teacher learning which is inquiry-oriented, ongoing and undertaken within specific contexts. In contrast to the considerable contestation at the pre-service level (Cochran-Smith, 2000; Darling-Hammond, 2000; Goodlad, 1990; 2002), Hawley and Valli (1999) speak of 'a new consensus' (p. 128) about the processes which constitute effective, change-oriented, teacher learning provision for practising teachers. Such a perspective demands that teachers in schools need to become 'serious learners' (Ball and Cohen, 1999, p. 4).

The logic of this consensus around effective teacher PD reveals a more democratic, context-responsive disposition on the part of advocates which opposes the individual, decontextualised workshop-approach typically adopted in schooling settings. The 'new doxa' of professional development practices encouraged is one which values PD which is collaborative, ongoing, site-based and focused upon inquiry into student learning (Hawley and Valli, 1999). In this vein, McLaughlin and Oberman (1996) refer to the need to reconceptualise the provision of teachers' learning, within an era of reform by moving from the 'program' approach of 'how-tos' and 'shoulds,' delivered by experts, after school or on weekends to a new approach which encourages habits of critical inquiry and deeper understanding on the part of students (p. x). Day (1999) points out how informal mechanisms for learning far outweigh formal mechanisms, and are heavily weighted towards the goals of teachers' work: 'a learner-focused perspective is much more important than a training-focused perspective' (p. 3). Such broad principles may be attained by engaging in a variety of practices, including by participating in professional development schools (Darling-Hammond, 1994), developing teacher portfolios (Retallick and Groundwater-Smith, 1999), supervising student teachers, inquiring in collaboration with other teachers (Cochran-Smith and Lytle, 1999a), analysing professional standards (Ingvarson, 1998; Mayer, Mitchell, McDonald and Bell, 2005), engaging in a community of learners at the workplace (Stoll, Bolam, McMahon, Wallace and Thomas, 2006), engaging in other forms of loosely termed 'teacher research' (Cochran-Smith and Lytle, 1999b) and adopting a 'researchly' disposition more generally (Lingard and Renshaw, 2009). There has also been a push for teachers to conduct research into the nature of student work as a mechanism for learning, although this is also influenced by broader, accountability-based, policy pressures to do so (Little, 2004).

This more active and activist disposition is similarly reflected in support for forms of teacher leadership. In their overview of the factors necessary for encouraging teacher leadership capacity for school improvement, Harris and Muijs (2005) advocate increased teacher involvement via multiple learning-related practices. A leading teacher habitus is characterised by a focus upon collaboration, partnerships, teacher and pupil leadership, a focus upon teaching and learning, and broad-based commitment on the part of teachers:

- It is important to foster *deep collaboration* and not superficial cooperation among the teaching staff;
- It is important to form *partnerships* within schools and to network with other schools and agencies;
- It is important to generate *teacher leadership and pupil leadership*;

- It is important to allocate time for personal reflection and opportunities for teachers to talk together about *teaching and learning*;
- It is important to generate the *collective capability*, expertise and commitment of teachers to ensure that all teachers are involved. (Harris and Muijs, 2005, p. 59; emphasis original)

Collaboration, networking, reflection, active involvement and commitment are flagged as essential for improving teacher and student learning.

While much of the literature advocating a consensus around PD is prescriptive in nature, some is based upon empirical research. Desimone (2009) draws upon multiple empirical studies to describe a 'research consensus' (p. 181) around studies of the impact of professional development on student learning. Desimone (2009) argues there is sufficient evidence within studies of the impact of PD—both qualitative and quantitative—to identify a consensus around key features or characteristics of the types of PD found to improve student learning outcomes, and which should therefore be promulgated. While acknowledging the difficulty of identifying direct causal evidence and links between PD and student outcomes (Guskey, 2000; 2002), and that there is insufficient evidence to identify categorically those features of PD which effect student learning (Wayne, Yoon, Zhu, Cronen and Garet, 2008), Desimone (2009) nevertheless suggests a 'core conceptual framework' (p. 183–184) which she describes as including five essential features: a focus upon subject matter content and how students learn this content; active learning, rather than passively listening to others; coherence between teachers' beliefs and PD, and between PD and broader school/district/state reforms; sufficient duration, including over both the time period in which PD is undertaken and the total amount of time involved; and collective participation, across a school, grade or department. These features lead to increased teacher knowledge and skills, and changes in attitudes and beliefs, resulting in changed instruction, and subsequent improved student learning.

In a similar vein, Adey (2004) draws upon multiple empirical accounts undertaken over his career researching professional development in England to argue that effective PD is not simple, has to be actively orchestrated rather than imposed, needs to be based upon actual teaching practices, and be undertaken in the knowledge that improvements are uncertain and occur over the long-term:

1. There is no such thing as a teacher-proof curriculum . . .
2. Change cannot be imposed. Teachers must be brought into the process of change as partners . . .
3. In-class coaching is essential. . . . coaching can take many forms, including demonstration lessons, classic observation-plus-feedback, team teaching, peer-coaching, and video-based feedback . . .
4. Change is slow, uncertain, and has many backward steps as well as forward ones. (pp. 15, 16)

Developed from the findings of several research projects into cognitive acceleration in science education in England, these findings imply a research disposition characterised by support for the participation of teachers in their own learning, engagement with everyday teaching practices through a variety of fora, and a patient, long-term approach to teachers' learning.

Reflective Practice and Workplace Learning

More recent efforts to promote active teacher PD practices and PD as a research process have often built upon, or been informed by, earlier work by influential educational researchers. Writing in the 1970s, Lawrence Stenhouse (1975) argued both the self-perception and conditions of work under which teachers laboured needed to change to enable much more active engagement on the part of educators in teaching and learning. In what he described as the 'curricular problem,' which he broadly conceived of as the practice of teaching, Stenhouse argued that teachers needed to take an active role in reflecting upon their practice in order to better inform this practice:

> I have argued, however, that the uniqueness of each classroom setting implies that any proposal—even at school level—needs to be tested and verified and adapted by each teacher in his [sic] own classroom. The ideal is that the curricular specification should feed a teacher's personal research and development programme through which he is progressively increasing his understanding of his own work and hence bettering his teaching . . .
>
> It is not enough that teachers' work should be studied: they need to study it themselves. (Stenhouse, 1975, p. 143)

Such an inclusive, inquiry-based disposition amongst researchers, supportive of a focus upon teachers' own practice, is also evident in earlier trends advocating the need for professionals to become more 'reflective practitioners' (Schön, 1983; 1987). This trend recognised that professionals make complex decisions *in situ*. This led to a push to foreground this context-specific knowledge as an important means of better understanding how complex decisions are made. Much of this earlier work emphasised the role of the individual professional in his/her own learning; the consequence of this was that teacher learning was often conceptualised as an individual rather than a collective endeavour.

Osterman and Kottkamp (2004) have framed their conception of reflective practice as a means of responding to failed efforts at school reform. For these authors, change at the organisational level also begins with the individual. Drawing upon earlier theorists of action, particularly Argyris and Schön (1974), Osterman and Kottkamp (2004) have argued for an approach to professional development which takes into account educators' espoused theories as well as their theories-in-use. It is the process of bringing the latter to light, rather than allowing them to remain uninterrogated, which informs reflective practice. Deep acculturation into particular practices influences educators' actions because of the long apprenticeship of schooling which they have experienced. Reflective practice is described as giving access to the everyday assumptions implicit in practice, foregrounding what is typically taken for granted, and thereby potentially enabling change in practice. Reflective practice involves articulating the taken-for-granted assumptions which frame everyday actions. Personal and/or organizational practices are foregrounded in an effort to alter entrenched practices. This frames the teacher as an active constructer of one's own knowledge, rather than as a passive recipient of other people's knowledge—the characteristic feature of more traditional, and typical, approaches to professional development.

To be most effective, this reflective practice is considered best undertaken within the context of teachers' everyday practices. Sparks and Hirsh (1997) refer to such site-specific learning as 'job-embedded.' Such learning is focused upon the particular contexts in which teachers work, and oriented towards addressing substantive challenges and concerns which occur within these contexts. In arguing for reflective practice as part of job-embedded learning, Sparks and Hirsh (1997) draw upon three cases of such learning in the United States—the San Diego Unified School District in California, Tucson Unified School District in Arizona, and the Carrollton Farmers Branch Independent School District in Texas. In the San Diego Unified School District, there was strong advocacy for five sets of practices to support job-embedded learning. These included colloquia, symposia, cadres of teacher leaders, a 'Common Ground Town Meeting,' and governance issues. Colloquia referred to gatherings of scholars who met to work with teachers on specific issues deemed important within schools or clusters of schools. Symposia involved staff meeting to determine how to make time available to engage in ongoing staff development. Cadres of teacher leaders received specialised training in group-work, how to facilitate learning, action research and implementing change. A 'Common Ground Town Meeting' involved developing common understandings about teaching and learning, and an overall vision to guide the work of job-embedded learning within the district. Finally, there was support for reconsideration of the district's professional development governance structures to assist in the facilitation of these other initiatives.

Support for job-embedded learning was also evident in efforts to facilitate ongoing, school-based learning in the Tucson Unified School District. This was apparent in the way in which a cadre of teachers had been developed to facilitate ongoing, school-based learning. Part of the role of this group was to assist school leadership teams to understand the qualities of high quality professional development, and how teacher learning could be utilised constructively to facilitate positive change within schools.

Within the Carrollton Farmers Branch Independent School District in Texas, cognitive coaching, an approach designed to foster teacher reflection, was introduced in place of the traditional teacher evaluation system. This initiative involved initial in-service into the process of cognitive coaching at the system level to assist teachers to improve their own metacognition skills, and as a precursor to cultivating such skills amongst their students. The program was then implemented at the school level, and involved teachers selecting a mentor/'coach,' and working with that person over a year to meet goals associated with professional competency standards established by the Texas Education Agency. A challenge to more traditional PD approaches was evident in the way this initiative involved regular meetings for a period of three years after the initial training. Collectively, advocacy for such approaches reflect a more democratic intervention and disposition within the field of PD practices.

Similarly, in their study of work-based learning, Almas and Krumsvik (2007) draw upon research into applications of ICTs in secondary school settings to reveal evidence of teachers' efforts to inquire into their own school-based practices. A more inquiry-oriented approach amongst teachers was evident in the active way digitally literate teachers in 'leading edge' schools—upper secondary schools which have been working systematically on integrating ICTs into classroom teaching and learning—engaged with policy demands for increased engagement in digital literacies across the curriculum. While initial insights into the nature and uses of ICTs may be elicited from external workshops, Almas and Krumsvik's (2007) research reveals ongoing collaborative work with colleagues in schools was seen as necessary for pedagogical knowledge about ICTs to become an integral part of practice. To be successful, adequate resourcing, leadership and the ascription of high status to digital learning were also seen as necessary for such initiatives to be successful.

A workplace-oriented disposition is also evident in Jones and Moreland's (2006) insights into how school-wide reform can be achieved via PD. Jones and Moreland (2006) drew upon an example of a school which implemented a model of pedagogical content knowledge in the area of science and technology education and how through professional development, improvements in teaching and learning were achieved in this subject area, as well as learning and assessment in other curriculum areas. An emphasis upon subject knowledge, knowledge of students, and knowledge of teaching approaches within the school informed teachers' learning. At the same time, sustained engagement in educational reform was also dependent upon the capacity for risk-taking within the school, the strategic choice of teachers involved in the project initially, and the way in which university-based researchers collaborated with teachers on common problems.

Drawing upon multiple case studies, Zepeda's (1999) support for approaches to teachers' learning which account for how adults learn best also reflects a more democratic disposition on the part of some researchers.

Trust is considered essential in situations of shared practice as participants shift from positions of the known to the unknown—a process which may engender considerable discomfort. This includes trusting both oneself—in terms of being open and honest, and being prepared to make mistakes and try again—trust in others, and trust in the process involved in participating as a member of a planning team endeavouring to improve teachers' practices. A safe environment in which people feel they can share ideas and criticism freely are described as essential. A quality facilitator under such circumstances is also considered important for ensuring equal participation of participants and to maximise effectiveness and efficiency. Tasks should be defined within set time parameters to ensure completion, and the group described as needing to be clear about the parameters of its authority to prevent inappropriate engagement in tasks. The allocation of some time to meet during school time is also considered important, as is the need to establish benchmarks by when certain objectives are to be achieved. Such benchmarks help participants to remain focused upon important goals guiding their work. Finally, Zepeda (1999) argues funding is also required, and that it should be derived from alternative sources, or by reallocating existing funds; either way, funding is construed as important to enable ongoing PD, rather than one-off activities.

Teachers-as-Researchers and Action Research

A collaborative, site specific and reflective disposition on the part of researchers of teachers' practice has perhaps been best expressed in support for the action research movement. Zeichner (2001) identifies five major traditions of action research, starting with the work of social psychologist Kurt Lewin in the 1940s, and introduced into schooling settings by Stephen Corey. This was followed by the British teacher-as-researcher movement of the 1960s and 1970s associated with Lawrence Stenhouse and John Elliott. A third tradition was the critical participatory action research movement in Australia in the 1980s advocated by Stephen Kemmis and Robin McTaggart, amongst others. A fourth tradition was associated with the North American teacher researcher movement involving teachers and researchers working together. Finally, Zeichner identifies the more recent 'self-study' approach to researching teaching and teacher education as a fifth tradition.

Reason and Bradbury (2008) employ a more holistic rather than analytic approach to understanding action research, arguing that action research constitutes a 'family of practices' which 'is not so much a *methodology* as an *orientation to inquiry*' (p. 1; emphasis original). Reason and Bradbury (2008) argue action research is a broad-based approach which should entail communication between different traditions to enable richer understandings of practice: 'there can never be one "right way" of doing action research' (p. 7). However, and at the same time, the political ends of action research need to be sustained. An example of such support is advocacy for more critical participatory approaches as a means of challenging more managerial and neoliberal logics. (See Hardy and Rönnerman (2011) for an elaboration of this argument in the context of a Swedish case study.)

Since its advocacy by Lewin in the late 1940s, action research has been applied to education settings, where it has been further developed and modified by various proponents. Elliott (1991), for example, argues that a generic model of action research cannot be somehow 'applied' to different educational settings; instead, action research needs to be considered as an integral part of teachers' daily practice. Altrichter, Kemmis, McTaggart and Zuber-Skerritt (1991) focus upon how action research means different things in different cultures and that part of the process of engaging with action research involves accommodating cultural adaptations. Carr (1995) attempts to describe the plurality of purposes of action research:

> Some regard action research primarily as a way of deepening teachers' understanding while others stress its role in stimulating practical improvement and change. Yet others see action research as an effective way of communicating research findings to teachers. For some, action research is a way of making teachers' professional knowledge more explicit; for others, it is a way of making teachers' professional knowledge more objective. (p. 102)

In general terms, action research is construed by advocates as encouraging more substantive interaction amongst teachers, and sometimes between teachers and other researchers, typically in relation to teachers' everyday teaching responsibilities and other elements of their work (Kemmis and McTaggart, 1988). Widely accepted definitions emphasise systematic knowledge production, for social and educational improvement (Carr and Kemmis, 1986; Kemmis and McTaggart, 1988). Kemmis and McTaggart (1988) highlight the importance of a social justice orientation in their conception of action research; for these authors, action research is:

> a form of collective self-reflective inquiry undertaken by participants in social situations in order to improve the rationality and justice of their own social or educational practices, as well as their understanding of these practices and the situations in which these practices are carried out. (p. 5)

Such conceptions of action research foreground teacher learning content oriented towards social improvement, not just the more technical aspects of teaching; this is what Reason and Bradbury (2008) refer to as the political ends of action research. For Noffke (2009), this political dimension sits alongside a more 'personal' and 'professional' dimension. The personal entails individual and collective growth amongst participants, while the professional encompasses a different way of 'knowing' practice by working with teachers and drawing upon their perspectives to understand teachers' learning from 'within' rather than 'beyond' practice. And it is the political which is most important.

Action research is also described as an approach to research which encourages teachers to theorise their own practice, such that the traditional division between theory and practice, and teaching and research—encouraged by positivism—is challenged (Carr, 1995). Elliott (2009) claims that while the action research movement has not been adopted in the whole-sale way in which it was originally intended, in the British version (deriving from Stenhouse) the original movement's aims to focus upon actual practical problems experienced by teachers in schools means that it is more likely to lead to research construed as relating to teachers' daily practices. Stenhouse's approach was seen as tapping into a form of educational research to enable schools to engage in innovative practices, rather than seeking to challenge the methodological orthodoxy within the academy, as occurred in German iterations of the movement (Elliott, 2009). That is, the foci of attention were qualitatively different between the two approaches to action research. Specifically, the more 'theoretically' oriented German tradition was seen as originating from epistemological and ontological problems which were the domain of the universities, rather than the practical problems confronted on a daily basis by those in schools.

An elaboration of one of the traditions identified by Zeichner—the critical participatory action research movement in the 1980s—is instructive for identifying the more democratic dispositions of some researchers in relation to substantive teacher research. Informed by Neo-Aristotelian, post-Hegelian and post-Marxian interpretations in practical philosophy and social theory, several researchers have advocated teachers as researchers of their own practice to inform and improve their own social circumstances, and that of the world beyond schools and schooling. Within the Anglo tradition of action research, the theorising of Wilfred Carr and Stephen Kemmis in the 1980s was seminal to this work. Through their call for a critical emancipatory approach to teachers' learning and development in their volume *Becoming Critical: Education, Knowledge and Action Research*, Carr and Kemmis (1986) exhorted a mode of teacher learning which placed teachers' material concerns and queries at the centre of attention. Only by inquiring into their specific, situated circumstances could teachers hope to engage in the forms of robust learning which would stand them in good stead in their efforts to make a substantial contribution to individual and collective social improvement. This stance was informed by Habermas' (1970) critical social science, particularly his call for the development of communicative spaces informed by the 'ideal speech situation,' with its emphasis upon intersubjective engagement to bring to light false understandings of the worlds which people inhabit. Carr and Kemmis (1986) advocated collaborative teacher inquiry as the principal means of improving teachers' knowledge of their circumstances, and as providing the tools to be able to change these circumstances for the better. Such knowledge construction served as a precursor to overcoming the obstacles which influenced educators' work, and resonated with the action-oriented emphasis upon teachers' learning advocated by Stenhouse (1975) a decade earlier.

Building upon their earlier work, a proactive, critical disposition is also evident in how Carr and Kemmis (2005) have subsequently argued any new edition of their original work *Becoming Critical* would necessarily need to be both a modern and a postmodern intervention. In modern terms, this would entail sustaining the commitment to critical action research as a way of responding proactively to the tensions between more emancipatory desires and current policies and practices which make it so difficult to ascribe to such values. Such an intervention would need to be postmodern in the sense that, epistemologically, it would need to rest on a shared conviction amongst proponents of the need to respond to the specific, ongoing injustices which characterise the world, rather than being based on 'any ahistorical standpoint' (Carr and Kemmis, 2005, p. 355).

Kemmis (2006) also recognises such work as incredibly difficult within the current context, characterised as it is by educational trends which have served to domesticate educational action research, thereby making it almost impossible for inquiry-oriented teacher learning—for teachers to think the very questions necessary to engage in truly socially critical research. This has significant implications for whether and how a more radical research-oriented disposition can be promulgated. With this in mind, Kemmis and Grootenboer (2008) refer to the need to reveal how institutions can create 'practice architectures'—specific structures which influence the nature of the subsequent practices in which people engage. It is only by seeking to understand the impact of these broader influences upon particular practices that it becomes possible to alter those practices.

This emphasis upon the tradition of practical philosophy has also proven popular amongst researchers in non-Anglo settings. In the opening chapter, of Moksnes Furu, Lund and Tiller's (2007) volume *Action Research: A Nordic Perspective*, Opdal (2007) refers to education as a practical discipline, thereby reinforcing the practical philosophical heritage underpinning much action research. The focus upon trying to understand teachers' actual practices reflects the valuing of active learning on the part of teachers, and a more activist research disposition on the part of researchers. The invocation of Aristotelian practical philosophy, particularly Aristotle's notion of *praxis*, to help ground his insights, also reinforces the ties between Anglo-authors on action research, and these Nordic researchers. Persson (2007) provides additional useful insights into how action research may serve to subvert dominant power relationships between those who typically engage in research, and the researched. However, Persson (2007) also makes some very useful cautionary remarks. While such learning is constructed as beneficial because it implies more active engagement on the part of educators, within the exercise of a democracy, the decision not to act, not to know, may also be a valid decision. To decide to do nothing may also be indicative of an active, learning-focused approach. Acting and knowing are not simply construed as unproblematic. Similarly, while such learning may be framed as a response to feelings of powerlessness within institutional settings, such learning also needs to be contextualised in order to promote change which challenges institutional barriers, lest it be co-opted. Also, while action learning as a form of action research in educational institutions purports to stimulate students' desire for knowledge, Persson (2007) asks whether this is actually the case. Finally, action learning implies risk-taking, but it is important that participants are actually aware of the risks they are taking. In this way, a critical, learning-oriented habitus is evident amongst researchers. Bjørndal (2007) draws upon Arthur Conan Doyle's Sherlock Holmes to make some useful analogies between the diagnostic approach employed by Holmes and his ability to draw inferences from the available evidence, and the action researcher's approach to the evidence before him/her. All of these approaches share a common desire to promote ongoing, reflective and active engagement in their own learning on the part of teachers.

Within this broader context of inquiry traditions, various authors, including Eilertsen (2007), Tiller (2007) and Lund (2007) in the Norwegian context, refer to action research initiatives involving collaboration between universities and schools. Leming (2007) refers more explicitly to action research as a mode of professional development in the context of teacher education, referring particularly to student teachers preparing to work in day-care centres. Zeichner (2003) refers to school-university partnerships in the Learning/Teaching Collaborative in Boston and Brookline, Massachusetts. This initiative is described as involving an 'Inquiry Seminar' in which teachers and academics meet together to discuss individual teachers' projects (Zeichner, 2003). The program had a direct influence upon students' learning and involved teachers applying knowledge, generated by staff members inquiring into their own teaching. Similarly, the School-Wide Action Research Program, operating out of the University of Georgia, involved an inquiry process, oriented towards reform, requiring participants to select a topic of interest, gather data, interpret it and take action as a result of the findings (Zeichner, 2003). All teachers from participating schools were involved and collected data from within and beyond their specific school sites. This study also demonstrates the uncertainty associated with inquiry approaches; the outcomes from the School-Wide Action Research Program were mixed with some participants experiencing improvements in students' in-class learning and better relationships between teachers, whilst others indicated no discernible improvements as a result of the program (Zeichner, 2003).

Broadly defined action research initiatives have also been endorsed by researchers, and described as being characterised by a focus upon a variety of different types of content, ranging from specific traditional subject matter, to topics of teachers' own choosing. The content of such initiatives range across the nature of student work, specific subject matter and techniques for teaching (Wilson and Berne, 1999), and assessment practices (O'Leary (2008)). Zeichner (2003) refers to the Lawrence School Teacher Study Groups, in Lawrence School, Massachusetts, in which members' learning improved as they focused specifically upon individual students' work samples, as well as specific curricular and assessment issues. The result was increased acknowledgement of teacher knowledge and specific changes in classroom practices. To achieve this, teachers maintained journals and gathered data from their classrooms. This is in contrast with the often generic content provided during short-term traditional workshop approaches to professional development (Feiman-Nemser and Norman, 2000).

Within the past decade, the terms 'evidence-based research' and 'knowledge-building schools,' together with the more general term 'practitioner inquiry,' have also been employed by researchers to describe instances of teachers inquiring into their own learning or collaborating with university personnel to do so (Groundwater-Smith and Dadds, 2004). The rubric of practitioner inquiry is preferred in some quarters to that of action research, which, it is claimed, has been appropriated by educational authorities and state educational bureaucracies as a means of implementing specific initiatives and programs such bodies deem to be valuable (Groundwater-Smith and Dadds, 2004).

The teacher-as-researcher movement has also been seen as an important contributor to efforts to dislodge less productive PD practices, and encourage action research amongst teachers. This movement involves teachers researching their practice in a variety of different ways and for a variety of purposes. Cochran-Smith and Lytle's (1999a) substantive support for this work is evident in their differentiation between teacher learning *for* practice, teacher learning *in* practice and teacher learning *of* practice. Teacher learning *for* practice involves teachers accessing information and investigations undertaken by other researchers (who are also sometimes teachers) into the nature of teachers' work and learning, and the types of learning which have proved beneficial for students (Cochran-Smith and Lytle, 1999a). Teacher learning *in* practice acknowledges the learning which occurs as teachers engage in everyday work processes (Cochran-Smith and Lytle, 1999a). Teacher learning *of* practice emphasises the role of teachers in investigating their own learning in a much more formal and structured manner (Cochran-Smith and Lytle, 1999a). The content of such learning is heavily focused upon teachers' daily work, in their classroom and schooling settings.

Collaborative Learning

Many of these initiatives involve teachers learning together, or with other people, on an ongoing basis. That is, from the perspective of PD as research, much of the teacher learning literature encourages teacher research as a collaborative process. Productive change is enhanced by teachers carefully inquiring together into their current practices, and the circumstances under which such practices are enacted. However, entrenched practices in schools have meant that collaborative practices have often been difficult to establish in schools as a vehicle for reform (Osterman and Kottkamp, 2004). Schools remain organised along traditional, bureaucratic lines, which typically involve teachers continuing to work in isolation from one another, despite calls for increased collaboration and the development of learning communities. The result is a lack of involvement by those affected by reform. Instead of including teachers in the development of new proposals for reform, these reforms are often simply imposed. Consequently, there is a lack of commitment to reform on the part of those affected, and a subsequent continuation of fragmented, individualistic approaches and emphases, which reinforce a conservative disposition amongst teachers. (See Chapter 4, this volume, for an elaboration of the nature of teachers' work and its effects upon teacher learning.)

Nevertheless, and in spite of these challenges, a democratic disposition is evident on the part of researchers in their support for teachers to inquire into their own practices together to improve student learning. This perspective is reinforced in an overview of research into teacher learning and whole-school change by Wilson and Berne (1999) who sought evidence of 'high-quality examples' (p. 176) of teacher learning—both the 'what' and 'how' of how teachers learn, as well as knowledge about subject matter, individual students, cultural differences, learning and pedagogy. The emphasis upon collaboration within Wilson and Berne's (1999) study is evident in the nature of the rubrics utilised to present their findings: 'opportunities to talk about subject matter,' 'opportunities to talk about students and learning' and 'opportunities to talk about teaching' (Wilson and Berne, 1999). As a result, the categories for organising this major review of literature indicate an emphasis upon promoting reform via teachers' learning with others. The practices most valued are collaborative, rather than individualistic. Explicit reference to knowledge production being a collaborative undertaking, rather than an individual activity, is also considered particularly important in some articulations of the action research movement. The work of the group only takes on its true meaning when individual reflections are shared with others (Kemmis and McTaggart, 1988).

In her review of professional development practices in the context of advocacy for more authentic professional learning in the workplace, Webster-Wright (2009) is explicit about the value of collaboration for effective professional learning, or what she describes as 'authentic PL':

> During the past two decades, empirical research has demonstrated that effective PL continues over the long-term and is best situated within a community that supports learning . . . Such situated learning at work

can engage individuals in actively working with others on genuine problems within their professional practice. (p. 703)

Webster-Wright's (2009) call for a shift from how to best provide professional development activities to a strong focus upon how professionals actually learn—with others in the workplace—further endorses more collaborative approaches, and is indicative of a more democratic disposition amongst researchers.

Similarly, and drawing upon Rosenholtz's (1991) earlier study of 'moving' and 'stuck' or 'learning impoverished' schools, Fullan (2007) advocates collaboration as a means of effecting sustained and sustainable change focused upon school-wide goals and objectives. 'Stuck' schools were those in which teachers were isolated and uncertain about their roles. Low job commitment, and commitment to their schools, characterised these school environments, influencing the nature of the teaching they provided, and subsequent student learning. In 'moving' schools, improvement in teaching was treated as a collective rather than an individual undertaking, and active involvement of colleagues in assisting teachers develop ideas, and provide feedback on instruction, provided the circumstances for improved and engaged teaching practice. The logics of practice which characterised research in this case involved advocacy for active engagement and interest in teachers' work, rather than passive engagement, or active avoidance of more interactive learning opportunities.

The significance of dialogue is emphasised by some researchers. For some researchers, this dialogue is considered most beneficial when it is critical rather than conciliatory in orientation; such dialogue does not foreclose on difficult but necessary engagement (Feiman-Nemser and Norman, 2000). Sustained dialogue is supported and considered imperative for effective social interactions (Isaacs, 1999; Yankelovich, 1999). Effective collaboration involves a focus upon cooperative strategies in which teachers go beyond typically fleeting, oral and intense interactions to more long-term, sustainable discussions characterised by more in-depth record keeping (Sachs, 2003). Such discussions are described as needing to be undertaken in the context of trust, such that members feel comfortable disclosing both failures and successes; consequently, effective teacher dialogue is dependent on sufficient time to develop this trust (Feiman-Nemser and Norman, 2000).

Some more collaborative approaches are overtly recognised as instances of action research, and involve collaboration between teachers and other educators, including specialist educators. Zeichner (2003) refers to the Madison, Wisconsin Classroom Action Research program as an example of an initiative involving teachers and researchers collaborating together. Eight to ten teachers collaborated with two teacher-education academics to formulate a specific research question which they explored over the course of a year. Participants kept journals and studied articles and handouts, as well as various 'exit responses' delivered by participants to the group, at the end of each of their meetings (Zeichner, 2003). Similarly, El-Haj (2003) reports upon how more collaborative logics were evident in a specific urban teacher network in a large city in the United States which focused upon the development of more equitable educational practices for students in members' respective schools. Teacher educators constituted part of the membership of this network and were involved in assisting teachers as they struggled to address specific concerns in their daily practices.

In the Australian context, support for collaboration as an integral part of teacher research was evident in the establishment and advocacy for the *National Schools Network* (NSN) during the early 1990s. The purpose of the NSN was to foster collaboration between academics and teachers to engage in action research projects designed to facilitate better understanding of the link between the organisation of teachers' work and student learning (Sachs, 2003). Such understanding was to serve as a precursor to assisting teachers to improve their teaching. The emphasis was upon teachers engaging in action research as a means of determining the factors inhibiting schools from instigating their own renewal and reform initiatives. There was much interest in how educators, across the schooling and tertiary sectors, could support one another to improve the learning of both teachers and students (Sachs, 2003). Sachs (2003) argues the NSN was also premised on the understanding that there was no single way of improving teaching and learning, and that the most effective means of doing so was to support teachers as they were engaged in researching their own activities to discern how to improve them. Importantly, these projects involved teachers working in conjunction with academics, in collaborative arrangements and were funded from a variety of sources, including the NSN, the then-federal government Department of Education Employment, Training and Youth Affairs, the tertiary sector and even some corporations (Sachs, 2003). The NSN also fostered teachers interacting with one another across systems, state and private, primary and secondary schools (Ladwig and White, 1996), and advocated teacher responsibility, involvement, learning, inquiry and decision-making (Sachs, 2003). Members had a considerable sense of commitment to the reforms being investigated, as they had greater control over the processes of reform which were influencing them (Ladwig and White, 1996).

At the same time, collaborative learning was evident in the federally supported *Innovative Links* project, which forged connections between schools and teacher education faculties in universities as a means of fostering teacher learning for renewing teacher professionalism (Sachs and Groundwater-Smith, 1999). Like the NSN, the *Innovative Links* project involved state, Catholic and independent schools. Part of the *Innovative Links* program was to promote whole-school reform by advocating the development of learning communities, which embraced students, teachers and academics as learners (Yeatman and Sachs, 1995). According to Sachs (2000), the underlying principle upon which the *Innovative Links* was developed was the notion of a 'learning society.' This is analogous to schools as 'learning organisations' (Senge, Cambron-McCabe, Lucas, Smith, Dutton and Kleiner, 2000) in which teachers, parents, students or other community members are engaged in addressing any of a myriad of school-related concerns. Within the *Innovative Links* program, student learning was only viewed as possible in an environment in which teachers were also learners, as were academics, or 'academic associates,' as they were known (Yeatman and Sachs, 1995). The *Innovative Links* program was essentially a policy supported, research-driven agenda which sought to challenge taken-for-granted assumptions about experience (Sachs, 2003). As it emphasised the importance of school-based and research-informed teacher learning, the program fostered an explicit link between schools engaged in reform and tertiary education faculties, which was seen as beneficial for both parties (Yeatman and Sachs, 1995).

Individualistic and isolated teacher learning practices have also been challenged by researchers' endorsement of the benefits of technological innovation. Lieberman (2000) refers to the influence of technology in helping to promote collaborative learning within networks existing beyond individual school sites. Such networks enable teacher educators to engage with teachers beyond bureaucratic schooling systems which struggle with change (Lieberman, 2000). These networks help to develop different and substantial modes of scholarship and enable a balance between the 'inside knowledge' produced by teachers and 'outside' knowledge developed through more traditional research and conceptualisation (Lieberman, 2000, p. 223). Similar examples include several of the networks reported upon by McDonald and Klein (2003), which involved writers, artists, scholars and scientists, some of whom were based in the university sector, who collaborated with teachers about their craft.

Some researchers nuance the nature and effects of collaborative learning by seeking to capture how contextual issues exert influence. Reflecting a more critical and democratic disposition, Avalos (2004) reveals how professional development across Latin American countries is characterised by a mix of deficit-based approaches to teachers' understanding, and more genuinely professionally responsive and empowering conceptions of teacher learning. This is due in part to the policies of lending agencies such as the World Bank and the Inter-American Development Bank which influence all aspects of these countries' public provision of services. The teacher learning which plays out reflects a variety of purposes including the implementation of major reforms, a focus upon issues of equity, for individual development, and social development more broadly. An example of more collective teacher learning approaches is provided by Cuba's push to encourage *colectivo pedagógico*—an initiative involving a group of teachers meeting to discuss teaching approaches, produce resources and plan teaching experiences. In other regions of the world, such as sub-Saharan Africa, contextual issues are also critical. Research by Christie, Harley and Penny

(2004) reveals how the lack of information about professional development practices reflects the capacity of these countries to resource teachers' learning initiatives. The PD which does exist in some countries is also difficult to identify because it may be part of initial teacher education programs, donor aid packages, and may be influenced by the quality of textbooks and teachers' guides. Under these circumstances, more research-oriented collaborative approaches exhorted in western settings do not typically guide PD decision-making. While more collaborative, research-oriented approaches are evident and supported in the PD practised in Europe, teachers' learning also trends towards individualisation, reflecting the influence of economic globalization, marketisation and the impact of information and communication technologies (Sugrue, 2004). Under such conditions, Little (2004) reveals how the increasingly popular emphasis upon 'looking at student work' is invoked for a multitude of reasons in the United States, including to improve teachers' pedagogical decision-making, promote teacher collaboration and community, promote school reform, and respond to public pressure for increased accountability. Multiple practices are evident in support for such PD, reflecting the myriad of purposes for the PD which transpires in different schooling settings.

A more democratic disposition on the part of researchers is also evident in their support for, and focus upon, collaborative learning provided through educational groups and organisations external to individual schools, but involving teachers organising and engaging in PD for and with other teachers. The PD associated with subject professional associations and networks is a particularly good example of such logics, and have received some attention in the relevant research literature. The PD practices associated with these groups may be both short-term and long-term in nature, and provide different benefits for teachers, depending upon the nature of the activities offered, and teachers' levels of participation. Research undertaken by the Queensland Consortium for Professional Development in Education (QCPDE) in Queensland, Australia, for example, reveals teacher associations and networks as an important source of professional development for many teachers (QCPDE, 2004). These networks provide a variety of modes of professional development to members, including conferences, seminars and workshops, journals and websites. A survey of subject professional associations in Queensland revealed that more than half of the 48 associations which responded to the survey construed conferences as the most successful means of professional development for members (QCPDE, 2004). These conferences were held on an annual or biennial basis and were considered successful because of the quality of keynotes speakers and individual paper presentations. Seminars and workshops were also construed as useful PD activities. While such responses reflect the influence of more traditional PD logics, the way in which such conferences were also seen as enabling teachers to exchange ideas and collaborate with one another revealed evidence of alternative, more collaborative logics on the part of participants. Some were held in the capital city of the state, Brisbane, while several associations also maintained regional branches which held events throughout the year, specifically for members in these areas. This literature also describes professional associations as developing their own journals which includes a mixture of academic and other articles submitted by teachers and other educators, as well as members of allied fields. Websites are also described as vehicles for teacher learning, although several associations have indicated disappointment with the level of forum use and other online discussions amongst members (QCPDE, 2004). Connections with non-teaching members, including parents, students and various other professionals, such as psychologists and members of the business community, are also recognised as important, and areas for further potential development.

Such a democratic disposition is also evident in support for more sustained collaborative teacher PD via formal academic study undertaken by teachers on a medium to long-term basis. Daly, Pachler, Pickering and Bezemer (2007), for example, argue in favour of the e-learning experiences of teachers enrolled in an online Master's program through the Institute of Education, London. Teacher narratives were employed as a research vehicle by teachers as part of the course. These narratives of teachers' experiences were then shared in an e-learning environment to serve as a means of building an online collaborative community for teachers' learning. These narratives also served as a means for teachers to evaluate the e-learning experiences in which teachers engaged. The various levels of engagement by teachers were reflective of a much more learner-focused approach to PD, and of collaborative research enabled by the development of this learning environment.

Teacher Professional Learning Communities

Researchers' exposure to, support for and advocacy of collaborative approaches—sometimes described as 'inquiry communities,' 'teacher professional learning communities,' 'teacher learning communities' or 'learning communities' (Cochran-Smith and Lytle, 2003)—also reveals a more democratic disposition. While Cochran-Smith and Lytle (2003) claim that these terms were not mentioned in the educational literature before the 1980s, they have become much more prominent recently.[1] Stoll, Bolam, McMahon, Wallace and Thomas (2006) provide a useful review of the literature on professional learning communities, arguing that while some of the empirical evidence which exists suggests such communities may be problematic, other empirical evidence points to improvements in teacher engagement. There is also some evidence of improvements in student learning (Louis and Marks, 1998; Lee and Smith, 1996), and that sustained collaborative PD can have positive effects upon both teachers and students, including student performance (Cordingley, Bell, Rundell and Evans, 2003).

Apart from some early and smaller studies into individual school communities, arguably, the research informing this approach gained in prominence as a result of the work of Louis, Kruse and Associates (1995). These researchers focused on individual school-based 'schoolwide professional communities,' a notion further developed by Louis, Kruse and Marks (1996). Forming part of Newmann and Associates' (1996) School Restructuring Study, based at the University of Wisconsin, the notion of schoolwide professional community was characterised by five elements: shared norms and values, a focus on student learning, reflective dialogue, deprivatization of practice and collaboration (Louis, Kruse and Marks, 1996). The focus upon learning communities was part of a broader project which placed student learning at the centre of a reform agenda which constructed teacher learning as an important part of broader school restructuring practices (Newmann and Wehlage, 1995; Newmann and Associates, 1996).

Since the mid 1990s, the term 'professional learning community' has been rearticulated by researchers and applied not only to within-school professional groups (usually teachers), but to broader groups of learners consisting of members from different schools, as well as other groups/institutions associated with schooling. Toole and Louis (2002), Louis, Kruse and Marks (1996) and Louis, Kruse and Associates' (1995) descriptions of professional communities typically refer to in-school groups consisting mostly of teachers. Cochran-Smith and Lytle (2003), however, refer to a myriad of types of professional communities including those established beyond individual school sites. The term has been applied to a variety of programs and initiatives involving new and experienced educators collaborating together for multiple purposes. These include:

> for the purpose of gaining new information, reconsidering previous knowledge and beliefs, and building on their own and others' ideas and experiences in order to work on a specific agenda intended to improve practice and enhance students' learning in K-12 schools and other educational settings. (Cochran-Smith and Lytle, 2003, p. 2462)

Such an entity is described as providing an 'intellectual space' to enable teachers' professional growth. This is achieved by organising time in particular ways, structuring talk and text and having a shared purpose (Cochran-Smith and Lytle, 2003). According to Toole and Louis (2002), a school-wide culture ' . . . makes collaboration expected, inclusive, genuine, ongoing, and focused on critically examining practice to improve student outcomes' (p. 247). In their summary of the key features of a functioning learning community, DuFour and Eaker (1998) emphasise collaboration; collaboration undergirds so many of the principles they believe should be guiding the development of such communities: shared mission, vision and values, collective inquiry, collaborative teams, action orientation and experimentation, continuous improvement and results orientation (Dufour

and Eaker, 1998). Louis, Kruse and Marks (1996) favour a broader conception of collaboration which involves members of the community beyond the
school; they invoke the African proverb, 'It takes a whole village to raise a
child,' to highlight the importance of a collaborative effort between all of
the adults with whom students come into contact (Louis, Kruse and Marks,
1996). The assumption is that the provision of teacher learning will result
in appropriate outcomes if it is heavily imbued with collaborative principles, which stands in stark contrast to the more individualistic approaches
to teachers' learning.

Critical engagements with collaborative learning

This exhortation to collaborate with other teachers is not advocated by
researchers unreservedly. As well as support for learning communities,
researchers' more descriptive, empirical accounts of some communities
also reveal a more critical disposition towards collaborative approaches to
professional development. However, even in this critical manifestation, the
very focus upon such communities is itself an indication that efforts by
teachers to inquire into their own practices constitute an important preoc-
cupation for many researchers within the broader field of teacher PD.

   More critical investigations have led to the development of a body of
research literature which problematises collaborative workplace based
learning and assumptions about its intrinsic value. Some researchers
have revealed that instead of collaborating with one another to improve
student learning outcomes, more collaborative, workplace-based learning initiatives have been shown to be shallow, serving to simply reinforce entrenched practices and prejudices, many of which serve to further
marginalise disadvantaged students or reinforce existing, conservative
learning regimes (Lipman, 1998; McLaughlin and Talbert, 2001; Supovitz, 2002; Westheimer, 1998; 1999). Some collaborative undertakings
may take a long time to even begin to become established, and are difficult to maintain (Grossman, Wineburg and Woolworth, 2001), while
the content of some may be questionable. Examples of the latter include
those communities which reinforce ingrained prejudices, such as racism
(Lipman, 1998), or traditional discipline-based teaching practices which
marginalise some students (McLaughlin and Talbert, 2001), or encourage a 'collective' form of individualism in which teachers all agree to
behave independently of one another (Westheimer, 1998; 1999). Studies
of specific communities of teacher learners provide in-depth empirical
analyses of actual communities. Researchers investigating these communities have not attempted to develop an overall 'model' of what such
communities could or should look like; rather, they provide insights into
the practices which characterise actual communities, including the content of the learning in which teachers engage. Such studies help to nuance
the more prescriptive literature associated with the provision of teacher

learning, which advocates collaboration without recourse to empirical research into the nature of actual communities. Studies of the micro-politics of actual communities provide insights into the difficulties of learning in conjunction with others, during periods of educational change (Achinstein, 2002). Researchers reveal how schools have struggled to focus upon the critical nexus between teacher and student learning. In the words of Hayes, Mills, Christie and Lingard (2006), '[t]he key point here is that schools need to become real learning organisations structured around the ongoing relationship between teacher learning and student learning' (p. 25).

Criticisms of the content of the provision of collaborative learning initiatives in teaching have also entailed critiques of the concept of 'community' more generally. The notion of 'community' invokes a logic of providing a solution to the fragmentation associated with modernity and 'the new work order' (Gee, Hull and Lankshear, 1996). In some ways, this builds upon earlier perceptions of the division between community and society in which community was proffered as a panacea to the ills of society more generally (Tönnies (1963/1887)). The problems of society, including inadequate, infrequent or inappropriate teacher learning, are simply the problem of a lack of sufficient engagement between those who comprise society. The atomistic individualism of our high modern/postmodern age gets in the way of a robust sense of community, which if evident, would serve to redress these shortcomings. This increased individualism and subsequent changes to traditional work patterns, typical of late modernity, are responsible for what has been described as a 'dystopia of exclusion' (Young, 1999) in society, in which different groups become alienated from one another. Under such conditions, notions of community are seen as a solution.

However, Sennett (1998) refers to current notions of 'we' associated with communities as the 'dangerous pronoun'; he argues that in the new work order, while communities typically connote a conception of inclusion, in reality, they effectively exclude members different from their constituent members (Sennett, 1998). This new work order is the product of neoliberalism, which has been responsible for a 'corrosion of character,' amongst those individuals affected (Sennett, 1998). This influences the types of communities which become established. The restrictions placed upon those in the 'really existing community' means such spaces become hard places indeed, for both members and non-members alike (Bauman, 2001). Actual communities are influenced by a lack of internal cohesion and are not necessarily established on the basis of altruistic grounds (Baumann, 2001; Renshaw, 2003). Bauman (2001) argues that for members, a community demands 'stern obedience in exchange for the services it renders or promises to render' (p. 4). For those who are not members, access is denied to what is perceived to be bodies which provide a degree of security, which individuals may not otherwise experience in harsher, more individualistic times.

Researchers have revealed that these tendencies toward exclusive, more corrosive and/or generally harsher conceptions of community are apparent in some of the narrower iterations of community which have become associated with the provision of teacher learning. Exposure to such communities reveals they may not be focused upon substantive inquiry into learning at all. Collaborative teacher learning may manifest itself in 'balkanised,' 'comfortable' or 'contrived' states (Fullan and Hargreaves, 1998). Balkanised teachers may associate with particular groups of colleagues only. These groups may be based on subject departmental affiliations (particularly in secondary schools (Little, 1993)) or other forms of segmentation and division. Their learning may become insular, ineffective or counterproductive. 'Comfortable collaborators' may interact and engage in forms of inquiry with one another, beyond their immediate subject department or year level affiliations but not in a substantive manner, preferring to ignore difficult issues (Fullan and Hargreaves, 1998). Their associations may be more social than professional, and their interactions may result in little of substance because of the propensity of such groups to maintain the status quo or to seek respite from broader and harsher political realities influencing teachers' work. Researchers argue the practices which dominate the work of these groups include a reluctance to enter into the disagreements and difficulties of accommodating difference which should characterise substantial inquiry processes. Contrived collegiality is typified by the implementation of bureaucratic processes to encourage further interaction between staff-members, but without any real substance (Hargreaves, 1994).

In contrast, researchers reveal effective communities of teacher learners are those characterised by an ability amongst members to appreciate differences of opinion, and to cultivate such understanding in order to generate a more informed and productive exchange of perspectives (Grossman, Wineburg and Woolworth, 2001). Instead of ignoring difference, mature communities are characterised by acceptance of different perspectives and the capacity of members to utilise these differences positively, in order to further the collective endeavours of the group. Differences become stimuli for the purposeful pursuit of agreement between different groups with a stake in education (Nixon, Martin, McKeown and Ranson, 1997). A propensity to ignore difference or to deny its existence is indicative of a community in its nascent phases or of one which has not yet begun to engage with a substantive function (Grossman, Wineburg and Woolworth, 2001).

The tensions which invariably arise within functioning communities of teacher learners, have led some researchers to propose that it is more important to move 'toward' the development of a theory of teacher community, rather than considering that there is such a thing as an effective theory of professional learning communities (Grossman, Wineburg and Woolworth, 2001). Exposure to such communities has given rise to a critical disposition encouraging continual critique, reflection and theorising about the nature of how teachers can learn effectively with others. Research in such communities reveals how the provision of effective teacher learning communities is difficult to develop and sustain, learning in conjunction with others is highly relational work, learning involves the interplay between individuals in context, and outcomes are always necessarily uncertain (Grossman, Wineburg and Woolworth, 2001). Even when institutionalised support is provided, such as the allocation of meeting time within the normal teaching timetable, and there is support from the principal and district office to enable teachers to engage with one another at their own work sites, establishing cultural support for such work is difficult (McLaughlin and Talbert, 2001).

To highlight the challenges of establishing functioning communities of teacher learners, Grossman, Wineburg and Woolworth (2001) reported on a two and a half year project involving the development of a community of teachers across the English and Social Studies departments in an urban high school in the Northwest of the United States. Their report on the first eighteen months of the project indicated that the community established did not conform to the descriptions of such communities in much of the existing, typically prescriptive and acritical literature about such bodies. Instead, the community established was beset by problems of both establishing and sustaining a group of individuals who were brought together by an external party, and who had no intrinsic desire to work with one another. Rather than assuming that a community of teacher learners would be easily achieved, the participants in Grossman, Wineburg and Woolworth's (2001) study came to realise that community building was difficult work. The community established was always tentative and in need of continual maintenance; the inquiries members engaged in were limited by the uncertainty about what could and couldn't be said when members met together. To overcome this impediment, the formation of a group identity and the establishment of norms for engaging with members were considered vital. One of the key characteristics of a functioning community was that members viewed themselves as members of a larger collective, rather than as members of a subgroup within the larger group, which is how the participants viewed themselves at the inception of the group (Grossman, Wineburg and Woolworth, 2001).

For Grossman, Wineburg and Woolworth (2001) exposure to such communities was productive of a critical habitus which characterised effective teacher communities as involving members accepting responsibility for not only their own, but for one another's continued growth and professional learning. Members of such communities also spent time on their own learning, and recognised that this would have benefits for students. Mature communities consisted of members who readily accepted that their work with students was fundamentally affected by the actions of their colleagues (Grossman, Wineburg and Woolworth, 2001). This led to recognition that it was important for teachers to spend time working with other teachers, as opposed to working solely with students, and recognising that this time was necessary. This is in opposition to a general belief amongst many teachers that all in-service activities should be explicitly directed towards student learning (Grossman, Wineburg and Woolworth, 2001); such an assumption implies that learning which is not geared exclusively and overtly towards improvement in student outcomes is misdirected. In those communities of teachers which were not fully developed, this perception dominated; time spent on teachers' own learning was not considered integral to enhanced student learning (Grossman, Wineburg and Woolworth, 2001; Wineburg and Grossman, 1998). Learning is something that both students and teachers engage in, but the essential nexus between the two is only recognised in mature communities. In Grossman, Wineburg and Woolworth's (2001) study, one particular community steadily matured as members took responsibility for the actions of other members of the group, and assisted one another in becoming comfortable with a more actively probing inquiry process within the group. This process required considerable time.

Experiences of more problematic communities of teacher learners have given rise to a more critical disposition amongst other researchers who have also revealed how collaboration can result in the legitimation of more individualistic dispositions, thereby reinforcing existing conservative teaching approaches. Westheimer's (1999) study of two different teacher professional communities provides insights into the difficulties of establishing sustainable and effective communities of teacher learners, particularly when more dominant approaches are drawn upon to reinforce existing practices. Communities that resulted from a 'liberal' and a 'collective' approach to community development were found to be very different. In one school, the community which was established was based upon a liberal ethos which emphasised the importance of the individual and of teachers' rights to conduct themselves as individuals, and in a manner which they considered appropriate, according to their own individual proclivities. This effectively isolated teachers from one another and encouraged them to work and engage in learning activities separately from one another. The consequence of this was not a weak community. On the contrary, the community which became established was one which was adamant that the individualistic philosophy to which the school had become beholden was worthwhile and should be maintained. Members guarded their individual choices jealously and worked together to ensure that they could continue to work in this way. In contrast, teachers in a second school embraced working together to improve student learning opportunities. While 'one school's professional community emphasise[d] teachers' individual autonomy, rights and responsibilities to colleagues, the other's was driven by a strong collective mission' (Westheimer, 1999, p. 71). A robust, collaborative community of learners did not eventuate as more sedimented practices continued to exert influence.

The nature of teacher learning communities have also been found to be culturally laden. In a cross-cultural study, Toole and Louis (2002) discovered that the broader cultural context in which they conducted their research led to different perceptions and tensions between more collectivist and individualist approaches within different teacher communities (Toole and Louis, 2002). The influence of a stronger culture of collegiality in China and Japan led to more authentic forms of collaborative inquiry because of the more pervasive influence of collaboration in the society at large; in the United States the influence of a more individualistic ethos meant such communities were less apparent. Again, such insights reflect a more critical disposition on the part of these researchers.

Strong communities of teachers have also been revealed by researchers as encouraging learning which may reinforce existing prejudices, doing little to challenge the established non-intrusiveness which often characterises teachers' work and learning (Campbell, 2005; Keddie and Niesche, 2011; Niesche and Keddie, 2011). In their work on the context of secondary school teachers' work, across sixteen schools in various localities in California and Michigan, McLaughlin and Talbert (2001) found that, in terms of both school-wide and departmental professional communities, when developed in isolation, strong communities did not necessarily lead to the sorts of classroom practices which were inclusive of the needs of all students. Several of the communities within their study effectively disenfranchised many of the students they were supposed to be assisting because these communities chose not to inquire into how traditional approaches to teaching marginalised some students. Instead, they actively promulgated entrenched divisions:

> Some strong department communities we observed developed elaborate policies for testing their students and sorting them into course sequences and achievement levels. These professional communities enforced 'traditional' methods of teaching, and teachers worked to transmit predetermined course material and to administer department tests that placed students in subsequent courses. (McLaughlin and Talbert, 2001, p. 10)

This situation contrasted with other departments in which very different practices were evident. In these departments, students' needs were taken into account and innovations in practice yielded both improved social and academic outcomes:

> In contrast, teachers in other strong department and school communities centred their work on students and shared responsibility for students' mastery of content and progress in the curriculum. They developed 'innovative' methods of instruction that achieved a better 'fit' of course work to students without compromising expectations for students' conceptual learning. Subject matter in these school or department contexts was not seen as 'given' but rather as material to be reviewed and revised

based on the needs and academic accomplishments of their particular students. (McLaughlin and Talbert, 2001, pp. 10–11)

While collaborative practices sometimes reinforced the status quo, the most successful communities were revealed as those in which teachers accepted responsibility for altering existing teaching practices which reproduced inequalities amongst students. Such communities were involved in continuously learning about the needs of students and conducting inquiries into how to make subject materials more relevant for those students most disenfranchised from schooling. The schools and departments in which teachers were most successful were those where there was an acceptance that teachers did need to engage with educational reform on an ongoing basis, and in which members felt they could draw upon one another to assist them in the process. Part of this process meant teachers within these communities also had to be open to critique into the effects of their activities (McLaughlin and Talbert, 2001). Successful communities of learners were described as those in which members were able to 'constantly ask and process troubling questions' (Fullan, 2003, p. 49). The restrictive individualism of Lortie's (1975) teachers was not present in these communities. Unfortunately, McLaughlin and Talbert's (2001) research reveals such transformative communities were not common.

A more critical disposition on the part of researchers is also evident in the uncovering of conservative, passive teacher learning approaches in the form of teacher learning communities which maintain the status quo and do not inquire too deeply into their interactions with students. Such practices were evident in Lipman's (1998) research into a school district in the American south. Lipman's (1998) work focused upon the city of 'Riverton,' which was characterised by entrenched racial discrimination and institutionalised prejudice. The professional communities established in Riverton's schools reflected many of the prejudices of the broader communities in which the schools were located, often exacerbating these difficulties. Consequently, these learning communities were not in the best interests of the students whom they were designed to serve. For example, in the 'Gates' school community, situated within a wealthy enclave and serving two distinct populations of students— local, predominantly white students, and a second group of African-American students who were bussed into Gates from neighbouring poorer districts under the auspices of desegregation legislation—teacher professional communities reinforced stereotypes about student achievement, thereby exacerbating ingrained racial prejudices. Members of this school did not view low student achievement as a central focus of their concerns. Instead, students were constructed as being responsible for their results and the pervasive view amongst their teachers was that there was relatively little which teachers could do to alter this situation. This passive approach on the part of teachers contributed to and reflected deeply rooted conservative prejudices within the community more generally.

Such findings were similar to research into teacher learning approaches encountered by McLaughlin and Talbert (2001) in the mathematics faculty of one of the schools in which they undertook research. McLaughlin and Talbert (2001) found that a strong, traditional, discipline-based culture amongst teachers resulted in increased 'tracking' (ability grouping) of students. The learning of teachers within these communities simply reinforced existing prejudices against those students considered least able. Again, this situation had the greatest impact upon minority students. The result was that those students most in need of effective organisational and cultural structures were the most disadvantaged. This lack of awareness constituted a key element of dysfunctional learning communities.

Researchers' more critical dispositions are also evident in critiques of collaborative action research practices where such practices have become domesticated by educational bureaucracies that have reframed action research as a method, rather than as a political project oriented towards increasing participants' awareness of the injustices which characterise their work (Carr and Kemmis, 2005; McWilliam, 2004; Groundwater-Smith and Dadds, 2004). McWilliam (2004) points out that action research as a method may often be construed as a default option for prospective researchers and teacher-researchers struggling to come to terms with the myriad of theoretical and methodological resources at their disposal. Under such circumstances, the philosophical underpinnings guiding genuine action research are jettisoned, and it becomes simply one more approach which may be applied for technical rather than emancipatory purposes.

Collectively, these studies offer important critiques of the provision of collaborative teacher learning. However, such insights are less a criticism of collaborative teacher learning approaches *per se* than a validation of the value of a more critical disposition on the part of researchers. Such a disposition is reflected in the push to remain cognisant of the nature and effects of such communities, and of the importance of not assuming that such approaches can resolve entrenched educational problems. Those instances in which teachers actively inquire together as part of a robust research process are supported. The disposition on the part of these researchers is one which encourages teachers to be researchers of their own practice, and not simply passive recipients of research undertaken elsewhere, but in a critical rather than passive manner. Active engagement on the part of teachers is foregrounded as the best means of ensuring productive PD, but this needs to be worked for if it is to succeed in improving both teacher and student learning.

TEACHER PD AS A RESEARCH PRODUCT

In spite of this strong history and advocacy for professional development as a research process, and support by researchers for teachers to engage in research into their own practice as a key mode of learning for improved practice, recent pressures within nation-states in the western world, in particular, have led to a resurgence in more traditional approaches to PD. That is, the logic of PD practices reflects more dominant, orthodox professional development approaches involving teachers passively consuming the findings of research undertaken by others. In large measure, this is part of a broader process of the privatisation of educational services, including the 'provision' of PD by various 'service-providers' (Ball, 2009). At the same time, increased centralisation has reduced advocacy for teachers-as-researchers—as researchers of their own practice—resulting in a push away from PD as a research process, to a greater focus upon research as an output, or 'product.'

Within this paradigm, research is construed as a specialist practice designed to inform practitioners, but not something which is part of the province of practitioners. Research is something to be 'delivered' by 'expert' researchers to practitioners, rather than an activity vital for the development of teachers. Indeed, conceptions of the 'good teacher' (Moore, 2004) may even be constructed in ways which are antithetical to teachers-as-researchers. The notion of teacher as researcher is not one which society immediately confers upon teachers. Rather, the opposite is often the case: 'the teacher as researcher is *not* an image our culture gives us. Rather, *teacher* and *researcher* are often constructed as figures in opposition, having very different traits, interests, and values' (Phillips and Carr, 2006, p. 7; emphasis original).

This shift is evident within educational practices more generally and is a product of the increasingly economistic, accountability-oriented context in which schooling is undertaken (see Chapter 1, this volume), leading to a realignment of the relationship between policy and research. In a context of significant criticism of educational research by those close to governments (Ozga and Lingard, 2007), the research which is most valued, and considered most valuable, is that which is construed as providing clear 'evidence' of the nature of educational practices and outcomes, and which can be readily translated into policies. These policies, in turn, should encourage further scrutiny of educational practices which are readily quantifiable to determine, through research, the effects of these policies. Within this cyclical process, research serves as both engine and instrument of educational change. At the same time as serving these accountability agenda, the broader discourses of the 'Knowledge Economy' within which education research is undertaken ensure that the 'researchly' disposition (Lingard and Renshaw, 2009) encouraged is one which is attuned to fostering economic growth. The knowledge/research of most value is that which is deemed most likely to result in improved economic productivity. This is further reinforced by the increasing trend of governments to outsource educational contracts to private consultancy firms, which are heavily involved in conducting research on particular policy-related issues and developing resources which can be on-sold to schools in the educational marketplace (Ball, 2009).

Within this broader economistic and accountability-oriented context, there is increasing pressure to ensure educational research contributes to the development of a systematic body of knowledge which can then be applied by teachers. Such an approach construes teachers as recipients of knowledge developed elsewhere rather than the originators of knowledge to inform their own practical judgments. Elliott (2007) argues that a strong focus upon 'outcomes' within paradigmatic forms of 'outcomes-based education' is founded upon positivistic assumptions which imply the capacity to develop and apply generalised laws which 'fit' on all occasions. Teachers' practices are assumed to be able to be manipulated to achieve pre-specified ends; indeed the capacity to specify the ends of education is implicit in such an approach. However, Elliott (2007) argues, such an approach downplays the inherently and necessarily complex, specific and contingent nature of teachers' practices, and proffers a 'solution' which makes little sense in light of the specificity of teachers' practices. Drawing upon MacIntyre's (1981) *After Virtue*, Elliott (2007) argues the only way to understand a practice is by participating in it, and it is only by seeking to understand the internal goods inherent within any given practice, and the standards of excellence which pertain to a particular practice, that it is possible to improve practice. To seek to do so via a means-end rationality is to achieve an understanding of something external to the actual goods inherent within a particular practice.

This is a particularly salient point at the moment when the push for improvements in students' outcomes via external teaching standards is so strong as to threaten the intrinsic qualities of education *per se*. Potentially, it becomes impossible to foster truly educational and educative practices (Connell, 2009). Under such circumstances, what is required is an approach to education research which provides insights into how teaching can be made more *educational*, that is, how to improve teaching practices in ways which encourage students to embrace the value of learning for its own sake, and to foster a particular way of life which seeks out the good for both the individual and society more generally.

More educational logics contrast with what Day (2002) describes as 'narrowly conceived "training" models designed to ensure effective compliance with externally initiated curriculum, assessment and teaching models' (p 51). Day (2002) argues such approaches dominate schooling settings at present, complementing the dominant logics of performance management, and constant auditing of student and teacher outcomes which skew the emphasis away from educational to more managerial outcomes. In this context, the research most valued is that which is construed as contributing to improvements in students' test scores: 'Research into ways of improving test and examination results increasingly brings into being a world where it is taken for granted that this is the main or even the sole point of education' (Smith, 2008, p. 185).

Within this context, the approach to research which is currently highly valued and validated is one based upon traditional randomized controlled trial approaches associated with the physical sciences. Such approaches are construed as informing advances in various professions, such as medicine, which are seen as amenable to these more 'objective' approaches. For researchers supportive of this paradigm, research is only of any value if it is construed as valid, reliable and replicable. Reflecting this more conservative and policy-responsive habitus, Slavin (2002) argues it is the emphasis upon randomized controlled trial approaches which have guided advances in various fields:

> The most important reasons for the extraordinary advances in medicine, agriculture, and other fields is the acceptance by practitioners of evidence as the basis for practice. In particular, it is the randomized clinical trial—more than any single medical breakthrough—that has transformed medicine. (2002, p. 16)

However, even though the field of PD practices is experiencing a resurgence of more traditional research approaches, Thomas (2004) argues that randomized controlled trials which undergird traditional positivist approaches to research are actually fairly mundane instruments which simply test the insights, often creative insights, of researchers. In refuting Slavin's (2002) argument, Thomas (2004) draws upon the example of the discovery that the bacterium *Helicobacter pylori* responsible for more than 90 percent of all peptic ulcers:

> RCTs [randomized controlled trials] merely confirmed the efficacy of antibiotic therapy in the killing of the bacteria. Once the discovery had been made that bacteria were the culprits (by the 'Aha! of an observant expert, not by a RCT) it required not a huge cognitive leap to get to the point that the bacteria needed killing in ulcer patients' stomachs. RCTs played a dull but important role in confirming the effectiveness of antibiotics in doing the killing. The point is that experiments and RCTs do not, as Slavin suggest, *lead to* 'extraordinary advances.' (Thomas, 2004, p. 12; emphasis original)

In spite of such refutation, randomized controlled trials represent a social practice, and possess a logic, which seems to accord with a level of prestige associated with traditional, positivistic research approaches which are construed as having a heritage of achievement and improvement in other (particularly medical) fields of endeavour. For a dominated field of inquiry, such as education in general and teacher professional development in particular, establishing an accord with a more prestigious field of endeavour (albeit one which is itself actually subordinate in terms of 'pure' knowledge hierarchies within the academy (Bourdieu, 1999)) seems a useful strategy, and one which gives additional credence, and accords additional symbolic capital, to traditional approaches to research. However, in doing so, such logics effectively dislodge a focus upon teachers as researchers of their own practice. The emphasis upon research as a 'product' taken up by teachers reinforces already passive dispositions towards teachers' own learning as part of their work (a point further elaborated in Chapter 4, this volume).

Calls to base practice on evidence—'evidence-based practice'—are associated with this more traditional 'medical' model, and work against facilitating more active teacher learning. Hammersley (2004) argues that the term 'evidence-based practice' is problematic because it seeks to silence debate about the nature of those dominant approaches associated with the term: ' . . . its name is a slogan whose rhetorical effect is to discredit opposition' (Hammersley, 2004, p. 134). While the term evidence-*informed* practice is also employed as a means of tempering this rhetorical closure, the effect is still to problematise any critique of what is construed as such practice. Hammersley (2004) is also particularly critical of the way in which this emphasis upon evidence-based practice reifies quantitative approaches to research, particularly as so much is now known about the value and validity of qualitative approaches which reveal why particular approaches unfold as they do, the varied ways in which they may be interpreted, and the unexpected effects and outcomes of particular initiatives. There is also the problem of the tendency to overlook accumulated professional experience, as the focus and locus of attention become more narrowly circumscribed and attenuated by more quantitative approaches. Narrowly conceived evidence-based practice approaches require professionals to make judgements which cannot be readily quantified, and professional goals are multi-faceted and have to be dealt with concurrently (Hammersley, 2004). Focused research by practitioners becomes marginalised as more dominant quantitative logics exert influence.

The influence of more dominant logics is also apparent in criticisms of qualitative educational research, including calls by some commentators for better quality research to contribute towards improved, evidence-based practice. David Hargreaves' (2007) 1996 Teacher Training Agency Lecture exemplifies this push for what is construed as more systematic, rigorous and objective research, rather than what is currently conceived of as inadequate research insufficiently oriented towards the needs of teachers in everyday situations. Indeed, Hargreaves' (2007, p. 3) opening comments convey his sense of a parlous state of affairs between educational research and practice, and reveal a traditional conception of the link between the two: 'Teaching is not at present a research-based profession. I have no doubt that if it were, teaching would be more effective and more satisfying.' He then goes on to make comparisons with medicine, a profession which he believes is better served by the research undertaken in the field, at least in so far as it is perceived within the broader community:

> The comparison I make now is with medicine, and in particular with doctors in hospitals. The medical profession has gained in public

prestige concurrently with the growth of its research. The teaching profession has not. We need to investigate why this is so and what can be done to change things. (Hargreaves, 2007, p. 4)

Again, an unfettered faith in the research approaches perceived to be undertaken within the medical profession challenges more grass-roots approaches to educational research which place teacher research at the centre of changed practice. In this way, more dominant research logics are construed as offering a panacea to the lack of rigour perceived to pervade the educational research community, and the teaching profession more generally.

These more dominant logics have also been associated with the outsourcing of research by governments to large commercial organisations. Ball (2009) describes how the consulting and accountancy firm PriceWaterhouseCoopers is intricately and intimately involved in the 'business' of education policy and research. Similarly, the Hay/McBer Report (2000), for example, with its list of criteria which teachers in England should be able to meet to improve their practice, exemplifies a more technicist approach to professional development which foregrounds the place and value of developing decontextualised criteria against which to critique the effectiveness or otherwise of teachers' practices. The McKinsey and Company (2007) report, *How the World's Best-Performing School Systems Come Out on Top*, similarly embraces such an approach. Its description of successful school systems belies a concern to distil a general set of criteria which can then be disseminated and applied by teachers. The report outlines two broad challenges which confront teachers. The first of these is described as defining excellent teaching practice and the second involves developing the capacity to 'deliver' this excellent teaching practice consistently and reliably across school systems. Successful school systems, such as Singapore, are put forward as models of how to improve practice, including the provision of 100 hours of professional development per year. However, this alone is seen as insufficient. Alongside this more traditional emphasis upon dissemination, the McKinsey Report also argues that change needs to occur at the level of the individual teacher in terms of greater awareness of particular weaknesses in his/her own practice, and involve having the opportunity to observe instances of best practice in real settings, and then undertake necessary improvements. The logic of individual learning dominates, and is valued above more collaborative approaches. While there is recognition that more teacher learning needs to take place in teachers' own classrooms, advocacy of four broad approaches to improve teachers' instructional capabilities appear to locate the capacity to identify and cultivate excellent educational practice at one step removed from teachers' actual practice. These approaches are described as: building practical skills during initial teacher training; placing coaches in schools to support teachers; selecting and developing effective instructional leaders and enabling teachers to learn from each other. While these initiatives are reported as beneficial in terms of improving elements of practice, the extent to which they foster a disposition amongst teachers to research their own practice, in context, is not immediately apparent.

This advocacy for external approaches to teachers' learning is extensive in spite of a lack of evidence of its benefits. In their research into the factors which enable and constrain the transfer of good practice between schools at the school and individual level, involving 120 schooling practitioners, Fielding, Bragg, Craig, Cunningham, Eraut, Gillinson and Horne (2005) caution that it is more beneficial to emphasise learning/transfer in terms of 'joint practice development' rather than as a process of simple transference of 'good practice.' Drawing upon Fielding et al.'s (2005) study, Pickering (2005) foregrounds the need for teachers to be active knowledge makers in such a process, rather than just passive recipients:

> In their study for the DfES, Fielding et al. (2005) challenged the view that transfer of good practice was the most effective form of professional development. In the study, teachers talk about the need for the mutuality of the CPD process and the need to see CPD as a learning partnership, not as the 'giving and receiving' relationship of transfer, but as what the research team came to call 'joint practice development.' Although not defined, joint practice development is seen as a validation of 'the existing practice of teachers who are trying to learn new ways of working and acknowledges the effort of those who are trying to support them' (Fielding et al., 2005, p. 3). This emerges from 'their having developed creative ways of working and the complex task of opening up and sharing practice with others' (ibid). (p. 197)

Similarly, but from a more sociological-analytical perspective, rather than an 'evidence-based' or 'evidence-informed' approach, Lingard and Renshaw (2009) argue that teaching should be a research-informed and research informing practice. Such an approach foregrounds the capacity and necessity of teachers to actively mediate how research informs their practice, and implies a trust-based professionalism which ascribes teachers with the authority to make value judgments about how this should occur. Such an approach validates more active inquiry approaches on the part of teachers, encouraging teacher research as a process to experience, rather than simply a product to be consumed. By doing so, it is hoped to avoid the temptation to seek out simple solutions—'what works'—which inevitably disappoint (Biesta, 2007). The research habitus both evident and encouraged is one which is imbued with a broad understanding of practice, rather than a narrowly conceived 'evidence-based' approach, limited to supporting teachers as the acquirers of research generated beyond their immediate contexts. However, the extent to which such a reflexive habitus can be cultivated remains an open question, particularly given strong advocacy for more simplistic solutions. (See Chapter 6, this volume, for a more hopeful take on this situation.)

THE INFLUENCE OF CHANGE IN UNIVERSITIES

Research in education does not only occur within the teaching profession, but is an institutionalised part of the work of academics in universities. Consequently, it is subject to changes in the tertiary sector, where there is both support for alternative approaches to teacher professional development research, and where more traditional research is undertaken and encouraged. Circumstances at the tertiary level affect the nature of the research which is supported, how it is undertaken, and consequently, the research trends which become apparent over time. While differences exist across different countries, with their specific approaches to university provision, there are also important similarities which have influenced research associated with teachers' professional development, and which become apparent when focusing attention upon the nature of research within specific nation-states.

In Australia, while schools are the constitutional responsibility of the states, since 1974, universities have been funded by the Commonwealth (Lingard and Porter, 1997). Beginning in the early 1990s in Australia, reductions in federal funding have had a significant impact upon the types of research considered of most value, and therefore funded (Lingard and Porter, 1997); this has occurred as the state has shifted responsibility and accountability for utilisation of funds to individual researchers, which has increased pressure on the tertiary sector as a whole, and the nature of the educational research which is supported and funded (Lingard and Blackmore, 1997). Divisions in labour between academics have also altered the way they go about doing their research, contributing to greater competitiveness (McCollow and Lingard, 1997). As in the United States, where the research of most value (and considered worthy of funding) is being rearticulated by the National Research Council as that which is deemed to contribute overtly to improvements in student outcomes, typically defined in narrow academic terms, there has been an increased focus upon commissioned research in Australia which 'tends to be very targeted, of a particular methodological kind, linked to immediate governmental policy interests and with short-term purposes in mind' (Lingard, 2001, p. 17). The latest federal government 'Smart School' initiative, which includes support for research into targeted areas of literacy, numeracy, socio-economic disadvantage and 'quality teaching,' exemplifies this focus upon immediate government priorities (DEEWR, 2010). Furthermore, recent moves to rank academic journals, with practitioner-oriented journals ranked more lowly, and increased pressure to produce improved internationally recognised research 'outputs,' is evidence of the increased metrification of research-related work. In Australia, such trends have had a deleterious effect upon more national-focused research, and have the potential to narrow the breadth of research undertaken, thereby recalibrating academic work (Hardy, Heimans and Lingard, 2011). Under such circumstances, support for action research and research into broader foci or initiatives which may be designed to better understand the circumstances of teachers' work, may not attract support.

The adoption of recommendations from policies such as the 'West Report' (Commonwealth of Australia, 1998), *Learning for Life, Review into Higher Education*, has led to a more quasi-marketised approach to research practices in the tertiary sector. Also, the rearticulation of students as 'clients' has meant universities have been expected to be 'more willing and able than ever before to respond quickly and flexibly to their diverse and changing needs' (Commonwealth of Australia, 1998, p. 67). As well, the shift to mass provision within the university sector, in conjunction with a more managerial approach, has led to increases in staff-student ratios (Karmel, 2003). This 'client' focus as the new orthodoxy, together with reductions in funding to the tertiary sector in real terms has influenced all facets of the academic habitus. While it is important to acknowledge additional funding to the tertiary sector since 2006, and ongoing discussions about various research compacts between the federal government and individual universities more recently, the tertiary sector is still under considerable pressure, with continued calls for increased efficiencies. Pressures upon universities to become more entrepreneurial affect how academics comport themselves (Marginson, 2002). All of these factors have affected engagement between academics and teachers, leading to a reduction in collaboration and research undertaken across the school and university sectors.

In the United Kingdom, similar performativity and accountability-oriented logics are perhaps most evident with the increased focus upon research quality and output as a result of the Research Assessment Exercise (RAE). Concerns about the impact of research have resulted in an increased interest in applied and 'practice-based' research (Furlong and Oancea, 2005). However, action research and other teacher-as-researcher logics have been found not to fit neatly into such categories. Practitioner research is not easily categorised as either practice oriented or a traditional form of research, but as drawing upon elements of both. In their efforts to provide greater conceptual understanding of applied and practice-based research, Furlong and Oancea (2005) defined applied and practice-based research as:

> an area situated between academia-led theoretical pursuits (e.g., historical research) and research-informed practice, and consisting of a multitude of models of research explicitly conducted in, with, and/or for practice. (p. 9)

In the context of the RAE, Furlong and Oancea (2005) developed a multi-dimensional approach to assessing the quality of research. Under this model, research was to conform to the following criteria: epistemic (methodological rigour), economic (cost-effectiveness), value for use (technological approach) and capacity building and value for people (fostering practical wisdom) (Furlong and Oancea, 2005). Apart from the inherent tensions within such an approach which endeavours to isolate practical wisdom as one amongst several 'criteria' (Carr, 2007), such criteria also serve as a regulatory framework which delimits what is considered 'quality' research. Carr (2007) points out how Furlong and Oancea developed their initial ideas further in a subsequent paper, arguing that it was not their intention to delimit a set of criteria which could be applied universally to determine quality in applied and practice-based research (see Oancea and Furlong (2007) for a further elaboration of this point). By drawing explicitly upon Aristotle's concepts of theoria, poesis and praxis, Oancea and Furlong (2007) endeavoured to reframe the issue of how to interpret practice-based research beyond a more technicist and piece-meal approach. This debate is significant because it reveals that the RAE influences what is construed as worthwhile research, and within this context, practitioner research and other alternative approaches to research, struggle for recognition within tighter, econometric research measurement frameworks.

Canadian researchers, like those in Australia and England, have also been influenced by governmental steering mechanisms via higher education policy. Metcalfe and Fenwick (2009) reveal how the Canadian government sought to develop research capacity within Canada which will contribute to national competitiveness. Under such circumstances, even discourses about knowledge for the sake of knowledge are intimately implicated in broader discourses of economic development. Metcalfe and Fenwick (2009) show how the Canadian government's 2002 policy, *Achieving Excellence: Investing in People, Knowledge and Opportunity* and three subsequent programs funded through the initiative—*Canada Foundation for Innovation,* the *Workplace Skills Strategy* and the *Canadian Council for Learning*—were oriented towards critiquing the extent to which Canada was being innovative in comparison with other countries. Discussions surrounding these initiatives were heavily influenced by economic discourses even as participants endeavoured to focus more strongly on community partnerships. Furthermore, a continued bias towards providing funds to recognised research-oriented institutions limits the nature of associations, and the distribution of resources which is possible. Canadian higher education is also characterised by increasing competition between universities, the application of market-oriented mechanisms, and increased accountability demands, including compacts between individual universities and provincial governments (who fund the higher education sector in Canada):

> At the institutional level, there are more 'ties that bind,' more targets to be met, more funds to be matched, more partners to be found and more accountability plans to be submitted, as the government expands its mechanisms of control. (Shanahan and Jones, 2007, p. 42)

This includes significantly increased pressure upon Canadian academics to secure external research income (Polster, 2007). Under these circumstances, alternative knowledge modes, such as those involving teachers adopting the role of knowledge producers, become increasingly difficult to be involved in and to support.

Added to this, within the competitive field of higher education, universities the world over are also positioned in a subordinate position to the elite American universities which effectively set the standard for what constitutes the leading model of university education. Marginson (2008) reveals various manifestations of American hegemony, including: the way in which American institutions have dominant research concentrations and are able to influence global flows of knowledge, the dominance of the English language, how American universities attract people to them and the way in which American universities serve as 'ideals' against which other universities measure their performance. These 'ideals' include the traditional, high-status, not-for-profit, private, research-intensive university, and the for-profit vocational university seen as responsive to the market. Both of these 'ideals' influence how the sector is construed in other nation states, and how the university sector takes shape within these countries. On the first model, teacher research and it variants lack prestige; on the second, such research is seen as irrelevant, and insufficiently attuned to perceptions of market need.

Furthermore, more serendipitous conditions also influence the place of educational research and the research which is supported at the university level at any given moment in time. In their reflections on when 'history happens to research,' Piquemal and Kouritzin (2006) highlight how broader political events influence what is deemed valuable and valid research. In their case, in deciding to undertake international comparative research into social suggestive norms in the context of language teaching and learning in Canadian, French and Japanese universities, Piquemal and Kouritzin (2006) found themselves engaged in research deemed important in a broader political context in which a relative lack of Arabic-English translators was construed as contributing to insufficient warning about the September 11 attacks. All of a sudden, research into cross-cultural issues became the new 'hot topic.' These researchers speculated that changed political circumstances probably contributed to the success of an application by two junior, untenured academic members of staff. Teachers' learning, a perennial issue, lacks the sense of immediacy and panache of some foci.

Under these collective circumstances, it is perhaps not surprising that modes of teacher learning which actively involve practitioners inquiring into their circumstances are residualised in relation to other pressures and demands within the academy. This is on top of more traditional reservations about the nature of knowledge developed through practitioner research. McWilliam (2004) asks the question 'W(h)ither practitioner research?' criticising the denigration of practitioner research in a tertiary environment tightly allied to conceptions of 'disinterestedness' as the dominant paradigm of knowledge production. The concept of practitioner inquiry, with its explicit focus upon the interests of those involved, is seen as anathema to the *esprit de corps* of the modern university. This is reinforced by the increased emphasis upon citation rates and the focus on measuring productivity in terms of research outputs. The capitals of most value in the current academic economy are large numbers of articles and citations in prestigious outlets—'tier 1'/'A-star'/'four-star' journals—and research-related grants. Such measuring serves as a proxy for the effectiveness of research, and ranks research along a 'global binary':

> A tight binary logic of inclusion/exclusion assigns worldwide academic labour to one of two categories: part of the global research circuit that uses the dominant language and publishes in the recognised outlets; or 'not global,' outside the hegemonic circuit, the bearer of knowledge obsolete or meaningless and doomed to be invisible. (Marginson, 2008, p. 314)

These conceptions of research are distant from the logics of teachers-as-researchers of their own practice. Under these circumstances, teacher research is not construed as likely to result in either products or knowledge which are able to be commercialised, research outputs construed as valuable within performative tertiary settings, or knowledge deemed valuable in and of itself within more traditional conceptions of knowledge development. Teacher-research is in real danger of invisibility.

Collectively, these pressures within university settings contribute to the continuation of research into PD as an external activity involving academic and commercial researchers inquiring into teachers' practices in schooling settings without comparable support for teachers to be researchers of their own practice. This has the potential to narrow the understanding of the provision of teacher learning, and to reduce it to an activity or series of activities designed to implement the findings of research undertaken in other contexts (Lingard, 2001). Such an approach marginalises teacher-initiated research and construes the findings of those engaged in teaching as being of lesser value than research undertaken by those beyond the school site; the notion of teacher-as-intellectual (Giroux, 1988) is steadily attenuated under such circumstances. The result of these pressures is a more conservative approach to teachers' learning, with decreased opportunity for school-university partnerships aimed at fostering action research and teacher-as-researcher approaches more generally. More dominant approaches are likely to characterise the field of PD practices, and contribute to the continuation of a conservative teacher habitus.

CONCLUSION

This chapter has revealed that teacher professional development exists as research, and that the nature of this research is heavily contested. In broad terms, there is strong pressure for approaches to educational research which construe teachers as the recipients of research undertaken on them, and by others removed from teachers' everyday work settings. Such research adopts a more passive approach to teachers' learning, and leaves little room for input into the nature of the research undertaken, and questions of whose knowledge is of most worth.

However, at the same time, the field of PD practices is also influenced by a considerable history of advocacy for more active involvement by teachers in their own learning. This has included calls for teachers to become action researchers, or teachers-as-researchers of their own practice. Where undertaken, such approaches construe teacher-led PD as an integral part of the work of teachers, even if relatively sketchily supported in comparison with more dominant practices. The failures and difficulties associated with such approaches have also sometimes called them into question, even as evidence of their successes have also ensured continued support. However, the more critical researcher habitus framed by experiences of the challenges of more teacher-centred, collaborative approaches is also one infused by experiences of the potential for such approaches.

More recently, these more active, teacher-centred approaches have faced more severe criticisms in the form of support for reductionist approaches to educational research which seek to foreground more traditional PD practices. The 'medical' model, in particular, has been drawn upon extensively to dismiss alternative approaches to teachers' learning. This process has been exacerbated by the push to quantify and measure educational outcomes, resulting in challenges to those logics which seek to focus more upon the individual learning of teachers *in situ*. Pressures in universities have made it difficult to foster this more profession-based teacher learning, as the push for quantification of outputs diminishes the ability of academics to work closely with those in schools.

Consequently, and as with PD as policy, PD as research is characterised by conflict and contestation. The field of PD practices is a site of tension between different proponents of teachers' learning as research—all of whom agree on the value of teacher PD, but are widely divergent in relation to whether and how teachers can or should be researchers of their own practice.

Part II

Professional Development in Practice

4 Professional Development in Practice
PD as Teachers' Work

[T]eachers in most schools were accustomed to showing up at professional-development sessions, listening respectfully, taking part in the day's assigned activities, leaving, and then continuing to do what they had always done in their classrooms. (Hubbard, Mehan and Stein, 2006, p. 247)

INTRODUCTION

The literature on teachers' professional development, teachers' work and the sociology of education, more generally, reveal teacher professional development as characterised by a plurality of practices. These practices are not uniform, and do not arise in isolation, but instead reflect the circumstances under which PD as part of teachers' work is undertaken. Often, these circumstances reflect the effects of more managerial and neoliberal logics within schooling settings, and the field of PD practices more generally. This chapter provides insights into the nature of PD as teachers' work, revealing the nature of contestation between different practices within the field of teacher professional development.

While there is advocacy for a much stronger focus upon enhancing learning rather than simply 'delivering' content across the professions (Webster-Wright, 2009), the dominant mode of teacher learning, undertaken as teachers' work, continues to be what has been described as the 'training model' (Zeichner, 2003), often manifesting itself in the form of individual one-off workshops (McRae et al., 2001). The content of such workshops reveal the influence of specific, typically instrumental approaches to teachers' learning, often supported by the state (Day and Sachs, 2004). Many of these short-term, state-sanctioned teacher learning or 'professional development' activities continue to dominate teachers' learning practices for a variety of reasons, including the busyness of teachers' work (Connell, 1985), teachers' desires for learning opportunities which are perceived as immediately applicable to their teaching situations (McRae et al., 2001), the increasing influence of managerial pressures upon principals (Thomson, 2001), and the nature of the cultural and structural fabric of schooling—or what Tyack and Cuban (1995) refer to as the 'grammar of schooling.' More active and productive professional development has also been adumbrated by work intensification in schools and schooling systems more generally (Easthope and Easthope, 2000; Hargreaves, 1994, 2003; Smyth, 2001; Tang and Choi,

2009). Such demands have often arisen in response to more managerial imperatives within schools, and the increasing individualisation of teachers' work (Groundwater-Smith and Mockler, 2009).

At the same time, it needs to be acknowledged that within the past three decades, these practices have been augmented by advocacy for more substantial, longer-term learning opportunities for teachers, as an integral part of teachers' work. This has been due, in part, to the influence of teachers taking a more active role in researching their own practices (see Chapter 3, this volume). Policy support for the action research movement, and other modes of teacher research, and the emphasis upon teachers collaborating together to better understand their work and learning practices, have all exerted influence over traditional approaches to the provision of teachers' learning (Cochran-Smith and Lytle, 1999). Over time, teacher learning initiatives involving teachers inquiring into their own circumstances at school sites have been recognised as increasingly important, such that the logics of practice which characterise the field of PD practices, as expressed as part of teachers' work, are increasingly varied between more active and passive approaches to PD. This is similarly reflected in the varying content supported as part of teachers' professional development.

However, in spite of this increased recognition and valuing of more substantial, ongoing modes of workplace learning—particularly as evident in research into how teachers learn best, and policy support for the results of such research—this has not yet translated into a significant and sustained change in the provision of teachers' learning as part of their work practices. Much PD content reflects the dominance of policy-makers' aspirations to ensure PD practices reflect what are perceived as the immediate needs of the state (Groundwater-Smith and Mockler, 2009); this submission to the doxa of the state reflects the influence of accrued statist capitals, emanating from the field of power. The PD practices which subsequently arise sometimes clash with those valued by teachers as part of their work in schools, and those supported by researchers. These tensions are reflective of a disjunction between the embodied capitals of teachers engaged in daily teaching practices in schools, and the often more economistic and bureaucratic capitals endorsed by the state. Consequently, while there is evidence of more sustained, workplace focused and intensive approaches, which engage teachers more actively in their own learning, over extended periods of time, such initiatives are still relatively uncommon. The short-term workshop approach is still the dominant mode of teacher learning, and much of the content of such workshops reflects pressures created by the immediacy of teachers' work and a narrowing interpretation of the learning needs of teachers (Day and Sachs, 2004). The result is an approach to teachers' professional development which does not reflect what is known about how teachers learn best, and is often described in disparaging terms. This is exemplified in the way in which Borko (2004) describes PD in the context of the United States:

Despite recognition of its importance, the professional development currently available to teachers is woefully inadequate. Each year, schools, districts, and the federal government spend millions, if not billions of dollars on in-service seminars and other forms of professional development that are fragmented, intellectually superficial, and do not take into account what we know about how teachers learn. (p. 3)

This information about what is known about how teachers learn is typically contained within a myriad of articles, reports and other texts into the nature and effects of PD practices, a sample of which were outlined in the previous chapter into professional development as research. In and of themselves, these sources represent one of the most significant forms of capital accumulated by researchers in school and university settings. However, within PD as practice, the extent to which this knowledge is understood, translated, and produced by practitioners, is problematic. Whether and how this occurs influences the nature of PD as part of teachers' work.

THE INFLUENCE OF MANAGERIAL AND NEOLIBERAL LOGICS UPON TEACHERS' WORK

Smyth, Dow, Hattam, Reid and Shacklock (2000) argue that the nature of teachers' work is heavily influenced by the broader context of globalization, and of global capital formation within uncertain times within which such work is undertaken. The economy, with its own logic of calculation and of profit (Bourdieu, 2005), influences teachers who are expected to respond to directives to engage in their work along more business-oriented lines, and in schools which have been increasingly influenced by increased competition and the commodification and marketisation of education. This is in spite of the very different histories, cultures and values which have guided decision-making in education in the past. Smyth et al. (2000) refer to the new circumstances influencing all aspects of work as characterised by:

1. flexible post-Fordist forms of production and restructured workplace organization;
2. a greater reliance on market forces as a mode of regulation, rather than rules, regulations, and centralized bureaucratic modes of organization;
3. more emphasis on image and impression management as a way of shaping consumers;
4. a re-centralization of control in contexts where responsibility for meeting production targets is devolved;
5. resorting to increasingly technicist ways of responding to uncertainty; and,

    6. a greater reliance on technology as the preferred means for resolving complex and intractable social, moral and political problems. (p. 3)

The dominant economistic logics of practice are evident in the way in which these authors construe the work of those in schools in relation to more traditional production processes (Fordist assembly lines), and the framing of education as a measurable entity which can be subject to the business tools of 'production targets' and impression management. This is occurring alongside administrative logics of increased technicisation of education, and efforts to manage the complexity of the educational process. Such processes are more in keeping with businesses and large bureaucracies than schools.

    As a result of the ascendency of these logics, schools have adopted more business-oriented models of workforce participation which have in turn influenced relationships, particularly between teachers and administrators in, and associated with, schools. Goals are increasingly set at a distance, and there is increased pressure upon those in schools to ensure that these goals are met (Lingard and Christie, 2003). As part of this process, the principalship has been rearticulated along more managerial lines, such that the work of principals is more like that of line-managers in a business enterprises, rather than collegial leading educators working with teachers in schools (Thomson, 2004). Much of this work involves 'selling' images and impressions of schools to prospective 'clients'—parents and students—and monitoring performance within schools in terms of increasingly narrowly conceived performance management tools and techniques.

    Such pressures are readily apparent across a variety of national contexts. In Australia, Smyth (2001) argues teachers have undertaken their work in challenging circumstances for some time. The ascendency of more administrative logics have fuelled a push since the 1990s to exclude teachers from more active engagement in the decision-making influencing their work. Rather, those beyond schools have made decisions and prescriptions about teachers' work. The result has been a sense of loss within the profession, at the same time as teaching has been construed as increasingly complex:

> There was a widespread feeling among teachers that their work was undervalued, and even more misunderstood as neither the public nor the media fully understood the increasing complexity of their work—increased retention at postcompulsory years, greater ethnic diversity, the demands for rapidly expanding new areas of study, requirements to accommodate to increasing centrally generated edicts and directives, and all of the complexities landed on schools through the wider breakdown of social capital. (Smyth, 2001, p. 65)

As an example of the complexity which attends the teaching habitus in high modern/postmodern schooling settings, Smyth (2001) refers to the difficulties of implementing the 'Advanced Skills Teacher' classification into schools in Australia as a vehicle to improve the status of teaching, and to challenge entrenched conditions. This initiative ultimately foundered because it was construed as inadequate for capturing the complexity of teachers' actual teaching practices. Bureaucratic logics were resisted as teachers balked at their work becoming part of a process of fabrication, designed to 'impress outsiders' (p. 68), rather than a more authentic, genuine engagement with the principles informing the Advanced Skills classification. The more bureaucratic game of having to account for performance dominated over more legitimate learning practices which should have been an integral part of this work. The individualistic nature of such initiatives was also criticised as not in keeping with the collaborative nature of actual teachers' work. While more administrative and bureaucratic logics were valued at the policy level, teachers' more contextualised habitus—a product of specific and local school settings—led to resistance to discursive support for the 'monopoly of the universal' (Bourdieu, 1998, p. 59) associated with the broader field of power, as sanctioned by the state.

More recently in Australia, the logics of practice of teachers' work have been characterised by increasing management pressures which have influenced the extent to which teachers feel they are able to fulfil their roles effectively. A recent survey by the Australian Secondary Principals' Association reveals that 25 percent of teachers in the first three years of service anticipate leaving the profession within five years. These pressures are associated with tensions between teaching and administrative responsibilities, as well as pressure to teach outside of teachers' subject areas:

1. There is a real tension between achieving a high quality of classroom teaching and progressing one's career through taking on additional-management and day to day administrative responsibilities;
2. A significant minority of beginning teachers are placed under extra pressure by having to provide classroom instruction in unfamiliar subject or year level contexts. (Australian Secondary Principals' Association, 2007, p. 2)

In this way, more administrative and bureaucratic capitals appear to be increasingly valued in a broader field in which the logics of practice of teachers' work are rearticulated in ways alien to many teachers' conceptions of how such work should be enacted.

Similarly, and from a Dutch perspective, van Veen (2008) argues that the rise of these more bureaucratic logics of practice have led to deprofessionalisation amongst Dutch high school teachers, and are evident in significant and widespread concerns about the quality of teaching and education in general. As in Australia, this situation will have significant ramifications for recruitment and retention:

This sense of concern is increased by predictions of enormous teacher shortages in the coming years as a result of not only retirements but also the departure of too many beginning teachers from the profession during the first five years. Furthermore, teachers' working conditions in terms of workload, autonomy, and influence are strongly declining. In other words, the attraction of teaching appears to be at an all time low. (van Veen, 2008, p. 91)

Reflecting Smyth et al.'s (2000) understanding of the new work order as involving increased devolution of responsibility for meeting already established 'production targets,' van Veen (2008) situates concerns about education in the Netherlands as the product of the way in which teachers are treated as the implementers of programs and activities designed by others. This shift in focus from more autonomous professionalism to a more regulated professionalism reflects the influence of more bureaucratic logics. The result is a valuing of more administrative capitals, at odds with the embodied capitals characterising a teaching habitus forged under circumstances of greater trust in teachers' professionalism, and at odds with a belief that teachers should exercise their judgment as part of their professional responsibilities. As the capacity for engaged and ongoing involvement is adumbrated, the teaching habitus which becomes systemically valued is one which complies with systemic requirements and which is prepared to sacrifice individual initiative and design.

These broader administrative and bureaucratic logics have been further exacerbated by other pressures within education. Drawing upon evidence from the United States, Esteve (2006) argues that the rapid rate of educational change, including the transformation from elite to mass education, has led to increasing stress and 'burnout' amongst teachers. Esteve (2006) identifies twelve factors which he believes have been responsible for increased pressure within teaching. Nine of these changes are related to external pressures upon teachers, while only three relate to the specific nature of the work undertaken within teachers' classrooms. These external changes include expectations that teachers will deal with an increased number of tasks associated with students' social and psychological needs, as well as issues related to drug and sex education, and a myriad of other concerns. Broader social and economic pressures for dramatic changes in curriculum content also place pressures upon teachers to keep abreast of the latest developments in particular subjects, and to engage with new disciplines, where necessary. Within schools, Esteve (2006) reveals a lack of adequate resources to undertake the educational renewal called for by educational authorities exacerbates teachers' working conditions. Such pressures contribute to the sense of individualism felt by teachers, exacerbate bureaucratic and administrative pressures upon teachers, and represent challenges to more educative logics.

Speaking from an English perspective, as well as more generally, Whitty (2006) reveals how changing conceptions of professionalism have altered teachers' work. In the earlier postwar period, teachers enjoyed considerable autonomy from the state. However, increased concerns about professionals as self-serving, together with changed economic times during the 1970s, 1980s and 1990s, led to a more restricted form of professionalism involving increased regulation on the part of the state. The broader field of power has exerted increased influence upon other fields, including the field of PD practices, and education more generally. The result is less autonomy than previously, and increased pressure to conform to specified mandates, but also an increased focus upon the individual teacher as responsible for educational outcomes, regardless of circumstances. A shift in notions of professionalism towards a more market-driven model has also seen a fragmentation of professionals into those more oriented towards traditional modes of engagement, often along more welfarist lines, and more managerial and market-oriented professionals whose habitus is reflective of current emphases upon explicit standards and measures of individual performance, and the adoption of market-type mechanisms to promote reform (such as performance-based pay). As an alternative, Whitty (2006) calls for a more democratic conception of professionalism (cf. Sachs (2003) notion of teaching as an 'activist profession') which takes into account the perspectives of the broader parent, student, business and citizen communities, but acknowledges the difficulty of establishing such a position in light of the more limited modes of professionalism endorsed by the state and teachers themselves.

Consequently, the logics of practice of teachers' work are characterised by increased expectations and a plethora of multi-faceted and typically uncoordinated reform efforts, alongside changing social norms, which have all combined to increase the complexity of teaching (Fullan, 2007). Instability, isolation, uncertainty, complexity and overload characterise current practices (Fullan, 2007), a situation which simply builds upon previous concerns, albeit from different sources (cf. Lortie's (1975), Goodlad (1984), Rosenholtz (1991) and Hargreaves's (1994) theorising and research about the challenges which have attended teachers' work over time). Such practices contribute towards explanations of the nature of current professional development practices.

PROFESSIONAL DEVELOPMENT AS TEACHERS' WORK

A broad raft of literature, including in the areas of the sociology of teaching, teachers' work, school reform, educational change and leadership studies, reveals how these broader pressures are manifest in the form of traditional, short-term, state sanctioned approaches to PD, with alternative, teacher-generated and more sustained PD approaches being relatively rare. Harris and Muijs' (2005) summary of some of the main barriers to more effective professional development resonate with these concerns:

- Conditions of service for most teachers mean that little time is available;
- Most teachers' learning is incidental, occurring in the classroom;
- Teachers' learning lives are characterized by fragmentation and discontinuity;
- Direct classroom experience seems to be the principal means for learning;
- Few schools or individual teachers routinely plan for intervention by others into their natural learning lives for the purpose of peer-assisted learning. (Harris and Muijs, 2005, p. 60)

These barriers reveal the dominance of unstructured, conservative, fragmented, immediate and individualistic logics of practice within the field of PD practices. Lock (2006) describes these dominant logics as resulting in the following practices:

(a) one-shot and one-size-fits-all workshops; (b) use of the transmission model from experts to teachers; (c) failure to address school-specific differences; (d) just-in-case training; and (e) system-wide presentations that do not provide sufficient time to plan or to learn new strategies to meet the reality of their own classrooms. (p. 665)

This précis resonates with many of the key features which characterise PD practices.

PD as Short-Term, Individualistic and State Sanctioned

Much professional development is dominated by short-term, individual activities, allied to state-sanctioned prerogatives (McRae et al., 2001; Zeichner, 2003). Such activities frequently serve as the 'default' mode for many teachers' learning. These initiatives lead to an acquiescent habitus amongst teachers, who consequently 'anticipate' themselves as passive recipients of information generated elsewhere (Eisner, 1992). The content of such initiatives is often very generalised in orientation and typically geared towards government-supported agenda, which have become increasingly allied to improving economic productivity in an increasingly competitive global environment (Day and Sachs, 2004). This content is typically delivered via educational departments to teachers who are seen as being in 'deficit'—as lacking in necessary skills to ensure improved, typically academic, outcomes for students (Day and Sachs, 2004). That is, the field of PD practices is one in which teachers' habitus are seen as inadequately disposed to statist conceptions of what should constitute worthwhile teachers' learning, and in need of intervention to address this deficit.

A large-scale Australian survey conducted by McRae et al. in 2000, involving more than 5800 teachers, revealed workshop attendance as the dominant practice for teacher PD for many teachers. Sixty-seven percent of respondents noted that, in the previous year, they had attended workshops involving an external speaker; 60.7 percent had attended workshop discussions with colleagues from their schools; 53.7 percent had attended workshop discussions with colleagues from a range of schools (McRae et al., 2001, p. 147). The content of many of these workshops revolved around particular state-endorsed programs or mandates, which bore no specific relevance to teachers' individual workplaces (McRae et al., 2001). Such days typically involved teachers listening to an external 'expert' (Eisner, 1992) and the content of such workshops was frequently validated in terms of what Sparks and Hirsh (1997) refer to as a 'happiness quotient'—a measure of participants' satisfaction with the particular PD they have just experienced (p.1). These days contribute to, and reflect, a teaching habitus consumed by immediate concerns, and demanding of 'tips and tricks' construed as applicable to teachers' current circumstances. However, given that these workshops are typically targeted at relatively large cohorts of teachers, their content is necessarily broad-based and, as a result, cannot respond to the peculiar local circumstances in which individuals and groups of teachers necessarily undertake their work. Within the McRae et al. (2001) study, more short-term learning dispositions amongst teachers were reflected in the way in which workshop participation dominated dramatically over the 18 percent of respondents who indicated they had been involved in some form of action research project over this same time (McRae et al., 2001).

Similarly, in the English context, these dominant logics are evident in the way Pickering (2007) describes how much PD involves 'delivering' what is considered requisite knowledge and skills to teachers via a mix of external experts, sanctioned by educational governing authorities, and often focused on instances of 'best practice':

> This highly technicist view of teacher development suggests that an increase is best achieved by a standardised approach to CPD [Continuing Professional Development], in which knowledge, skills and understanding are 'delivered' to teachers, and thereby transferred, by a combination of top-down experts and examples of best practice. (Pickering, 2007, p. 193)

These still-dominant practices exacerbate already problematic practices which characterise the nature of teachers' work and lives. Waller (1932) and Lortie's (1975) earlier and influential studies into the sociology of teachers and teaching indicated how all elements of teachers' practice, including their learning, were influenced by the intensity of the role of the teacher. According to Waller (1932), the teacher's role was not sufficiently conducive to learning in general. Instead, the nature of the role meant learning, for all involved in schooling, became 'a sad and serious business' (p. 391). Teachers' habitus were dominated by concerns about the particular circumstances in which they were working, and a belief that learning was a necessarily difficult enterprise. Furthermore, the 'individualism,' 'conservativism' and 'presentism' of Lortie's (1975) Dade County teachers influenced all elements of their professional practice, and what they believed to be possible. The 'egg-crate' structure of an individual teacher, administering to a single class of students, encouraged such an outlook (Lortie, 1975). The doxa of individualism, conservatism and presentism framed teachers' conceptions of what was possible, reducing their sense of efficacy in relation to how learning could be different. All other activities, including the learning teachers experienced, were made to 'fit around' these dominant practices within schools.

This disposition towards conservative, individualistic, short-term PD practices is the product of a relative lack of attention to teachers' needs over time. Drawing upon approaches to PD in the Australian context, Connell (1993) reveals how the provision of teachers' learning needs, typically described in terms of 'in-service' education, have been addressed in a limited range of formats. This has been the case since the inception of such initiatives:

> In-service education was in its infancy in Australia in the early 1960s. It involved little more than an occasional visit to an experimental school if one happened to be reasonably available, lecture-demonstration sessions for teachers at a school or group of schools by a curriculum specialist, and perhaps a day or weekend course at a teachers' college or some other appropriate location. Such activities appear to have had little impact. (Connell, 1993, p. 153)

Such a process was an individual undertaking, involving teachers being 'in-serviced' in specific programs or initiatives relating to content knowledge, classroom management strategies or teaching strategies (Grundy and Robison, 2004). These events typically took one day or half a day to complete and were organised by professional associations or state educational authorities. A strong history of such practices reinforced their doxic status amongst teachers, and teachers' conservative habitus.

Inconsistent focus upon teachers' existing understandings also characterises many learning opportunities for teachers. This is the case for state support for PD for Information and Communications Technologies (ICTs). Drawing on two case studies of PD related to ICTs in the UK, Holmes, Gardner and Galanouli (2007) show how such PD does not always take sufficient account of the existing circumstances prior to such interventions, such as teachers' initial interest in and commitment to engaging with ICTs, or how to encourage teachers to continue to engage with ICTs after initial support is no longer available. The Virtual Learning Environment (VLE) for Citizenship Project involved six teachers in three schools who were all working to establish virtual learning environments in the area of citizenship education. This initiative revealed the importance of discerning teachers' initial values and attitude towards ICTs as a precursor to engaging in professional development activities associated with such initiatives. The initiative was not considered as successful as it may have been because of a lack of awareness of the values and attitudes towards ICTs by some teachers. In contrast, a second case study, the Social Assistance for and with the Visually Impaired (SAVI) initiative, was designed to assist teachers improve their capacity to provide inclusive classrooms in mainstream schooling settings. This case revealed the significance of sustaining engagement with ICTs after the initial support was no longer available. In this instance, the development of an e-community of teachers enabled participants to maintain contact and share ideas on an ongoing basis.

Conservative learning was also evident in the research reported by Slaouti and Barton (2007) who revealed how ICTs were used in the context of modern language teaching by newly qualified teachers in northern England. The research reported that while there was evidence of use of the Internet and word processing as part of the repertoire of teaching practices by these teachers, participants tended not to make as much use of other technologies such as data bases, video-conferencing or other forms of communication. Concerns about technical support to use such resources, as well as behaviour management, meant more traditional learning approaches were employed when using ICTs.

Rae and O'Brien (2007) revealed how ICTs in Scottish primary schools were engaged differentially by teachers. While broader, national prerogatives influenced the nature of ICT professional development undertaken by teachers, the way in which they engaged with these foci was also more in keeping with their own immediate needs and circumstances. Fragkouli and Hammond (2007) also revealed how engagement with ICTs by philology teachers in Greece had variable outcomes. Teacher leaders who had been involved in a previous ICT initiative served as teacher leaders for groups of teachers across multiple school sites. The research revealed that while teachers developed technological skills, and curricula-building skills in relation to the use of ICTs in the context of teaching philology, their engagement in this PD did not influence classroom practice. Lack of time, support and access to technology, as well as a sense in which the curriculum was constraining, were suggested as reasons.

Time

As well as a strong focus upon the immediate, advocacy for more sustainable, ongoing learning opportunities for teachers is also stymied by a teaching habitus which reflects and encourages minimal time allocation to address teachers' learning needs. The myriad of responsibilities typically associated with the role of the teacher all create pressures upon teachers' time (Connell, 1985). Teachers' time-poor dispositions are forged from conditions of having to provide instruction to large numbers of students (particularly in a secondary context). As a result, teachers have minimal structured time, what Little (1999) describes as ' . . . the crowded interstices of the day and week' (p. 234), to devote to formal learning and planning. As Goodlad (1984) reported more than two decades ago, this means that 'teachers who seek to plan very carefully, to create alternative kinds of classroom activities, or to assign and read essays regularly cannot do what they expect of themselves within a normal work week' (p. 170). Consequently, teachers are always seeking ways to manage this work in the most effective manner. Under these circumstances, a teaching habitus is forged which pushes teachers' learning needs to the boundaries of their work. The end result of this is that PD receives less attention than it should.

This doxa of marginalisation of teachers' learning within the field of PD practices is exacerbated by the way in which teachers' work extends well beyond formal teaching duties. A learning-impoverished habitus is also the consequence of teachers' engagement in a host of extra-curricular activities, ranging from such daily or weekly activities as playground duty, bus supervision, sports coaching and training and staff meetings for all manner of matters, to more intermittent, yet still ongoing commitments throughout the year (Connell, 1985). The latter may include parent-teacher interviews, attendance at official functions, school plays, recitals, debating events and public speaking events (Connell, 1985). Such pressures militate against the desire to learn (Wineburg and Grossman, 1998), and encourage a disposition responsive to immediate 'quick fixes,' rather than long-term approaches to the provision of teachers' learning.

This proclivity towards the immediate is further exacerbated by the pressures imposed by more bureaucratic, state-sanctioned demands for reform. Day (2002) argues time constraints have been further exacerbated by the current managerial conditions under which professional development is undertaken. The emphasis upon implementing external programs and initiatives, as well as new curricula or other educational reforms, have reduced the capacity and space to engage in PD oriented towards more localised needs and demands. This narrowing of attention to more immediate foci has detrimental effects upon the capacity of professionals to operate beyond prescribed, functionary roles: 'Concentration of finance and effort on short professional learning opportunities which predominantly focus upon institutionally defined needs may well, in the long term, result in cultural *isolation* and *parochialism*' (Day, 2002, p. 65; emphasis original). For an already conservative teaching habitus, such concerns are particularly problematic.

Day, Sammons, Stobart, Kington and Gu's (2007) investigation into the Variations in Teachers' Work, Lives and their Effects on Pupils (VITAE) project commissioned by the Department for Education and Skills (DfES) in England provides useful insights into teachers' lives, work and effectiveness in different stages of their careers. This research revealed how teachers were particularly concerned about the lack of time to collaborate with colleagues and engage in more reflective practices. This was attributed in part to the valuing of a policy-responsive disposition which foregrounded those issues valued by the state rather than individual schools and teachers. The time of the study, between 2001 and 2005, was a period in which funding for teachers' professional development was devolved directly to schools, but was simultaneously characterised by considerable central direction about how such funds were to be used. This included a focus upon the *Induction Support Program for Newly Qualified Teachers*. Also, the *Teachers' Standards Framework*, which outlines the appropriate standards of practice at specific career stages and associated developmental activities, determined much of the professional development deemed valuable. At the same time, and in spite of efforts to reduce the amount of administrative tasks which teachers undertook as a result of the findings of a major study into teachers' workload by PriceWaterhouseCoopers (2001), the VITAE project revealed teachers' administrative workloads had not reduced. The result was PD practices reflective of policy prerogatives, and a valuing of PD capitals attuned to specific and dominant policies. This was in the context of teachers desirous of alternative, more long-term, collaborative and reflective practices.

Also in the English context, Hodkinson (2009) reports how teachers' professional development as teachers' work is similarly affected by current managerial conditions, and how these conditions affect the amount of time and resources able to be allocated to teachers' learning. In longitudinal, qualitative case studies of four subject departments (Information Technology, Art, Music and History), Hodkinson (2009) reveals how time was considered a major impediment by teachers. This was exacerbated by working in a more managerial context in which concerns about performance management, league tables and classroom inspections took up considerable time and energy. Under such circumstances, a teaching habitus dominated which was reflective of PD initiatives as 'add-ons,' and the most valued capitals being improved standardised test scores. Both teachers and their managers were reported as reluctant to allocate time to engage in PD. Teachers were expected to give up their own time to participate in initiatives beyond the five mandatory allocated PD days designated as such in school calendars. There was also a tendency to allocate resources only to those activities which related to schools' annual development plans—local school-based manifestations of particular government priority areas. Those initiatives which were overtly associated with such foci attracted funding while alternative approaches and foci were neglected.

From a Dutch perspective, van Veen (2008) argues that while teachers' work necessarily requires autonomy on the part of teachers to be able to respond to the specificity of their situations, government regulations and requirements inhibit the extent of this autonomy. Under these circumstances, high work loads make it difficult for teachers to make time to engage in the forms of work which foster professional growth:

> Dutch high school teachers have numerous teaching hours and school days in the year, considerable time pressures, limited possibilities to design their own work, and a high probability of emotional overload and burn out . . . Secondary school teachers thus encounter major time problems when they work in the manner that they prefer and try to grow professionally . . . lack of time seems to be a serious problem for high school teachers in the Netherlands. (van Veen, 2008, p. 104)

Again, the habitus produced by these circumstances is one which is complicit in the marginalisation of substantive allocations of time to teachers' learning, and characterised by conflict over the desired and actual logics of practice associated with the field.

Change

The increasingly rapid rate of change in schools has influenced all facets of teachers' work (Fullan, 1993; 2000; 2007; Fullan and Hargreaves, 1991), further encouraging more superficial learning dispositions amongst teachers. The provision of genuine teacher learning initiatives is difficult to achieve in schooling contexts because of work intensification within schools and schooling systems more generally (Easthope and Easthope, 2000; Hargreaves, 1994; 2003; Smyth, 2001). An increase in the administrative burden upon those in schools means responsibilities traditionally undertaken by heads of department, in secondary schools, for example, are being increasingly taken up by experienced/'advanced' teachers (Easthope and Easthope, 2000). There is also a feeling that those teachers who are not prepared to undertake such responsibilities, but who instead concentrate their efforts upon their classroom activities, are seen as failing to contribute to the full range of roles within their school. Such responses are evidence of teachers' struggles to engage with multiple educational reform agendas which have been added to their purview (Hargreaves, 2003; Smyth, 2001; Smyth et al., 2000). Collectively, these pressures foster a teacher habitus resistant to reflecting upon teaching practice, resulting in the substitution of intellectual creativity with cultures of compliance (Hargreaves, 2003). There is also some evidence that it is permanent, female teachers most committed to their work who are most disadvantaged by time and work-load pressures, as they undertake a plethora of different activities (Easthope and Easthope, 2000). The focus upon establishing a 'culture of care,' which should pervade schooling (Noddings, 1992), falls heavily upon these members. Under these circumstances, the embodied capitals arising from focused teacher learning are resisted. Instead, teachers' dispositions are inclined towards those learning options which are seen as able to be undertaken quickly and which are perceived as immediately relevant to the particular change process at hand.

Elliott (2009) argues that tighter control over the purposes of education in more managerial times also leads to a narrowing of autonomy, with the dominant focus being upon improved standardised test scores, resulting in teachers' learning being increasingly limited in scope and focus. With the increased push for improved standardised test results, professional development has been rearticulated away from more active and teacher-centred modes of learning focused on educational needs in specific settings:

> What is now called 'practitioner research' tends to be understood as an inquiry into how to drive up standards in the classroom. 'Standards' in this context refer to what standardized tests of attainment measure rather than qualities inherent in learning processes that are deemed to be educationally worthwhile in themselves. 'Practitioner research' of this kind is shaped by an objectivist and instrumentalist rationality as opposed to the deliberative and democratic rationality embedded in the idea of research-based teaching to improve the ethical quality of teachers' interactions with students in the teaching-learning process. (Elliott, 2009, p. 179)

The logic of practice which prevails is that of instrumental rationality, as teachers are recast as implementers of state-sanctioned programs, rather than as original contributors to knowledge development. From Elliott's (2009) description, a teaching habitus is forged which is increasingly responsive to standardised state-sanctioned conceptions of student learning. This contrasts with educators such as Elliott's efforts to foster more active engagement on the part of teachers in their own learning. These more active inclinations are also reflective of a more 'researchly' disposition amongst proponents of genuinely student centred action research initiatives (see Chapter 3, this volume, for an elaboration of this 'researchly' disposition). This emphasis upon state-sanctioned programs as vehicles to foster change is also evident in Hustler, McNamara, Jarvis, Londra and Campbell's (2003) report into teachers' perceptions of teacher professional development in England. Of 2,259 survey respondents in the research, 72 percent believed that too many PD days were driven by national agenda.

Individualism

More instrumental logics also exacerbate the individualism which already characterises teachers' learning. While teachers consider collaboration important, a more individualistic disposition is also evident in their belief that they should be able to make decisions in isolation from their colleagues (Grundy and Bonser, 2000). This is a perspective shared by both teachers and principals, although teachers express stronger views about the importance of individual decision-making than do principals. This is in direct contrast with teachers' expressed desire to also engage with colleagues rather than to work in isolation (Grundy and Bonser, 2000)! The weak collaboration which results contributes to feelings of uncertainty amongst teachers, impinging upon teachers' self-concept and their ability to engage in productive work for students' benefit (Rosenholtz, 1991). Such pressures contribute to the continuation of a conservative teaching habitus, and are reflective of the individualistic nature of teachers' work in general: 'Teaching, by and large, in both elementary and secondary schools is a lonely activity' (Eisner, 1992, p. 613).

Darling-Hammond (1998) believes this tendency towards isolation pervades the whole career of teachers. Teachers' individualistic dispositions are a product of the way in which their habitus is forged from being socialised to work alone from the beginning years of many of their careers:

> Most ... teachers start their careers in disadvantaged schools where turnover is highest, are assigned the most educationally needy students whom no one else wants to teach, are given the most demanding teaching loads with the greatest number of extra duties, and receive few curriculum materials and no mentoring. (Darling-Hammond, 1998, p. 10)

Little (1990) refers to this tendency to work alone as the 'persistence of privacy.' Such experiences encourage the 'lone wolf' scenario which sees teachers relying upon their own initiative and resources, rather than seeking to expand their horizons and opportunities for further learning with others (Huberman, 1995). Such individuality complements the conservative logics of practice which have been isolated as typical of the culture of teaching (Lortie, 1975). An example of individualistic cultures of teachers working in their own classrooms in isolation from colleagues is revealed by Hodkinson (2009). In the English faculty in one school in England, teachers' individualistic habitus was forged out of having few opportunities to work with colleagues in their own school, in other subject areas, or other schools. The result was a teaching disposition which construed that there was inadequate time to engage in learning activities, to problematise practice or to alter practice accordingly. The doxa of teacher learning as an individualistic activity also meant that teachers' learning was an incidental activity which arose from teachers' interactions with students, rather than the product of explicit learning initiatives focused upon critiquing teachers' actual practices.

School Cultures and Structures

A more conservative teacher habitus in relation to teachers' learning is also exacerbated by the way in which schools are structured and the cultures which arise within them. The 'grammar of schooling,' the taken-for-granted ways in which schools are organised, affect what occurs within them (Tyack and Cuban, 1995). Within secondary schools, for example, subject departments constitute 'a naturally occurring ground for teachers' interactions and satisfactions' (Little, 1993, p. 149). Such structures can lead to balkanisation within departments, as teachers limit their associations within the school. The teaching habitus arising from such socialisation leads to a lack of participation in substantial learning communities, which can prove difficult to establish (Fullan, 2007). As Fullan (2001) argues, creating purposeful and sustainable communities in high schools is highly problematic: 'I must say, as others have, that they need major surgery . . . Put positively, we need whatever it will take to create purposeful learning communities' (p. 129). Barth (1991) is similarly critical of the norms which become established because of the structural and cultural impediments associated with teachers' isolation within secondary schools: 'God didn't create self-contained classrooms, fifty minute periods, and subjects taught in isolation. We did—because we find working alone safer than and preferable to working together' (p. 128). The more conservative logics of practice encouraged by such practices foster a less reflective teacher habitus which is in turn reflective of these dominant schooling practices.

Schlechty (1997) refers to the need to address both cultural and structural factors to challenge entrenched practices within schools because 'structural change that is not supported by cultural change will eventually be overwhelmed by the culture, for it is in the culture that any organisation finds meaning and stability' (p. 136). A coherent approach within the field of PD practices, so necessary for educational reform, is possible only if both structural and cultural factors are addressed concurrently (Fullan, 2003; Fullan, 2007; Newmann and Associates, 1996; Schlechty, 1997; Sizer, 1994; 1997; Sykes, 1999). The interactions which transpire as a result of structural and cultural limitations are often contrived in nature, typically short-lived and considered relatively ineffectual (Hargreaves, 1994). Also, even where structural changes are introduced, more substantive learning practices are likely to be expunged by conflicting conservative approaches associated with a long acculturation into such practices within the field. Conservative, doxic practices are in danger of eclipsing alternative, emergent practices.

This is particularly the case during those instances of the implementation of complex educational reforms across whole districts, rather than just within individual schools. Hubbard, Mehan and Stein (2006) provide useful insights into the complex logics of teachers' learning within the context of a whole-of-district reform effort in the San Diego City Schools (SDCS) district in southern California. The authors reveal how a fast-paced, centralised and comprehensive reform initiative focused upon improving students' literacy (the 'Balanced Literacy' program) in schools in San Diego conflicted with established norms within the district:

> Despite their familiarity with the literature on the cultural and political dimensions of reform, district leaders seem to have *miscalculated* the potency of the effects of students' background characteristics; local relationships; teacher buy-in; past histories; habits, beliefs, routines, and standard operating procedures; cultural norms; and politics. All influence the fate of a district-wide reform effort. (Hubbard, Mehan and Stein, 2006, p. 241; emphasis original)

The introduction of a reform initiative which was seen as top-down and imposed led to resistance amongst principals and teachers within the district, whose conservative habitus resulted in inadequate 'buy-in' by those most affected by these reforms, and upon whom implementation success or failure depended. These specific cultural and structural influences worked against the enculturation of alternative and more substantive learning logics which have the potential to challenge these more entrenched practices.

Recognising Research

In spite of ongoing attempts and some evidence to the contrary, teacher professional development practices are also influenced by a lack of recognition of the validity of educational research findings, and a subsequent lack of widespread advocacy for alternatives to traditional approaches to teacher learning within the field. The unrelenting, interactive nature of teaching and teachers' work and the lack of systemic support is productive of a conservative teaching habitus predominantly interested in learning experiences believed to be immediately applicable to teachers' own classroom situations (McRae et al., 2001). Shulman's (1986; 1987) 'pedagogical content knowledge' is often left underdeveloped in schooling settings because ' . . . there is little time, encouragement or expectation for such knowledge of practice to be developed or shared within the profession' (Ballet, Kelchtermans and Loughran, 2006, p. 221).

Educational research or research approaches developed in the academy, which are seen by teachers as being characterised by more analytical concerns, are in contestation with the more normative logics of the work of teachers in classrooms, and are consequently often ignored (Labaree, 2003). Within schools, it is 'valued outcomes' which are given greater legitimacy than 'valid explanations' (Labaree, 2003, p. 17). Teachers are constantly and rapidly 'taking decisions in the classroom based upon their view of what is in the best interest of the student' (Day, 1999, p. 12). Under these circumstances, research is perceived as not being sufficiently 'practical, contextual, credible, or accessible'(Gore and Gitlin, 2004, p. 35). The pressures upon teachers create misunderstandings between academic researchers seeking to challenge teachers' emphasis upon immediate concerns, and teachers whose habitus is forged in an environment which makes them predisposed to the immediate. The result is that while more research-oriented logics emphasise the importance of teachers as students of their own professional practice, and of the need for teachers to be aware of more formal research findings undertaken within universities and other educational fora, this is not always borne out by the logics which characterise teacher learning as part of teachers' work. This situation is further complicated by the logic of conflict/contestation necessarily associated with debates within universities about the relative value and validity of research undertaken by teachers, and research on teaching undertaken by university researchers (Cochran-Smith and Lytle, 1990). It is also complicated by recent reforms within education faculties in universities which have seen an increased emphasis upon the practical components of the role of the teacher and a diminution of the role of traditional educational disciplines (Goodson, 2003).

Under these pressures, it is little wonder that teachers' learning struggles to be 'done differently.'

ALTERNATIVE APPROACHES TO PROFESSIONAL DEVELOPMENT AS PART OF TEACHERS' WORK

At the same time, and in spite of the effects of these dominant logics, there is evidence of alternative teacher learning initiatives enjoying some success, both within and beyond individual school sites. Subject-specific networks, for example, have provided opportunities for teachers to reflect more systematically together upon their work and learning. In the state of Queensland, Australia, the Queensland Consortium for Professional Development in Education has documented several case studies of subject-specific networks from across the state, within which teachers took an active role (QCPDE, 2002). The ALEA: Meanjin Brisbane Local Council network was associated with the Australian Literacy Educators' Association and dedicated to fostering collaboration between different groups and individuals with a particular interest in language and literacy in the Brisbane region (QCPDE, 2002). The Queensland Art Teachers' Association was a more longstanding and formalised professional association consisting of primary, secondary and tertiary art teachers established to promote the Visual Arts (QCPDE, 2002). The Cairns Consortium of Schools consisted of a cluster of primary schools which were interested in how they could share human and physical resources to improve the learning opportunities in their respective schools. The Establishing Teachers' Network was developed to provide professional development support for new teachers in the northern part of the Gold Coast. The group was open to teachers returning to the profession after an extended absence, as well as new teachers. Finally, the TAFE Children's Services Network was developed to provide support for teachers involved in the delivery of TAFE courses for the child care industry (QCPDE, 2002). All of these consortia constitute sites for alternative learning opportunities to the more traditional workshop approaches which characterise the field of PD practices. As such, they serve as sites for the production of a teaching habitus quite different from that which currently dominates.

Other alternative teacher learning practices undertaken by teachers include action research projects, the development and maintenance of professional portfolios, formal studies through higher education institutions, school-university partnerships and the beginnings of more substantial engagement with professional standards, and subject-specific teacher networks. At their best, these alternative practices encourage and provide the opportunity for teachers to engage in learning activities with one another, academics and others engaged in schooling processes, in a much more structured fashion. They also involve more input from teachers and are undertaken over longer time frames than is usually the case with most teacher learning events (McRae et al., 2001; Groundwater-Smith and Mockler, 2009). While they acknowledge the continued dominance of short-term workshops, researchers such as McRae et al. (2001) refer to the general trend towards 'embedding professional development activity into standard workplace activities' (p. 166), and provide evidence of what they describe as 'significant conformity' (p. 166) to the general principles of more effective, collaborative teacher learning. Active, ongoing PD focused upon building teachers' content knowledge, facilitating collaborative learning, and providing regular feedback to teachers are found to positively influence student learning (Meiers and Ingvarson, 2005).

Some effort has also been made to utilise standards for more genuinely professional development purposes. Such an approach challenges more reductionist logics often associated with the use of teaching standards. A recent survey and focus interviews of teachers involved in a pilot of professional standards and case studies of representative groups of teachers engaged in utilising these standards for professional learning purposes in Queensland has revealed that such standards have proved beneficial, even if engagement with colleagues has proved difficult because of time constraints (Mayer, Mitchell, Macdonald and Bell, 2005). Teachers' endorsement of the standards for professional learning indicate a more reflective and professionally grounded habitus responsive to conceptions of professional standards which foster the opportunity for more substantive teacher learning (Mayer, Mitchell, Macdonald and Bell, 2005). The use of standards can facilitate genuine teacher learning, and improved practice (Ingvarson, 2005).

Pickering, Daly and Pachler (2007) also provide useful insights into alternative approaches to teacher learning via the Master of Teaching ('MTeach') program through the Institute of Education, University of London. This program was designed to encourage more innovative and effective approaches to teachers' professional development than is typically the case. Rather than treating education as a disciplinary study, the program fostered a much more active approach to teachers' learning:

The Master of Teaching is similar to other Master's-level provision in the field of education in that it aims to provide award bearing professional development for teachers in line with the expectations of the relevant national qualifications framework level descriptors. It is quite different, though, in so far as it does not treat the students' engagement with education as the intellectual study of an academic discipline. Instead, it foregrounds critical reflection on professional practice as well as educational research literacy, i.e., the ability to read, interpret and implement educational policies in a critical and context-sensitive manner as well as to understand, apply and be able to produce educational research and enquiry. (Pickering et al., p. 2)

Drawing on interviews with a group of 20 MTeach graduates, Pickering et al. (2007) reveal how the course fostered alternative approaches to PD which overtly valued teachers' input into their own learning. While acknowledging that those teachers who undertake courses such as the MTeach are highly motivated with 'strong personal and professional drive' (Pickering et al., 2007, p. 199), these teachers' viewpoints provide useful insights into PD practices more generally. Reflecting an overtly critical habitus forged from many years participation in PD activities, one participant, 'Andrew,' described the PD he had experienced in the following terms: 'I have sat through so much bad INSET, that I actually find it difficult to differentiate the merely boring from the utterly intolerable' (in Pickering et al., 2007, p. 200). Pickering et al. (2007) also provide a useful summary of the logics which characterise what they describe as 'good' and 'bad' PD from the perspectives of the teachers interviewed in his research. 'Good PD' is characterised by a focus on learning, the co-construction of knowledge, relates to specific schooling practices, is interactive, challenging, not forced upon teachers, demanding/high level, caters for individual/group needs, is ongoing, and provides information which is novel and insightful. In contrast, 'Bad PD' emphasises teaching rather than learning, is judgemental, superficially entertaining/performance focused, external to schooling practices/needs, encourages passivity (especially through use of PowerPoint), is patronising/forced/low level, addresses mass needs, typically 'one-off' and repeats previously known knowledge (adapted from Pickering et al.,2007, p. 200). The contrasting labels provide cogent insights into the intrinsic contestation which attend teacher PD within the field of PD practices.

In more general terms, and reflective of teacher agency in spite of the nature of much of teachers' work, Ballet, Kelchtermans and Loughran (2006) argue for a refinement of what they describe, drawing upon Apple (1986), as the 'intensification thesis.' Apple (1986) argues teachers' work has become increasingly intensified as they become the targets of increasingly specified curricular, prescribed texts, which effectively limit their capacity to influence the aims and content of the educational practices in which they engage. However, while acknowledging the salience and evidence of the intensification of teachers' work over time, including through increased accountability pressures, Ballet, et al. (2006) suggest a refinement of this argument. Intensification can be mediated by teachers themselves by engaging in more productive professional development practices. Such an approach is an instance of the socio-analysis possible when teachers become attuned to their immediate teaching responsibilities, thereby cultivating more developmental rather than accountability logics.

CHANGING CONCEPTIONS OF SCHOOL LEADERSHIP

The continued reliance upon traditional approaches to the provision of teacher learning is also a product of the nature of the leadership which exists within schools and institutions associated with schooling. Within schools, leadership is recognised as having significant impact upon all elements of practice (King, Ladwig and Lingard, 2001; King and Newmann, 2000; Lingard, Hayes, Mills and Christie, 2003).

The pressures upon principals are multifaceted and complex and influence all aspects of schooling (Leithwood, Jantzi and Steinbeck, 1999). Recent pressures upon the principalship have had a marked, and sometimes deleterious, impact upon the provision of teachers' learning and educational reform processes. The 'principalling' habitus has become increasingly reflective of increased pressures of managerialism within schools, which has led to a culture of hierarchical decision-making. In the English context, Gunter (2001) refers to principals undertaking their work in a neoliberal context within what she describes as 'performing' schools. In Australia, Thomson (2002) argues more technicist approaches to leadership make it difficult to foster the sorts of context-specific work and learning so necessary in schools serving socio-economically struggling communities. Schooling is being increasingly influenced by pressures for increased planning, auditing and accountability. It is these pressures which are rearticulating principals' work, rather than more intrinsically educational issues (Thomson, 2004):

> There is widespread agreement in the scholarly and professional communities that principals' work has become more removed from educational matters, and much more concerned with accounting, 'human relations' and planning and accountability. (Thomson, 2004, p. 50)

Such pressures have meant that decisions are often made at the upper echelons of schools and schooling units, with relatively little input from teachers or other personnel within schools (Grundy and Bonser, 2000). This is in contrast with earlier efforts to promote school management and leadership via more democratic logics.

This influence of more administrative logics has had an impact upon the content of the learning undertaken by staff. Not only do dominant, traditional decision-making practices militate against teachers adopting a more active stance in relation to their own learning needs in schools, but the learning which is supported reflects broad administrative and state-sanctioned logics, many of which may not be associated with fostering teacher learning for student learning (Grundy and Bonser, 2000). Managerial pressure to ensure that teachers are exposed to specific information or approaches deemed valuable within the broader state apparatus, attenuates the capacity of teachers to contribute to addressing their own learning needs. While the increased prevalence of school-based management has resulted in an increased tendency to devolve responsibility to schools, further devolution has not necessarily occurred within schools (Grundy and Bonser, 2000).

This means the content and processes of teacher learning advocated may be oriented towards satisfying managerial prerogatives, rather than addressing students or teachers' learning needs. Hargreaves (1994) comments on the immorality of administrators utilising collaborative time with teachers to achieve administrative functions, typically associated with central mandates. Under these circumstances, alternative learning practices, characterised by more substantial content and genuine collaboration, are marginalised (Hargreaves, 1994). However, the best schools are those in which leadership practices are focused upon improving classroom pedagogies (Hayes, Christie, Mills and Lingard, 2004; Lingard et al., 2003). Dispersed leadership amongst teachers, rather than 'heroic' individual leadership residing with a principal, is necessary for the development of productive modes of teaching and assessment across individual schools (Hayes et al., 2004). In spite of this, while individuals in administrative positions are exhorted to focus upon 'leading learning,' (Lingard et al., 2003) and to engage in more 'sustainable' approaches beyond managerial imperatives (Hargreaves and Fink, 2006), more managerial concerns typically dominate such efforts. Managerial and neoliberal conditions ensure that the lived practices of principals are intricate, complex and often contradictory (Niesche, 2011). This makes it difficult for principals to embrace negotiation, engagement and pedagogically related learning, rather than more administrative functions (Thomson, 2001; 2004). Consequently, the nature of the teacher learning which results may be disconnected from the needs of teachers and students.

CONCLUSION

Teacher learning as part of teachers' work remains heavily influenced by pressure to engage in teacher learning practices which are construed as applicable to teachers' immediate circumstances, and reflect the broader cultural and structural conditions under which such learning occurs. However, and at the same time, there is also evidence of teachers engaging in more substantive learning initiatives, and of teachers taking a more active role in their own learning. Under these circumstances, the teacher habitus evident is one which challenges the passivity of the dominant logics of practice which characterise so much PD at present. Alternative practices involve teachers engaging proactively and critically with evidence of student learning, collaborating with others, and undertaking formalised study as a vehicle to more deeply engage with their work and learning.

While recognised as important, these alternative approaches to teachers' learning have proven difficult to foster within the field of PD practices. More resilient, short-term, externally provided professional development initiatives have continued to exert influence in schooling settings. Such practices are abetted by more bureaucratic and managerial logics, which clash against more intrinsically educational practices, and which have proven so resilient in the context of continuous educational reform. The way in which educational leadership has been rearticulated around more managerial and administrative matters contributes to the resilience of conservative PD practices. The result is a continued emphasis upon more traditional approaches to the delivery of teacher professional development, and a tendency to foreground PD content focused on specific state reforms and initiatives.

5 Professional Development in Practice
PD in Australia, Canada and England

The endless tick-boxes and 'administrivia' associated with quality assurance provide a wealth of 'evidence,' which in turn reportedly has the capacity to build public confidence (as well as contribute to the intensification of teachers' work), but we posit that the real issue of quality lies well beyond the public relations exercise of quality assurance, in the core business of teaching and learning and providing care and support for young people. There is no 'quick fix' in the provision of quality in these quarters—rather, quality teaching and learning is underwritten by sound teacher professional judgement, critical professional discourse between colleagues and access to professional development and learning, which is engaging, situated and relevant to teachers' needs and those of their students. (Groundwater-Smith and Mockler, 2009, p. 10)

INTRODUCTION: UNDERSTANDING PRACTICE IN CONTEXT

The only way to understand educational practices is to study them in context. That is, educational practices need to be understood as intrinsically social activities. They become part of a practitioner's way of being through ongoing engagement with other practitioners involved in a similar practice. The process of 'being' involves the acquisition of specific dispositions through exposure to particular experiences, as well as active strategising on the part of individuals within these contexts (Bourdieu, 1998). Resultant practices have a particular history, such that actual practices are a manifestation of history-in-action, of living history.

Chapter 5 of this volume endeavours to reveal the nature of educational practices as they pertain to teachers' professional development under current policy, research and work conditions, and across selected national contexts. To do so, the chapter reveals in-depth insights into how teachers and other educators influenced by or influencing professional development practices actually understand such practices. However, and at the same time, while allowing teachers and other educators to 'speak for themselves,' it is necessary to simultaneously explore these interpretations in light of the possible practices, and conditions, which exist at any given moment. While the particular practices which arise are possibilities within a potentially infinite array of approaches to PD, these possible practices do not simply exist in isolation from their circumstances, but are instead influenced by these circumstances. Consequently, these practices are construed as possibilities which are structured and influenced by a context which implicitly or explicitly supports and inhibits particular approaches over others, at the same time as they are subject to change by those engaged in them. These practices are understood as possibilities within a specific social context, or 'field,' which is characterised by competition over the resources, or 'capitals' of most value (Bourdieu, 1990; 1998). Such approaches are always in contestation and tension with one another.

To try to understand the dominant PD practices, as well as competing emergent or residual PD practices, it is necessary to focus upon actual professional development practices themselves. To this end, and in the hope of shedding light upon PD practices under more global conditions, this chapter loosely adopts what Stake (2006) describes as a 'multiple case study analysis' of actual professional development practices, within different national contexts. Such an approach explores a particular phenomenon in diverse settings; Stake (2006) describes the collection of cases as a 'quintain.' While each case has its own particular circumstances, details, concerns and sets of relationships, it is the particular phenomenon under investigation which makes the multiple case study approach so valuable:

> Each case to be studied has its own problems and relationships. The cases have their stories to tell, and some of them are included in the multicase report, but the official interest is in the collection of these cases or in the phenomenon exhibited in those cases. We seek to understand better how this whole (in this book, I am going to call the whole—the entity having cases or examples—a 'quintain') operates in different situations. The unique life of the case is interesting for what it can reveal about the quintain. (Stake, 2006, p. vi)

In this chapter, the 'quintain' being referred to is not an individual organisation, group of educators or a policy, but teachers' professional development practices. It is the interest in how professional development is enacted in particular settings, within and across national contexts, which unifies the cases presented. Furthermore, under global conditions, some of the common themes evident across these varying national contexts are worthy of further investigation for what they reveal about the field of PD practices as a globalized field of policy and practice.

CONTEXTUALISING PD IN QUEENSLAND, ONTARIO AND ENGLAND

The cases presented are drawn from research undertaken in regions in three different but related settings—the British Midlands of England, the Canadian province of Ontario and the Australian state of Queensland. Within traditional Euro-centric discourses, Australia and Canada are framed as former dominions of the British Empire with broad historical ties which link them to one another, and to England. While each of these countries have very specific histories, and have evolved differently over time, within these Euro-centric discourses they share a common institutional history, evident in the commensurate parliamentary systems of government, legal systems and democratic governance practices which have developed in each nation. Arguably, there are sufficient commonalities between these to make it possible to profitably explore the resonances which exist across them in relation to public provision of services, including education. It is an exploration of how the professional development practices are currently enacted in specific schooling sites and systems, within and across national contexts, to which this chapter is devoted.

The data presented in this chapter is drawn from ten years of empirical research, beginning in 2001. This includes: a three-year study of the professional development practices of teachers working across a cluster of six schools in the southeast corner of Queensland, Australia, in the early years of the decade; a six-month study of the professional development practices supported and enacted by principals and senior provincial administrators in the Canadian province of Ontario, Canada, in the middle of the decade; and a six-week study of the professional development practices of teachers from a specialist languages college in the British Midlands region, England, during the latter part of the decade. This research has been published widely, or is under review for publication, and only brief contextual details, sufficient to make sense of the broader argument presented in this book, are provided here. (For more detailed expositions on the Australian research, see Hardy and Lingard (2008) and Hardy (2008), and for the Canadian research, see Hardy (2009) and Hardy (2010)).

Queensland

The Australian study, undertaken in a regional community in southeast Queensland between 2001 and 2003, involved exploring the PD practices of a group of ten teachers and school-based administrators who sought to respond proactively to calls for educational reform in Queensland. A large-scale study of teaching practices in Queensland public schools—the Queensland School Reform Longitudinal Study (QSRLS)—revealed that teachers in Queensland provided a socially supportive environment for students, but that there were relatively few connections made between schooling practices and students' experiences beyond school, few instances of the active recognition of social difference in classrooms, and a need to improve the intellectual quality of students' classroom experiences (Lingard, Ladwig, Luke, Mills, Hayes and Gore, 2000). At the same time, and in an effort to foster more engaged and rigorous teaching practices, the public educational authority, Education Queensland, implemented a new curriculum, the 'New Basics,' as an alternative to more traditional disciplinary-based curricula. The New Basics was designed around the fulfilment of various 'rich tasks' as the culminating learning experiences in which students engaged (Education Queensland, 2000). These curricula and assessment reforms were also complemented by an increased focus upon teachers' pedagogical practices. This took the form of teachers being encouraged to critique, individually and collaboratively, their teaching practices. To assist in this process, teachers were encouraged to interrogate and compare their teaching practices with a list of 'productive' practices used originally to research the nature of teachers' pedagogies as part of the QSRLS. These 'Productive Pedagogies'[1] were also conveyed to teachers in more traditional workshops as part of the process of fostering reform in Queensland.

Within this broader context of calls for reform, administrators from a cluster of schools in a regional community in south-east Queensland orchestrated the formation of a group of teachers to work together to help facilitate curriculum, pedagogical and assessment reform across their respective school sites. The group of teachers was composed of experienced teachers from four primary schools, one secondary school and an environmental education centre, and became known collectively the 'Curriculum Board' The cluster of six schools from which these teachers were drawn was described as the 'Future Schools Cluster.'

The Queensland research reported in this chapter reveals how membership of the Curriculum Board served as a vehicle for the professional development of members. Mention is also made of the nature of the professional development opportunities this group sought to facilitate within and across the schools which constituted the Future Schools Cluster more generally. That is, there is a focus on the PD experienced and endorsed by a group of teachers during a period of flux and significant pressure and support for educational reform.

Ontario

The Ontario study, undertaken in the first half of 2007, reveals the insights of senior educators from Ontario, Canada, into the nature of professional development practices in the province during a similar period of rapid educational change. The research draws on the perspectives of twelve principals, six academics with various backgrounds (full-time tenured professors to part-time lecturers seconded from local education authorities/school boards), six senior Ministry of Education officials, as well as representatives from other peak educational authorities in Ontario, including the Elementary Teachers' Federation of Ontario, and the Ontario College of Teachers.

These senior educators were reflecting upon teachers' PD practices during a period of strong support for education in their province, following an earlier period of significant criticism of teachers, and of dramatic cuts in resourcing to all areas of public funding, including education. Since 2003, the provincial government had injected substantial additional funds into education. This included $50 million in 2004 for a new body within the

Ministry of Education, the Literacy and Numeracy Secretariat, which was charged with oversighting improvements in students' literacy and numeracy practices throughout the province. As part of this process, the province set in place an educational improvement regime which included a target of ensuring that 75 percent of students achieved 'level 3' on a four-point scale. These improvements were to be tracked through the province's Education Quality and Accountability Office (EQAO), a body established in 1998 in response to earlier calls for increased attention to the quality of students' literacy and numeracy outcomes in the province.

The Canadian data reveal the nature of the professional development practices supported by these senior administrators, principals and academics, at this time.

England

The English study, undertaken in the latter half of 2009, reports on the PD practices of teachers working in an inner-city comprehensive 11–18 secondary school and languages college, distributed across two campuses in a mid-sized city in the British Midlands. The city and surrounding suburbs were undergoing a slow process of gentrification after a long history as an important manufacturing and industrial centre in England, and indeed the world. A school had originally been established at the site of 'Midlands High' in the late medieval period. During much of the nineteenth century, the school at this site was a privileged religious boys' school, which had transformed into a grammar school by the early twentieth century. By the late 1960s, and reflecting broader demographic trends within the city, the school had become a comprehensive co-educational state college.

At the time of the research, the school had a student population of approximately 1600–1700 students, and catered for students from a range of ethnic and socio-economic backgrounds. Indeed, the school's website described the school as catering for a diverse student population reflecting the diversity to be found within the city more generally. Reflecting its status as a senior languages specialist college, one-third of students were in the sixth form. Half of these students originated from the lower school (which catered for students aged 11–14), with the remainder drawn from schools throughout the city and surrounding suburbs, towns and villages.

The school was generally acknowledged within the broader community as a 'good school.' During interviews, several teachers were at pains to point out that the experiences of students and teachers at this school were different from other, more 'struggling' schools in the city, and England more generally. A recent Ofsted inspection, undertaken during the data collection phase of the research, described the school as 'a good school where all students are valued; they achieve well and their attainment is above average' (Ofsted inspection report, September, 2009). Indeed, the report goes on to describe the school in glowing terms:

All in school share a common goal to achieve excellence for all students. The impact of the specialist language capacity ensures that some of the provision and outcomes for students are extremely good. The school's language specialism prepares students very well for their future. Partnerships with businesses and universities both here and abroad provide real life events and activities for students to experience the world of work. The curriculum is enriched by creative courses which are nationally and internationally recognised. The large numbers of home languages spoken by the students is celebrated with a resulting notable impact on the school's cohesion as a whole. Equality of opportunities is promoted, with students indicating a good comprehension of human rights concerns, and a clear sense of issues pertaining to racial equality.[2]

On both traditional and more progressive measures, this school was considered to provide students with a beneficial educational experience, relevant to the wider world.

Eighteen teachers were interviewed about the nature of the professional development practices they experienced and which they found most beneficial in terms of their students' social and academic learning. Interviewees occupied a number of positions, and included Newly Qualified Teachers (NQTs) and Recently Qualified Teachers (RQTs) in their first and second year, mid-career teachers, and more experienced and later-career teachers. Interviewees were drawn from across multiple faculties/discipline areas. Several had a range of administrative experiences, including as year-level/pastoral advisers, deputy heads of department, heads of department and assistant deputy principals. The deputy principal, who was serving as acting-principal at the time of the research, was also interviewed in relation to his current responsibilities overseeing professional development of staff within the school as a whole.

PD WITHIN AND ACROSS CONTEXTS

Although educators from each of these sites differed significantly from one another, and were located in varied institutional and national/state positions and situations, a number of common themes are evident across their experiences, reflecting, in part, the broader neoliberal and managerial conditions within which their work and learning were undertaken, and challenges to these conditions. These themes also provide useful insights into the interplay between broader policy, research and work conditions within which these educators worked and learned, and the competing logics which attend this process. These themes relate to how educators conceptualised teacher PD, the nature of curriculum-based PD, the influence of the quantification of educational outcomes on teachers' learning, the modes of PD in which teachers engaged and the extent to which teachers felt in control of their PD. Conflicted and varied practices within these themes provide evidence of the field of PD practices as a site of complex and contested logics, and of educators' individual and collective habitus reflective and productive of these tensions and intricacies. These contested practices reveal evidence of the influence of policy support for particular types of PD and resistance to such support, as well as evidence of the dominant and dominated relationship of teacher research to PD, and of the nature of the work practices which characterise teachers' professional development.

Conceptualising PD

The way in which PD is conceptualised by teachers and other educators reveals evidence of the policy, research and work arena on teachers' practices, and of competing neoliberal and managerial logics alongside more educational foci. There was sometimes strong support for particular types of PD, as evident in some senior Ontario educators' propensity to strongly support PD associated with the implementation of centralised policy prerogatives. A more policy-responsive as well as a more learning-focused habitus was evident in the way in which an academic, who acted as an advisor on educational issues to the Ontario government, described how efforts were being made to encourage a shift from more traditional professional development practices to a more substantive 'professional learning' approach:

> Well, in the past, I think [PD] has been a limited notion, which is professional development days, professional development workshops. So we're trying to get away from that; not eliminate them, because they can be valuable for stimulation and new ideas, but we're trying to replace that concept of professional development with—I'll put it in capitals— 'PL,' 'Professional Learning,' and to have that learning grounded in the kind of day-to-day capacity building at the school level, and linked to policy. So people can still do their individual professional development, which they might do at a conference or course, or taking a Masters' degree or whatever. So that's all there, but I think the new conception of Professional Learning is to integrate PD in two ways—one is integrated into the culture of the organisation and what they're trying to accomplish, and the other is to interrelate it with policy. So that it's more purposeful and more collective. (Dyson[3], Professor and government advisor, Ontario)

In this way, there is support for PD, but for PD of a particular ilk. Educators in Ontario were 'trying to get away from' typical PD days and workshops, thereby revealing a strategy to challenge dominant logics of practice within the field of PD practices (see 'Modes of Teacher Learning' later in this chapter for a more specific focus on particular modes of PD). These more dominant practices were construed as competing with efforts to foster more ongoing teacher learning, described as 'professional learning.' The discursive appropriation of the term 'professional learning' in place of professional development could be taken as a strategy to emphasise the value of teachers' learning. For an educator well-versed in the academic research literature, the focus on professional learning as 'grounded in the day-to-day capacity building at the school level' also resonates with the push for localised learning as part of the 'research consensus' (Desimone, 2009), or 'new consensus' (Hawley and Valli, 1999), amongst educational researchers, about the need for PD to be relevant to educators' daily practice and circumstances.

However, and at the same time, explicit efforts to link PD practice with broad conceptions of both organisational culture, and idealised versions of current policy also reveal how the PD valued is that which is consistent with centralised conceptions of policy and practice (see 'Controlling PD' later in this chapter for a more explicit elaboration of the power relations attending teacher PD). While PD was recognised and validated, and there was evidence of, and advocacy for, a 'researchly habitus' (Lingard and Renshaw, 2009) attuned to a desire to cultivate learning at the local level, for PD to be useful, the PD supported had to be linked to more uniform provincial conceptions of whole-school approaches (capacity-building), and the unquestioning implementation of province-wide educational policy. The implication of this push towards 'more purposeful and more collective' PD practices is that a focus on the school as an organisation, and on current educational policy, will lead to improved student learning. In this way, a policy and politically oriented disposition is evident in the valuing of teacher learning as the handmaiden of a dominant, idealised conception of policy and practice, even as there are concurrent efforts to simultaneously recognise more localised and alternative PD practices, at least at the discursive level.

Similarly, in Queensland, the PD supported is heavily influenced by dominant conceptions of teachers as acritical implementers of policy, as well as more active approaches to such learning. The reforms being implemented in Queensland were based on reconstituting the curriculum away from traditional disciplines to a more trans-disciplinary approach, and were qualitatively different than those in Ontario, which focused strongly on more traditional literacy and numeracy curricula. However, in both contexts, a habitus was evident which was influenced by and supported PD focused on centralised policy implementation. This was apparent in the way members of the Curriculum Board accepted the task of working with teachers across the six school sites which constituted the Future Schools Cluster:

> I recall that, from a principal's meeting, the deputy from Cresswell High, Tom . . . they were having concerns with the New Basics that . . . the school was going to be having to do . . . And they were wanting the feeder primary schools to be talking the same language that the

kids will be hearing in Grade Eight. (Hilary, environmental education centre teacher, Queensland)

Well, I think from the point of view of New Basics, we (secondary staff) had certain things we had to do. There were these Year 9 Rich Tasks that we had to implement so we, as a school, had to come up with a way of doing that within our school setting. So [Education Queensland] Departmental requirements led to change, in our theme structure and the way we had to operate. (Lisa, Chair of the Curriculum Board, Queensland)

The PD which was valued and which transpired in Queensland appeared to be dominated by broader policy guidelines. Such a stance reflects not only the dominance of centralised policy pushes for reform—as in Ontario—but also how those positioned in a more dominated position within the field adopt a passive approach in relation to the broader policy logics influencing them. Such a stance reflects the influence of a more managerial approach to organising teachers' work, and of the effects of such practices (namely, how teachers construe themselves as implementers of initiatives developed elsewhere (Day and Sachs, 2004; Eisner, 1992)). Unlike the academic advisor to the Ontario government, these teachers were not intimately acquainted with the policy-making process, and construed themselves primarily as respondents to the push for educational reform within Queensland. Ironically, in Queensland, this more passive habitus was evident in the context of the development of the New Basics curriculum as a more inclusive, essentially more democratic alternative to more traditional curricula, and which sought to challenge more entrenched and less educative learning practices.

Reflecting the relative absence of attention to PD practice in policy-making, and a centralised-policy habitus more generally, several Ministry officials in Ontario conceptualised policy as something which was generated at the provincial/Ministry level, and which was then interpreted by those engaged in PD at the school board/district and school levels. PD practice was marginalised by being conceptualised as something which was more of a concern for those in school boards and schools, rather than the Ministry itself:

So, when I think of it in terms of what's going on out there right now, I would say that in terms of policy direction, it's pretty high level at this point . . . [And] as it filters down, there's more and more room for interpretation by the boards, by the schools, by the teachers themselves. The policies that we put in place tend to be more around higher level curriculum issues or directions as opposed to . . . the PD that then resolves (sic). (William, Ministry official, Ontario)

PD practices were construed as something which resulted from a process of 'filtering' policy from above. While it was recognised that policy 'interpretation' occurred at the board/district level, a conservative educational habitus influenced by more administrative logics was also evident in the unquestioning approach to PD as something specified in policy which was then interpreted at lower levels of the educational bureaucracy. The province determined the policy agenda, and schools implemented the policies.

This process of conceptualising PD 'from above,' and as something to which teachers responded, is also evident in England, where teachers are exhorted to comply with particular policies and strategies. Again, PD is generally devalued. A more critical habitus was evident in the way one experienced teacher described much of the teacher professional development which he had experienced, and experienced by colleagues more generally, as 'death by Powerpoint.' (Nick, Chemistry teacher, England)

In the English context, specific accountability-oriented policy regimes, such as those associated with Ofsted inspections, also add to the administrative tasks which need to be undertaken in schools. As a result, a compliant habitus is evident amongst educators in which there seems to be considerable emphasis upon the superficial as well as the substantive. For the head of the Art department, under these circumstances, what was learnt, in part, was how to comply with such regulations and to produce appropriate paper reports/plans:

> I think what Ofsted did was enabled us as a department to have to quickly galvanise ourselves from an administrative point of view. I mean everything was in—you can see here the set-up [points to draws and filing cabinets]. Everything here is labelled in draws and all the rest of it. But what was really interesting was we've got an NQT [newly qualified teacher] who's just come through all the lesson planning. Very, very tight. Every 'i' has to be 'dotted'; every 't' crossed. So she was able to input a lot of information as regards what was a good paper piece of lesson planning. It enabled me, as the head of department, to sort of have a look at the framework that we have as a department, and help me refine and galvanise more, the annual plan that's in place. (Leonard, Head of Art, England)

Under these conditions, administrative logics in response to government policies requiring periodic Ofsted inspections cultivated a teacher habitus reflective of more managerial concerns. Compliance with administrative requirements seemed to encourage learning about managerial processes rather than about how to effect more substantive reform. Under such circumstances, PD is marginalised.

However, and at the same time, there is recognition that PD is and could be important, and that those within school boards/districts/authorities and schools could exercise agency in relation to the PD 'that then resolves' (William, Ministry official, Ontario), thereby simultaneously challenging these broader managerial logics. There is at least some recognition of teachers and other educators as 'policy-makers' and policy actors themselves as they actively negotiate the parameters and constraints within which their work is framed (Taylor, Rizvi, Lingard and Henry, 1997; Rizvi and Lingard, 2010).

Alongside more managerial logics, agentic responses are construed as possible, and as contributing to the policy parameters which then ensue. The sense of PD as important and as being able to be influenced from within the profession is evident in the way senior members of the Ontario College of Teachers (OCT) sought to construe the relationship between the regulatory and more developmental aspects of the Ontario College of Teachers, and the role of teachers in developing the guidelines to guide learning within the profession. The sheer volume of initiatives associated with teachers' PD in the form of various programs/courses described as 'Additional Qualifications' also reflects a systemic focus on PD:

> [Regulatory and developmental components of the OCT] often support one another. For instance, if you looked at the Additional Qualifications courses and programs—there are over 200 of them—and the development of those guidelines occurred in consultation with practitioners, members of the public, educational partners, community groups, so they were developed collaboratively, to ensure that the knowledge and skills in them are necessary, that those courses do reflect the needs in the field, that they do respond to the current profiles of learners. (Olivia, senior member of OCT, Ontario)

> For each course that Olivia is talking about, there will be approximately 10 pages of guidelines, developed collaboratively, you know, with colleagues in the profession and public, regarding the length of those courses, the content in those courses and the framing of those courses, and those courses need to be framed and reflect the professional standards. (Elizabeth, senior member of OCT, Ontario)

While the regulations/guidelines associated with the formal AQ courses clearly influenced the nature of the PD practices advocated in Ontario, and while a compliant habitus is evident on the part of two senior members of the OCT who were formerly teachers but had been employed in an administrative role with the OCT for several years, at the same time, the existence of these courses is also indicative of a valuing of more profession-oriented PD in general.

Support for specific standards of practice by members of the OCT also reflects a valuing of teachers' learning. Such standards were seen as explicitly focused upon what teachers should know and be able to do:

> Let's use the examples of the standards. One of the requirements of a regulatory body is to define the nature of the profession—what are the standards for the profession—what do teachers need to know, or what

does the profession need to know and be able to do, and so that's been there since the very beginning, and I think we've expanded the number of people, and the variety of ways that we've gathered data from engaged members of the profession, over a 10-year period. (Olivia, senior member of OCT)

The way in which teachers engaged with these standards more generally was somewhat more complex, though, than might first appear to be the case. While these standards had a significant regulatory effect upon the profession, whether and how teachers engaged with them was dependent upon the nature of the PD in which teachers participated:

> I'm not sure the College [OCT] has had a big influence [on PD]. They would, if you talk to them; they'll sound like they have. Teachers in general don't really use the standards of practice. The only time a teacher would hear about the standards of practice is if they were taking an AQ course, and even in the AQ course, it would depend upon who was teaching that course, whether a lot of time, or a tiny bit of time was spent on the standards. (Linda, Ontario Elementary Teachers' Federation, Ontario)

While the standards of practice were significant managerial policy levers, influencing how Additional Qualifications were framed, and therefore how PD was conceptualised within the province, for a member of staff of one of the largest teachers' federations/unions in Canada, and who worked regularly with teachers in applying new curricula and understanding provincial reforms, actual engagement with the standards as part of teachers' PD was a much more haphazard affair. A more active and activist disposition problematised a simple process of acquiescence to more managerially oriented, policy-informed logics focused on the standards of practice. Again, and in a different way, a more agentic, critical policy-responsive habitus is evident, arising from active engagement with professional standards.

In England, at the same time that managerial foci exert influence, there is also a valuing of PD which goes beyond more managerial conceptions of policy and practice. A more active habitus, forged from ongoing focus on discipline-specific teaching practice, led to PD being construed as relevant when responsive to teachers' perceived and actual needs:

> I used to have a sinking feeling when CPD was mentioned because I hadn't any real deep sense that I needed developing. I was really more concerned with the day to day workings of my job and trying to do what I was doing well and better rather than perhaps differently. Now obviously CPD should help make you do the job you're doing better, but I felt that I was really wanting to spend all my energy

getting my behaviour sorted out in class rooms, which is probably similar to a lot of teachers; they can have CPD for that, that's no doubt. So I did shy away from it early on. But because I became involved in sort of a wide range of Chemistry through the Royal Society of Chemistry, I've realised what CPD can actually be, and that it can be really beneficial to teachers. So through the RSC, I'm involved in delivering CPD—a slight irony—and I realise now the value that it has. And that it doesn't need to have a sense that the teachers are there just to have 'a jolly' out of school—if anybody ever feels that CPD is 'a jolly,' I'm not sure—but it leaves people feeling empowered to do their job. So I guess I now see professional development in several ways, in that it leads to a development of the individual from a subject appreciation, appreciation for education, appreciation for young people. It also perhaps gives them the tools that help to go back into their school and do the job. So I guess CPD is different for different people and I guess it depends on the type of CPD. (Clinton, Chemistry teacher, England)

From initial experiences of PD as an external imposition upon teachers' time, PD came to be seen as an opportunity to further develop one's own and other teachers' understandings of their work, from a variety of perspectives. Arguably, by engaging in a process of reflective socio-analysis in relation to his own specific circumstances, this teacher came to see PD as valuable for his own, and others' learning. Participation in the Royal Society of Chemistry led to an understanding of how PD could be different from perhaps dominant approaches—approaches which led to 'a sinking feeling' whenever the term PD was mentioned. Such involvement reveals a more reflective habitus on the part of a teacher who, by his own admission, began his career in a reactive rather than proactive relationship to his own learning. That more active involvement in his own learning led to a change in his perspective, including active advocacy of more productive PD practices, is evidence of the power of an alternative to more neoliberal and managerial logics within the field of PD practices.

PD and the Curriculum

The existence of more neoliberal and economistic logics alongside more educative logics in policy, research and practice is also reflected in the way PD is enacted in relation to the curriculum. From the outset in Queensland, the curriculum was considered a key area of intervention for teachers' learning. This focus upon the curriculum was in keeping with support for curriculum renewal within the key state policy at the time, *Queensland State Education 2010* (QSE2010), and was integral to securing federal government funding through the Australian federal government *Quality Teacher Programme* (QTP):

> In aligning with QSE2010, the Future Schools Cluster is developing a seamless curriculum through the implementation of a middle school project. (Proposal submitted for QTP funding by Deputy-Principal of the secondary school)

This emphasis upon the curriculum was a response to research-informed policy concerns in Queensland arising out of the Queensland School Reform Longitudinal Study (QSRLS) about the relatively poor quality of classroom practices for students in the middle (particularly lower secondary) years of schooling. It was also a response to national QTP policies which required a focus upon particular disciplinary areas:

> The main focus of the project is the development of the middle school through teacher networks in the areas of Technology, Literacy, Numeracy and Science. A Curriculum Board comprising teachers from each school coordinates teacher networks and provides leadership and direction for that section of the project. (Proposal submitted for QTP funding by deputy-principal of the secondary school)

The focus upon teacher learning within the disciplinary areas of literacy, numeracy, science and ICTs reflects a more utilitarian conception of education, as these are areas deemed more likely to lead to improvements in economic productivity (Smyth et al., 2000). Such foci reflect a field of PD practices characterised by increased alignment between education and the economy, a situation which has become increasingly prevalent more recently (Hartley, 2003; Smyth, 2001). The PD practices most valued under these circumstances are those groupings, networks and associations deemed most likely to facilitate teacher learning for student learning closely associated with improved economic output.

The influence of more economistic logics are also apparent in the Ontario context, with its focus on literacy and numeracy. This was reflected in principals' comments:

> Certainly, the [Literacy and Numeracy] Secretariat has been, I think, part of the biggest driver [for PD] ... so in every school, and in all directions—you would be getting it from the board office—it would be around literacy and numeracy initiatives in your school. (Richard, elementary principal, Ontario)

> ... from the system ... [our] School Effectiveness Plan has to be in the area of literacy, numeracy, climate/culture. (Tricia, elementary principal, Ontario)

In England, while teachers' learning focused less overtly upon the dominance of some disciplines over others, PD dominated by discipline-specific initiatives reflects more conservative department-centric teacher learning practices. In the Chemistry department for example, discipline-specific knowledge was the dominant focus:

> [PD] tends to be quite department-centric to be honest, I mean, there are things we have to buy into, as part of the whole school development, but off the top of my head, it tends to be things that actually might impact on our lessons in the department . . . The problem we've had is just that we've had so much change in the last couple of years with implementing a new Triple Award, Science GCSEs[4] to Year 9—so take it down a year group—and then, obviously, we restructured in Key Stage 3. We've had a new syllabus and scheme, AS1 and 2[5]. So just trying to keep up with that, and do our core business, has been difficult enough. (Jason, Chemistry teacher, England)

> We feel as a department that most of our professional development occurs really within, between ourselves. I'd say we're very tight knit. There are 6 A-level Chemistry teachers within our Chemistry department, and a Chemistry technician who's a PHD chemist in his 50s, and between the 7 of us, we talk about Chemistry a lot and learn a lot from each other. (Clinton, Chemistry teacher, England)

> So, staff have certainly looked at ways of teaching the [Chemistry] syllabus and different activities that have enabled kids to achieve improved results. I've actually been to some training courses to look at different specifications from a different board. (Nick, Chemistry teacher, England)

Reflecting the effects of subject specialisation in secondary schools, teachers' ongoing work as members of a busy Chemistry department was productive of a conservative habitus focused primarily on PD associated with changes to disciplinary syllabi. This conservative habitus was fostered by a strong and coherent culture of learning from colleagues within the discipline.

In Queensland, the name of the coordinating body responsible for orchestrating the various teacher networks within the Future Schools Cluster—the 'Curriculum Board'—reflects how issues pertaining to curriculum, management and teacher learning coalesced. The term evokes notions of a 'board of directors' in the commercial world, and intimates that the group was responsible for 'overseeing' or supervising the activities, or 'productivity' of teachers engaging in curriculum reform. At a discursive level, the Curriculum Board is indicative of those policy and broader social pressures around management issues and more managerial logics, with their concerns about maximising outcomes at least cost, more typical of private enterprise than the public sector. This is in keeping with earlier emphases upon managerialism within the public sector as a whole (Cerny, 1990; Painter, 1997; Yeatman, 1993).

In the context of these more managerial logics, there was also evidence of teachers being appropriated for the purposes of facilitating curriculum renewal, at least initially. This was readily recognised within the group:

> So the principal group had met, I know at least on one occasion and then they'd chosen key teachers in the schools to go along to a day and from that the Board was formed. (Lisa, Chair of the Curriculum Board, Queensland)

Policy pressure for curriculum renewal upon those in schools led to a relatively rapid response amongst administrators as they sought to respond to concerns about student outcomes in the middle years. The way in which the administrators encouraged the development of the Curriculum Board, and an acquiescent habitus on the part of members, also reflects the tendency for educational authorities to strategically appropriate the energies of teachers for their own purposes (Grundy and Bonser, 2000; Hargreaves, 1994)—a situation exacerbated by short time frames associated with government policy implementation cycles.

Board members' compliant habitus is evident in how they construed their work as a vehicle to assist administrators to explicitly address specific state policies and initiatives:

> I think the success of the Board is the fact that the principals' association is extremely keen for it to continue. They see that as something, an initiative of theirs in a way, that actually helps them meet departmental and district office and state government sorts of guidelines and things that they need to do. It's made it easier on them. (Kim, primary teacher, Queensland)

A submissive disposition on the part of members of the Board appeared evident, and helps explain how the administrators were able to be policy-responsive under conditions which prohibit the sorts of long-term, inquiry-development processes necessary for more sustainable teacher learning practices. A conservative policy-responsive habitus, attuned to responding to policy directives for improved curriculum, typically in specified, traditional disciplines, is evident on the part of administrators, and on the part of teachers.

At the same time, the focus on curriculum reform in the Future Schools Cluster constitutes part of a broader set of competitive pressures upon schools within Queensland at this time. In the context of more neoliberal logics, the formation of the Curriculum Board was designed to stimulate teachers' learning for its members and other teachers in the Future Schools Cluster to ensure a marketing edge in a broader competitive school market place. The work and learning of the group were a reflection of increased pressures of marketisation—of the normalisation of the 'citizen-consumers'

(Clarke, Newman, Smith, Vidler and Westmarland, 2007), and the redefinition of citizens as consumers—a key marker of neoliberalism (Peters and
McDonagh, 2007). This was particularly evident in the way in which the
focus on curriculum enabled improved working and learning opportunities
between the secondary school and their feeder primary schools. There was
recognition amongst teachers that more neoliberal logics made it necessary
to increase the 'market-share' of the secondary school in the context of a
significant increase in competition in the form of private education provision in Australia during the past two decades:

> I think it was probably a concern that there really wasn't any con-
> nection between our feeder schools and ourselves . . . The high school
> had decided to go into a publicity exercise promoting itself in the
> community and yet we weren't going into our primary schools and
> doing anything with them. If we had primary schools coming in and
> using our facilities, or our teachers going out and helping the primary
> schools, then we would get that natural progression amongst the kids
> that Cresswell High was the place to come . . . And we were noticing
> a drop off in the numbers in the primary schools. As early as Year 4
> and 5, they were starting to move over to the private schools, so it was
> seen, yeah, we had to start working very early on in the piece. (Terry,
> secondary school curriculum co-ordinator, Queensland)

In this way, more marketised logics exerted influence, as the school sought
to promote itself as the 'place to be' amongst the schools within its catch-
ment. More neoliberal logics were evident in the desire to promote stronger
links between the primary schools and secondary school in the region to
arrest declines in its own numbers, particularly to the private system—all
part of a broader trend of increased private activity within education (Ball,
2009). Sharing resources, and fostering traditional disciplinary-based collaborative learning networks between primary and secondary teachers,
were seen as vehicles to assist in this process.

These competitive logics were complemented by more managerial logics
which construed the focus on curriculum renewal as being responsive to
calls for the local District Office, and Department of Education more generally, to be actively involved in facilitating educational reform:

> [Information about the teacher networks] also goes to the District
> Office because it's an initiative and it's something that doesn't happen
> in very many places in the state, so it gives District Office a little bit
> of kudos as well. And it also means then that it probably helps, if you
> think about the state head office . . . that they can then get to say to the
> Minister, and that, 'We've got these little networks. In this district, this
> is what's happening. This is where teachers and principals are work-
> ing together and this is how this runs.' And it suits them, that they've

actually done something themselves to meet a need, which was KLA[6] and New Basics. (Kim, primary teacher, Queensland)

The existence of the Board, and members' efforts to engage in teacher learning for curriculum renewal, were proof of the District Office having 'done something themselves to meet a need,' and therefore able to satisfy accountability concerns associated with political pressure for more sustainable modes of teacher learning.

However, as well as recognition of the value of PD for curriculum renewal for performative purposes (Lyotard, 1984), there is also evidence of curriculum-focused PD practices for more substantive purposes— practices which still remain atypical within the field of PD more generally (McRae, 2001; Zeichner, 2003). That curriculum reform was to be facilitated through various networks is evidence of the influence of more research-informed logics—evident in support for such networks within the federal *Quality Teacher Programme*, and QSE2010 policies—as well as the more collaborative learning practices which sometimes characterise teachers' work. Such practices emphasise the need for teachers to take a much more proactive, professional stance in addressing their own learning needs; this is reflective of calls for teachers to become 'serious learners' (Ball and Cohen, 1999, p. 4)—a sympathy evident not only within relevant policies, but also recognised through the efforts of Board members.

Also, in terms of the focus upon the middle-years schooling curriculum, the application and initial efforts to establish the Board are also simultaneously indicative of the effects of more educative logics arising from research into educational practices in Queensland, and which inform policy developments in this state. The Queensland School Reform Longitudinal Study (QSRLS) research indicated a need for an increased focus upon the curriculum, assessment and pedagogical practices which constituted the middle years (see Carrington, 2002; QSRLS, 2001). This area of middle schooling had gained considerable attention within Education Queensland, particularly as a result of the QSRLS findings, and the findings from earlier research about disengagement amongst students in the middle years (Education Queensland, 2000). Concerns about the quality of the curriculum in the middle years served as an important stimulus to change, and were felt particularly by the administrators associated with the Future Schools Cluster:

Originally, from the Future School's Cluster, it started off as administrators meeting together to have a look—the middle school issues were a concern for us—looking at cross-campus activities. (Rachel, primary deputy-principal, Queensland)

A focus upon cross-school curriculum renewal as a vehicle for teacher learning, rather than only focusing upon learning within individual schools, was considered essential.

Similarly, in Ontario, strong foci upon specific areas of the curriculum alone, and more managerial logics associated with implementation issues, are also challenged by teachers and educators themselves. Reflecting a more critical habitus, educators questioned the provincial focus upon literacy and numeracy, arguing instead for a broader approach to teachers' PD. For a senior member of the Ontario Elementary Teachers' Federation, and reflecting a broader educative disposition to teachers' learning needs, PD needed to address not only issues of literacy and numeracy, but other educational matters as well. While literacy and numeracy were heavily resourced, other curriculum areas, including the Arts, and a broader conception of curriculum related to issues of equality and the concerns of specific constituencies, were all deemed important and worthy of support:

> We actually tended to focus a lot of our small professional development budget on issues that the government wasn't. So we've done some things on literacy and numeracy; we've written some books, but we tend to do a lot on the Arts, on the idea of the whole child. We also do a lot of professional development around equality. We have a whole department that's an equality and women's services department, and they do a lot about erasing prejudices. And they do run quite a few series of workshops across the province. (Linda, Ontario Elementary Teachers' Federation, Ontario)

This push to ensure that other domains were addressed adequately in schools is also evident in how principals within the province related to the focus upon literacy and numeracy. While most were overt in their support for an increased emphasis upon students' literacy and numeracy practices, and endorsed PD initiatives focused upon improving students' literacy and numeracy capabilities, a more critical disposition was evident in concerns about PD-support for other curriculum areas:

> We talk about, right now, the arts, in Ontario, and what's happening to the arts, because we're so focused on literacy and numeracy. And there's a danger in having that focus. So I think there're other things that schools have to continue to value, . . . other, you know, critical and creative problem solving. How are those important skills and thinking processes part of all curriculum, not just literacy and numeracy, and how do we ensure that the dollars and the resources are still spent on other ways that kids learn, so the arts is a big part of that? And our board to date, . . . the Ministry, too, has valued the arts, but we're starting to see a decline in that, in terms of the dollars that are, that are allocated to that. So it will be interesting to see what happens. . . . So I can keep it going here, because this is a school—it has some dollars. We can raise money— 'non-board funds' we call it. I have been in schools that have not been so resource rich. (Rita, elementary principal, Ontario)

Working in a relatively wealthy school meant this principal was able to sustain PD on curricula areas beyond those funded by the province. A more situated, broadly educational habitus, influenced by earlier ongoing support at the Ministry and board/district level more conducive to broader conceptions of student learning was evident, and challenged narrower curriculum renewal foci emphasising reductionist approaches to literacy and numeracy.

Such concerns were similarly reflected in the way in which a former literacy consultant seconded to work in the pre-service program of a local university described support for PD practices in the province:

> I think where it's also a real disconnect is for classroom teachers who are in areas of speciality or are in areas where there hasn't been the same kind of resource allocation and funding to support the learning that they need. (Nancy, seconded board consultant, Ontario)

As a former elementary teacher, the consultant's concerns reflect a more situated habitus—both product and productive of ensuring that the PD enacted within the province took into account all aspects of teachers' curricula practices, not just those associated with literacy and numeracy.

While the provincial focus upon literacy and numeracy is readily apparent, alternative logics in the form of a more broadly based, context-specific conception of curriculum are also evident. In one new school, the demands of working in a new environment in which teachers did not necessarily know one another, and needed to have the opportunity to share their experiences, led to the use of time created by the focus upon literacy and numeracy to engage in PD related to a much broader conception of curriculum associated with the needs of this school:

> Our board made a decision a few years ago . . . to do early dismissal days. . . . So at that time our board said that every school, as part of their 'School Effectiveness Plan' would have a focus on literacy and on numeracy and school culture. . . . We had four of them each year, and the kids would be dismissed early, . . . and then you would have an afternoon session with your staff that you could facilitate. That was absolutely critical to me in a brand new school where you didn't have time with huge growth to sit and talk about just the day to day things to say, 'How are things going? What experiences have you had?' Because I had staff who didn't know each other, having just met together, let alone for the things that my board was asking me to do. So we did a balance of both. We felt it was really important to record and experience and listen to the thoughts and special opportunities that staff had and do that kind of sharing. (James, elementary principal, Ontario)

A more situated, site-specific habitus, reflective of teachers' actual work circumstances, exerted influence. While literacy and numeracy curriculum foci were supported, more school-specific circumstances also influenced the teacher learning which occurred.

Educators' comments also reveal a habitus forged out of experiences of alignment between provincial foci on literacy and numeracy curricula, and more local concerns about the curriculum enacted in schools. This was the case when the emphasis upon literacy and numeracy curriculum areas were deemed beneficial when construed as relevant to teachers' work and helpful to teachers' learning:

> . . . you don't always hear me complimenting the Ministry, but I have to say, the expert panel documents that they put forth, really gave us the momentum, to bring the initiatives to life. They were really outstanding in putting forth documents for early reading, middle grade reading and for the intermediate levels . . . Then they had the same for numeracy. (Michelle, elementary principal, Ontario)

This alignment gave rise to a more compliant disposition which construed the testing of these curriculum areas to be improving over time, and subsequent resources produced as increasingly beneficial to teachers' learning:

> There was a lot of controversy, has always been a lot of controversy, around EQAO and standardised tests and that kind of thing. And I think the work that the [Literacy and Numeracy] Secretariat is doing, is making the validity of the testing—it's improving the validity of the, not of the testing *per se*, more of the reason for testing, and the use of the data, and how to use the data in an appropriate manner . . . The documents that they're producing are very helpful. (Reggie, elementary principal, Ontario)

However, while this more compliant disposition was evident, the emphasis upon using data 'appropriately,' 'bringing initiatives to life' and 'use of data in an appropriate manner' also reveal a bias towards ensuring curriculum reform made sense in context. Even as educators acquiesced to the push for particular types of student and teacher learning, a more situated, reflective and critical habitus was evident amongst educators as they articulated the PD and PD-related resources considered more genuinely educative.

Similarly, in England, there is also evidence of a habitus arising from and productive of efforts to foster teacher learning initiatives more broadly, across disciplinary boundaries at local sites, and not simply to be responsive to managerial calls for curriculum reform, or attention to a narrow range of curricula issues. Geography, Physical Education (PE) and languages teachers at Midlands High were all engaged in ongoing collaboration to develop a more integrated curriculum which assisted students to understand both the nature of disciplinary knowledge, and how such knowledge can be usefully drawn upon to better understand the wider world:

It's put these words into context. So we do a lot of Geography using coordinates in Spanish and map symbols, and all those things—sort of reinforcing place using Geography. There's a lot of Geography actually because we look at the physical geography (maps and all those other things), then looking at countries that speak Spanish, countries that speak French. That's one of our priorities this year, to get that embedded. I mean I'm doing a research project on teaching French through sport with my Year 9 pupils. So I've just got a little bit of funding to do that just to see if that can raise attainment in both PE and languages, and if it helps maintain motivation and enthusiasm for both those subjects.

. . . and I've spoken to the English department a lot about meta-language so we're using the same terminology in French and Spanish and German when we're talking about the building blocks of language that they're using in English. So we can sort of enhance what each other are doing, rather than confusing them with just different words . . . So we're trying to work with lots of departments to make it more interesting but also to support their broader learning so it's not just, 'Here we go again. Here's a list of French words they need to learn.' (Clarissa, Head of Languages, England)

Teachers' learning entailed engaging with one another to develop curricula experiences more responsive to students' needs. A more orthodox teaching habitus, heavily influenced by disciplinary-based learning logics, was challenged by a push to ensure teachers had the opportunity to work with colleagues across disciplinary boundaries. Such an approach was construed as the best way to build upon students' existing understandings, and minimise confusion to ensure improved student learning. A more collaborative disposition was similarly evident in relation to another program within the same school which encouraged interactions between teachers, albeit in the context of a desire to ensure individual disciplines retained their *sui generis*:

It's not a regular occurrence, but one thing which Geography has been involved in is the 'Opening Minds' project . . . Since the beginning of last year, we have undertaken 2 ½ term projects with History and Religious Education in Year 7. And I know that Anika [PD coordinator] is expanding that into Year 8 with other subjects to try and get the balance between allowing subjects to have their own identity still. Because there have been some schools which have gone completely to the cross-curricula end and have lost any substance of what subjects are about. So when they get to GCSE, they have their problems with those students knowing what bits were Geography, which bits were History and so on. So we were very careful to make sure that we kept our [subject] identity, but at certain points in the year, have that crossover link. And that has meant people have been working together, designing lessons, planning them, evaluating them and extra curricula resources. And actually even been sharing field work between those departments, which has been very useful, very collective. (Keith, Head of Geography, England)

While existing schooling structures and concerns about how to address entrenched assessment regimes (such as GCSEs) meant PD remained strongly focused on individual disciplines, more cross-curricula initiatives were recognised as being valuable learning opportunities for teachers in context.

In these ways, the focus upon specific curriculum issues in different national/state/provincial contexts reveal evidence of a teacher habitus forged from more neoliberal and managerial PD logics, and narrow conceptions of teachers' work. However, and at the same time, the learning which developed also reveals evidence of alternative logics at play, and of a more 'agentic,' strategising habitus on the part of educators as they seek to support PD beyond a narrow focus on literacy and numeracy, including incorporating more school-based conceptions of curriculum.

Teacher Learning and the Quantification of Education

The push to quantify educational outcomes, and for teachers to focus their learning on improving quantifiable measures, is also indicative of the influence of broader managerial and neoliberal logics as part of teachers' PD practices. This push to quantification was evident in Queensland, where there had been concerns about students' results in the middle years (students aged 11–14), in particular. In light of the findings of the QSRLS, teachers and principals in schools in Queensland were under pressure to improve their results on literacy and numeracy-based 'Basic Skills' tests:

> And it was again, I suppose, Education Queensland's influence in that ... they were the ones pushing the, 'Are your marks up to scratch? Are you doing this, that and the other?' And no matter what we think of their testing and all the rest of it—I must say I'm very much against it—but still it ... they were producing things, producing results and all those other sorts of things that said, 'You should concentrate on this area. ... ' (Mike, primary principal, Queensland)

This 'trust in numbers' (Porter, 1995) approach influences educational policy and, in turn, the way in which those in schools construe what is deemed possible at the school level, including in terms of teachers' learning. Even as a critical habitus, borne of concerns about an increased focus upon students' test scores, was evident, there was a realization that such measures were considered important within the educational administrative arm of the state, and that teachers' learning was expected to be allied towards improving such measures as indicators of student learning.

The influence of this 'education as numbers' approach was also apparent in an administrative habitus characterised by concern that teachers in Queensland should be able to identify the progress they had made in respect of students' marks as a direct result of the professional development in which they engaged. For members of the Curriculum Board, this included how membership of this group, and the learning they sought to orchestrate across member schools, played out in terms of student academic outcomes. This more administrative habitus was evident in the need to be able to justify resource expenditure on PD to date. Such a habitus was apparent in a deputy-principal's concern about whether and how PD focused upon the 'Productive Pedagogies' had had an impact:

> Is there the capacity to meet one of our needs to, you know, in the vein of revisiting . . . Can we do it as a view of where we've progressed? . . . getting people to reflect on where they were and where they are, and then in doing that, they're reflecting on the Productive Pedagogies. But it's also providing some data which is a bit thin on the ground in relation to well . . . where have we moved? Where have you as individual teachers moved as a result of us spending 18 months, you know, a considerable amount of effort in Productive Pedagogies? (Tom, intermittent Board member and high school deputy principal, Curriculum Board meeting, 28 August, 2002)

> The emphasis upon quantifiable improvements by teachers as individuals also resonates with broader neoliberal logics and trends towards construing education as a cost, and, in this case, teachers as consumers of resources (Clarke et al., 2007; Peters and McDonagh, 2007).

Concerns about quantifying educational outcomes are pervasive. In Queensland, quantifiable outcomes were the most valued capitals. Such capitals were construed as evidence of teachers' learning within the Curriculum Board, and the Future Schools Cluster more generally. This was reflected in how one principal construed such indicators in comparison with more qualitative evidence of student learning:

> I have seen more involvement in kids and their learning in the last couple of years than I've seen for many a day in secondary. I think there should be more emphasis on the pedagogies . . . you know. Why are kids interested in learning whereas three years ago they weren't? This is what the Board has done or what . . . ? [We need] more intense survey approaches rather than the fairly bland survey approach that we have tended to do. Coupled with fairly intense observations about what is going on. I don't think we observe classes very well and we don't have that skill [at high levels]. Now, that's not really good quantitative data, I know. I need teachers . . . who will tell me that the kids are going

much better. But what I would really like is someone to show me that that is the case, so that I can say to the Director-General, 'These kids ... their critical thinking skills have gone from there, to there, as a result of the program.' Now I don't have that information from people here at the moment. All they can tell me is that critical thinking has improved a hell of a lot because of the approach that is adopted. And I'm not sure that I really know what that means if I am trying to convey the success of the Board. (Andy, secondary principal, Queensland)

While there was a recognition of the value and need for more qualitative approaches to discern whether and how PD was influencing classroom practices, the capitals most valued were quantitative. Concerns about how to convey the success of teachers' learning to the Director-General of Education Queensland reflects the influence of these accountability pressures, and an administrative habitus positioned to be responsive to bureaucratic demands for such evidence.

This push towards quantification created similar pressures in Ontario. As in Queensland, the doxic practices of quantification and increased pressures of accountability went hand-in-hand, and this had a direct influence on the PD supported within the province. That the specific school board under investigation set itself a higher benchmark than the rest of the province as a marker of distinction attests to the prestige associated with these quantifiable capitals:

[W]e know that [PD] was driven by the provincial assessments and that whole accountability issue, that the public, or at least the politicians are saying is so important in Ontario, in other places obviously. So, that's how it started, that's how it played out. And certainly in our board, our goal is 80 percent, whereas the Ministry goal is 75 percent students achieving 'level three.' So, I think what that meant was boards of education started to focus their dollars, in terms of resources, and support for supply days and professional learning, around those initiatives. (Cynthia, elementary principal, Ontario)

The demand for such capitals as the principal currency of the day was evident in the way in which schools within this school board were expected to develop school-based 'SMART' goals (—goals which were 'specific,' 'measurable,' 'attainable,' 'realistic' and 'timely'—) based on a variety of data including data from diagnostic reading programs, and students' report cards, but with particular emphasis upon EQAO literacy and numeracy scores:

One of the areas that [the school board] has been exploring the last few years is the development of SMART goals—goals that are specific and measurable, with clear targets ... we developed SMART goals, related to our School Effectiveness Plans, and the data that we were analysing of our student achievement levels. And we as a whole staff have worked through some targets that we wanted to achieve by the end of an 8-week learning block . . . From the system, we have to have directions—a School Effectiveness Plan has to be in the areas of literacy, numeracy, climate/culture . . . And our director has a goal of 80 percent of our students achieving level Three or Four by 2008 in the areas of reading; those are very big goals. So we, first of all, narrowed it down by looking at our school data, and created our SMART goal for the school, but then within that context—within the context of the SMART goal for our school, it was going to look different at kindergarten, in Grade Four, in Grade Eight. So that's where the individual piece came in, but I know that with each of those individual pieces, we are targeting our school's SMART goal. . . . (Susan, elementary principal, Ontario)

Policy pressure to ensure improved outcomes on measurable educational outputs reflect the push for 'policy as numbers' (Ozga and Lingard, 2007) with its emphasis upon quantifiable educational outcomes as the capitals of most value. As a more prosperous school board within Ontario, the decision to increase the proportion of students who achieved Level Three or above on province-wide literacy and numeracy tests (from 75 percent to 80 percent) reflects how this 'avalanche of numbers' (Rose, 1999) has been actively engaged by educators who are seeking to present their work in the best possible light. While teachers and principals seek to respond to local needs, this is within the parameters of a field of practice already dominated by more managerial logics focused on education as intrinsically quantifiable.

That high test scores are the capitals of most value is apparent even when there is evidence of efforts to downplay what are perceived as some of the more negative effects of the push to quantify evidence of student learning outcomes:

> . . . the threat [of sanctions because of low EQAO scores] seems to be lifted. We do have that 75 percent number, but nobody has come to say we're going to close your school, or you're going to lose your job if you don't meet that. It's just information. So we're starting to use that information, and, as I said, the [Literacy and Numeracy] Secretariat has put up some professional learning programs based on the results across the province and where they think teachers need some professional learning to improve the results, and I think it's working. We'll see. We'll see when these results, when this year's results, come out. (Elsa, elementary principal, Ontario)

While there is evidence of efforts to downplay the less educative effects of quantifying student learning, policy pressures to ensure that students achieve specified targets also clearly influence perceptions of the nature and value of PD. In this way, the professional development which characterises the field is heavily influenced by the push for PD designed to secure improved test scores as the capitals of most value. While educators, such as this principal, are at pains to point out how the focus on quantifiable learning outcomes has ameliorated in comparison with earlier concerns, a 'principalling' habitus reflective of more quantifiable logics is evident, even as it seeks to resist such logics.

This influence of the policy push for PD responsive to this data is also evident in the way those in schools argue it is not the data which is problematic, but how teachers respond to it:

> The problem with it is that most people don't know how to use it. So they've got all this evidence and they become overwhelmed with it, and they try to figure out how to use it, and in the end, they become inactive because it's just too overwhelming. So they don't do anything. (Graham, elementary principal, Ontario)

The availability and use of such data has become naturalised, an accepted part of the educational landscape. Such responses are evidence of a disposition productive of and responsive to provincial emphases upon the value and validity of quantifiable data. Acceptance of teacher learning associated with broader policy foci reflect a policy-responsive habitus on the part of principals as educators occupying positions closer to the administrative arm of the state. This naturalisation of the use of quantifiable indicators of achievement is also evident in efforts to secure ever-higher measures of student achievement, and a focus upon data-management related goals:

> EQAO is also getting better at giving us very rich information. It used to be you'd get a 'Level 4' and 'Level 4' doesn't tell you much about data-management, but now they break it down into what questions your kids got right, what questions your kids got wrong. So you can really focus in on what about data-management that's not working for them. So you can really target your goal. (Kandice, elementary principal, Ontario)

In this way, the field of PD practices is heavily influenced by a particular conception of education which affords much value to evidence of learning which can be quantified.

This emphasis upon data as a valued capital, and of teacher learning focused upon quantitative measures of student learning, is similarly overt in England. Teachers commented on the way in which students' exam results/A levels influenced the learning in which teachers participated:

> Yes. So, for example, we use English literature—we have English literature, English language and combined A-levels. And we use 'AQA Board.'[7] And especially because it's a new one, they'll have training

sessions on what the examiners are looking for. They'll give you example essays. They'll talk about the kind of common mistakes. They'll give you a pack as well, so kind of teaching resources and things like that. So, someone from our department will go to a course from AQA and then they'll come back and feed back to us. So it's supposed to give us a really good kind of understanding of what they're looking for. Well, we had a few issues with A-levels [results] last year, because the training sessions were quite vague, and so, the syllabus was quite vague as a whole. But sometimes you get that when there's a new syllabus. It takes a while before it's really clear exactly what they're asking for. (Katerina, English teacher, England)

This focus upon quantitative evidence of students' learning reflects a field in which the capitals most valued are quantitative measures of student performance. The teacher learning most valued is that which leads to improvements in such results. Indeed, the pressure for improved performance is palpable:

> . . . as a curriculum leader I am under quite a lot of pressure to ensure that targets are met. . . . Grades are always compared to specific target grades that we are given, which are very 'aspirational' anyway. So even by meeting them, we are actually doing very well, never mind exceeding them. But one thing that I am very careful of is not to put too much pressure on the people within my team, other than on the first training day of the year when we'll go through the exam results for each person, so they can actually see how well their classes have done. (Keith, Head of Geography, England)

Such pressure leads to problematic practices, such as seeking out particular examination boards for the express purpose of improving quantitative outcomes:

> [We've] actually been to some training courses to look at different specifications from a different board, . . . because we believe the language in the question makes the content more accessible to students. . . . Results this year showed that there was a big jump in results. (Nick, Chemistry teacher, England)

Such is the pervasiveness of the focus on improved test results as the most valued capitals that the dominant disposition evident amongst teachers is one which takes it as natural that the professional development offered—typically 'training sessions' and 'training days,' such as those for exam board courses—should deliver/focus upon the knowledge required to secure such capitals. Under these circumstances, broader conceptions of teacher learning for student learning are challenged.

However, and at the same time, while PD practices in schools are clearly influenced by broader pressures for increased quantification of education to address accountability concerns, this emphasis upon the generation and use of data as valued capitals to inform teachers' learning is also engaged more educatively. More educative logics were evident in the way principals and other educators from Ontario, for example, critiqued the emphasis upon quantification. Such logics were apparent in Ontario educators' critique of relying too heavily on EQAO scores to inform professional development and educational decisions more generally:

> I don't want to see us get to the point that we're completely driven by standardised tests because I think that's, I think that's a mistake they made kind of south of the [Canadian] border. . . . (Reggie, elementary principal, Ontario)

While the focus upon EQAO and particular literacy and numeracy foci might be expected to cultivate an administrative habitus dominated by concerns about how to develop PD focused on measurable outcomes, this principal's response also reveals a more critical disposition arising from experiences of the negative effects of test-centred practices in the United States.

Educators also applauded efforts by the EQAO to provide data in ways which were more readily applicable to enhancing students' learning, and which could be more constructively employed to improve teachers' practices. Such an approach challenges the deprofessionalisation of teaching associated with the use of standardised testing to determine the effectiveness or otherwise of teaching practices (Day and Sachs, 2004). Endorsement of the use of EQAO results for what Webster-Wright (2009) describes as more 'authentic' teacher learning purposes, to cultivate a more research-informed teacher disposition (Lingard and Renshaw, 2009), reflects how more educative logics can deflect more accountability-oriented practices. A more student-oriented disposition was evident amongst Canadian educators for whom EQAO results represented a starting point for more informed professional development:

> But there are some good things that's coming out of it . . . some teams in schools are doing a really good job of looking at a small piece of the data. So they're taking something that's really small, starting small. For example, maybe they . . . they're just taking the reading . . . they're just taking the writing piece . . . And that's informing their instruction on how to move the kids towards other goals, that they've set for them, whether it's grade appropriate or beyond. . . . (Graham, elementary principal, Ontario)

Rather than simply being dominated by narrow prescriptive interpretations of policy, there was evidence of teachers using EQAO data in a more active way in relation to 'other goals'—goals beyond those associated with literacy and numeracy, which they believed students should strive for and attain. A more student-oriented habitus was evident amongst educators as they elaborated upon how more generic measures of learning could be used to inform students' specific learning needs. While the field of PD practices is dominated by the push to secure increased test scores as valued capitals in and of themselves, it is also simultaneously a site conducive to the development of more localised practices, at least some of which are explicit about the need to take students' particular needs into account.

More educative logics were also evident in the way EQAO data was construed as enabling a common language about teaching practice which was generative in instigating professional dialogue amongst teachers about their practice:

> Well, definitely—EQAO has had an influence on teacher PD, and we heard about this a lot when it first came out, that it actually changed the face of PD in Ontario, and not all for the bad. I felt from the Math education perspective that it was the first time where it actually opened up professional dialogue, and it changed the dialogue because there were some common elements that people all across the province were talking about—communication and math, for example. It was the very first time where teachers all across Ontario were hearing about the importance of having kids talk about what they're thinking. That's pretty significant, and I think it was the same in literacy. It really changed the face of professional development and professional dialogue. (Linda, Ontario Elementary Teachers' Federation, Ontario)

The way in which teachers were engaged in talking about the nature of specific curricula areas to which students were exposed reveals an alternative to more independent and privatised approaches to teachers' learning which typically characterises all aspects of teachers' work (Lortie, 1975; Rosenholtz, 1991; McRae et al., 2001). Also, support for the more nuanced use of EQAO results serves as evidence of more educative logics to challenge more performative pressures within the field of PD practices.

Similarly, more holistic, student-centred logics are evident in how those forms of standardised data collected through diagnostic reading programs are considered valueless in and of themselves for teachers' learning, unless they are explicitly connected to broader understandings of students' capacities and learnings. This is particularly the case in new schools:

> When you're starting with a population completely from scratch, it's really hard . . . you spend so much time getting to know your kids. You don't have that history of going to the teacher next door and saying, 'Hey, you taught so-and-so last year. What can you tell me about his skills from last year compared to this year?' So while we have . . .

report cards, and we have their scores from [diagnostic reading pro-
grams] from their last school, we don't have that anecdotal piece—the
history with the kids—and when you also don't have that history as a
staff, you really don't know. If you're just looking at report cards, do
we have a common understanding about what an 'A' looks like, or a 'B'
looks like? So I take the report card information with a grain of salt . . .
Friday will be a really great day to just spend some time talking about
this . . . Because, if you're just talking about numbers, and you're never
connecting it to the kids, then there's a loss of meaning there. (Kandice,
elementary principal, Ontario)

Reflecting a habitus grounded in experiences of collaborative dialogue over
extended periods of time, worthwhile teacher learning is seen as most likely
to occur when teachers have the opportunity to build understandings of the
whole child together. Such localised learning is indicative of more active
research-informed approaches to PD, and of a habitus which challenges
singular emphases upon standardised testing, and more typical and traditional PD as part of teachers' work. Sustained dialogue is understood as
crucial for improved understanding of practice (Isaacs, 1999; Yankelovich,
1999). A focus upon a broader conception of students' learning rather than
data *per se* reveals a habitus reflective of, and which values, more student-
centred approaches to teachers' learning.

While the use of 'data walls' to visually display individual student
achievement in relation to EQAO data benchmarks (and those associated
with other standardised reading measures) clearly reflects the influence of
more performative logics, these technologies can also serve as a productive
vehicle for teachers' learning by serving as an additional means of information about the learning difficulties experienced by some students:

It was very powerful to see, for instance, a Grade 7 student on the same
board as the Grade 4 students. And the Grade 4—you could see they
were up one end, and you know, a couple of Grade 7 students were at
the lower end. And while you might know, in the confines of your own
classroom, that you've got a couple of students lagging behind, when
you see it on a board—multigrade—it's really powerful to see how far
those students are behind. So there's that motivation to invest in them
to move them up. And then it's also a very powerful experience to move
them up physically—to take the tab and move them along the board as
they gain success. (Kandice, elementary principal, Ontario)

The experience of the use of such walls to build students' self esteem, indicates
how more managerial logics can be reframed for more productive purposes.[8]
There is also evidence of educators' efforts to resist teachers' or students'
learning practices becoming dominated by standardised testing practices,
even as they are heavily influenced by such practices:

> I personally have not been driven by EQAO scores . . . What we don't want to do is start focusing just on the kinds of the questions that we're going to see and the kind of assessment, because it's paper pencil, so, you know—now we lose the 'multiple intelligences,' the ability to perform in different ways of learning. So that's the danger . . . And teachers are doing some really nice things. This is a whole pile of pieces of writing that teachers are bringing me. I know that it's test oriented— it's responses to reading—but they're trying to help them develop their ideas and do it more independently, . . . help our kids a lot, and nurture, and accommodate. (Cynthia, elementary principal, Ontario)

Within the context of increased pressure for improvements on standardised measures of student outcomes, a more student-centred disposition is evident which values students' capacities to fulfil higher-order and more elaborate cognitive tasks, and to work independently. While as Little (2004) reveals in the United States, the focus upon teachers inquiring into their students' work to inform their teaching sometimes reflects managerial concerns, such an emphasis also has the potential to encourage more substantive, student-centred logics reflective of experiences of teachers striving to personalise students' learning.

There is also evidence of teacher learning oriented towards more substantive conceptions of student learning in Queensland, rather than simply compliance with performative pressures to respond to standardised measurements of student learning. This was evident in critical and robust reflections upon whether and how the work and learning of Board members led to student learning:

> So, if we're looking at outcomes from kids' work, I don't know that we yet have the data to say, 'Yes, this worked for the kids.' We can certainly see from the end product of units of work that the kids have been able to articulate—'What have you done? Why have you done that? What does that mean?' They've been able to articulate that, and thinking about the presentation of the Year 7 students using skills like PowerPoint presentation—they've got a number of skills there, and are motivated pretty well. (Cilla, primary teacher, Queensland)

> I just know here with the [Year] 7s, that we are much clearer in our own minds, . . . about what we want to achieve and what we're going to get the kids to do, to . . . to achieve those outcomes. And that we're expecting a higher standard of work and that we're probably teaching better because we want a better standard of work . . . They're actually working to a higher standard overall . . . . . . than what I would normally expect of Year 7s at this stage in the year . . . Just because we've changed our approach, you're actually getting better work. . . . And we are getting tougher on our standards. (Kim, primary teacher, Queensland)

Teachers' attention to evidence of students' learning reflects a more situated, critical habitus focused upon broader conceptions of learning than those associated with test scores alone. Greater introspection on the part of teachers into their students' learning, and the capacity to identify improved student learning as a result of changed expectations on the part of teachers, constitute more active logics than is typically the case. In this way, more neoliberal and managerial logics are at least partially resisted, and potentially rearticulated towards more educative ends.

These more critical, introspective logics as alternatives to unthinking compliance are similarly evident in England. While Ofsted inspections are seen as a dominant influence upon teaching and learning practices, there is also a more nuanced understanding of the problems associated with too much emphasis upon test results and testing as a proxy for learning. That teachers elaborated extensively on these concerns reveals a more critical habitus on the part of some educators:

> And league tables have focused [teachers'] minds probably more than anything else . . . The down-side, which, I think, really is a significant one, is that we teach to the test more than we've ever done before. I know people at the university that I speak to say we've taught to the test forever; we've always taught the test. It's probably true, but we've never focussed as much on the test as we do now. And it's led to students turning around to us regularly in any subject saying this, 'Do I need to know that? If not, can we just skip that?' Kids don't use textbooks. They use course guides! (Clinton, Chemistry teacher, England)

Effective strategising to contest these more test-focused logics involves providing opportunities for more substantive PD oriented to a broader conception of learning, which can involve a variety of approaches:

> So I guess in terms of how may CPD affect or what CPD can do to change that: Well, I hope stuff like 'Chemistry for Non-Specialists' [a course offered through the Royal Society of Chemistry with which this teacher was associated] does allow those teachers to deliver a more rounded approach to Chemistry. . . . I'm an intelligent person; I know what's on the exam paper. I can groom them to just answer the questions. I think with the greater depth of knowledge, [teachers] can give a much more robust [response]. Kids can tell when teachers don't know their stuff. It's incredible, and even if the kids can't actually say that openly, they can tell, and they give teachers a hard time. So I think that type of CPD to empower teachers is really useful. Doing a Master's in Education, looking at particular ways in which pupils learn and different types of learning styles—I'm sure they're useful as well. We all know there are different types of learning cycles. Teachers usually end up going down the path that they feel most comfortable with, but

perhaps getting them out of that by exposing them to other things in CPD might be the thing that makes them realise that, actually, 'I do need to mix it up a bit.' (Clinton, Chemistry teacher, England)

While a continued focus upon testing, and concerns about the effects of unsatisfactory performance on Ofsted inspections are reflective of a habitus heavily influenced by managerial pressures to ensure compliance with standardised, numeric measures of success, the way in which multiple approaches to PD are endorsed as a vehicle to assist teachers to move beyond a focus on 'teaching to the test' also reveals a habitus reflective of alternative experiences. A more reflexive stance, and a socio-analytical capacity to not only critique the circumstances under which such testing is occurring, and its deleterious effects upon the long-term learning of students, is evident, as is a desire to actively embrace alternative strategies which contest more performative logics.

Modes of Teacher Learning

The ways in which teacher learning is enacted in school and system settings also reveal evidence of the influence of more accountability-oriented logics, as well as a more progressive disposition on the part of educators to teachers' learning. Modes of teacher learning also reflect the influence of more conservative logics, and how these are fostered by policy-supported, managerial logics.

More accountability-oriented logics are evident in the adoption of short-term approaches to teachers' learning, rather than the cultivation of more sustained, site-specific approaches. The superficial way in which some school-wide reforms are adopted within school systems reflects the influence of such logics. Such superficiality, and subsequent disenchantment, were evident in the decision not to continue to implement a particular literacy program, 'First Steps,' introduced to a school-board in Ontario:

> The Board, about five years ago, mandated that all students, Grades One to Eight, get plotted on 'First Steps,' and that the information is tracked electronically and on paper, and handed from teacher to teacher, year after year after year. So again, we went into a whole implementation—creating awareness, developing teams at the school level, getting them trained, not just on how to use the program, but, more importantly, how to influence teaching practice to move kids along the continuum, which we never got to because we got stuck on how do we mange plotting kids. . . .
>
> This September, the Board said, 'We're not doing "First Steps" anymore. So it's voluntary. If you want to use it as a reference, you may, but we will no longer be electronically tracking it, and requiring teachers to pass it on from year to year, and school to school.' So, as principal,

you just spent four or five years trying to get people on board—why is this important and what's the value for kids and what are we going to get out of this, and it's all good—to: 'We're not doing them anymore.' So when you say to them [teachers] next time . . . their immediate reaction is, 'Oh, this is going to be just like "First Steps",' you know, 'We're going to learn it; we're going to start to implement it, and then that's going to be pulled.' (Kandice, elementary principal, Ontario)

More managerial logics were evident in the decision not to continue the program. This fostered considerable caution on the part of those affected. For a principal struggling to discern how best to foster teacher learning amongst her staff, the superficial way in which broad-based reform initiatives were implemented made it difficult to encourage teachers to adopt an active stance towards improving their practice in the future. Such decisions, in conjunction with persistent pressures of time (Little, 1999)—'time is always a huge barrier . . . ' (Kandice, elementary principal, Ontario)—potentially limit more inquiry-oriented practices, making it difficult to effect an alternative to these more managerial practices. Such experiences can also cultivate a culture of cynicism in response to the failure to properly implement such initiatives.

Also, the cultivation of more individualistic dispositions encourage teachers to attend various workshops individually in an effort to improve their practice. As a result, in England, PD is construed as something which involves individual teachers attending particular courses, rather than more sustained inquiries into specific students and teachers' needs:

Well, for me, [PD is] information courses to help me deliver my subject, or develop my role as a pastoral leader, and also training courses and assessment courses. . . . (Nick, Chemistry teacher, England)

Importantly, this emphasis upon short courses and workshops goes hand-in-hand with a conception of PD as a cost—as a practice or set of practices which need to be actively understood as inherently limited by budgetary constraints. PD involves teachers taking courses, and being absent from their school:

[The PD] training group decide on the amounts of money available to various people, and obviously, they have a limited budget, and that's been pared down in recent years. (Nick, Chemistry teacher, England)

. . . and of course CPD is costly—it's costly in terms of provision, if you send people on courses, they cost money. And we also are now much more sensitive to the fact that the absence of a teacher requires cover and therefore it costs money. So there are external pressures now, and internal pressures. (Clinton, Chemistry teacher, England)

A more managerial habitus, imbued with a sense of PD as a cost, influences decision-making about the PD which is promoted, and discourses and practices around teacher PD in general. Such approaches to PD reflect the continuation of dominant, passive approaches to teacher learning. Given that this orthodoxy characterises much of the PD teachers experience, a more active, inquiry-focused disposition seems difficult to engender within the field.

In Ontario, a similarly conservative habitus, influenced by a long history of policy support for traditional dissemination approaches to PD, is evident on the part of educators. Professional development is about working 'on' rather than 'with' teachers:

> [PD] means making teachers better at their job in order that they can impact students and student learning, so giving them the skill set and the philosophy, in order that they'll be able to help students achieve the best that they can. (Graham, elementary principal, Ontario)

At the same time as there is an important and explicit focus upon student learning, the dominant disposition appears consumed by more traditional dissemination approaches. A habitus heavily inscribed with traditional conceptions of 'making' teachers engage in specified activities, and 'giving them the skill set' reflects those instances of PD schooling practices which involve PD as something 'done' to teachers. (Eisner, 1992; Day and Sachs, 2004)

A similarly conservative disposition is evident in Queensland in the way in which a senior member of staff in the high school (and member of the Curriculum Board) explained how the pattern which had already been established around 'providing' PD would continue to characterise the activities of the group:

> We now have a reputation that has developed for providing professional development for staff and so on, so I think that can just continue on through normal school funding. . . . (Terry, secondary school curriculum co-ordinator, Queensland)

This conservative disposition was reinforced by policy-related administrative barriers on the use of federal government *Quality Teacher Programme* (QTP) funds by members of the Curriculum Board:

> A lot of the QTP money had to go on consultant fees and those sorts of things. Very little could be used for the relief of teachers in classrooms . . . it basically had to go into consultants' fees. (Mike, primary principal, Queensland)

This is not to say that teachers did not seek to resist such conservatism:

> I think if we, within the Board, if we could have used the QTP money more for TRS [teacher release] and to get our teachers together in school time, we could have made more use of it for our purposes. But because we had to use it to employ someone who is a non-Education Queensland staff [member], and there are only very limited circumstances you can use the TRS [teacher-release funding], it meant we really had to pay someone to come in. And then if you do it in school time, the schools have to apply for TRS and schools don't have sufficient funds. So the downside is we were kind of making ... we weren't making up reasons, but we were finding it difficult to work out how to spend money. (Lisa, Chair of the Curriculum Board)

While administrative restrictions upon how funds can be used encourage the continuation of orthodox practices within the field of PD practices, a more context-responsive habitus is also evident which critiques and criticises the peculiar situation in which teachers find themselves as they struggle to determine how to best use the funds provided for PD purposes.

At the same time, the linear way in which professional development is often experienced by teachers also signals the continuation of more traditional approaches:

> I think that assessment is the next step. It's the next way and it comes around and that's in line with what the Department is sort of expecting and is doing, so that's the next ... stage that has to come around as well. And possibly, teachers would be able ... would be looking at that as the next little bit. (Kim, primary teacher, Queensland)

> So we had an afternoon that involved Year 7 staff and we targeted our learning coaches here at Cresswell High [teachers in Years 8 and 9] and had them meet to share across the Cluster the work that they've been doing in classrooms ... And then we said, 'Well, we've done the 7 to 9s [teachers in Years 7, 8 and 9], so the next time we meet, let's look at the 4 to 6s [teachers in Years 4 to 6] or let's look at P to 3 [teachers in Preparatory to Year 3].' So we had a student-free day later in the year when we had those different groups meet at different times of the day. (Lisa, secondary teacher, Queensland)

A more conservative habitus, influenced by many years' experience of more traditional workshop approaches is evident in teachers' sense that they needed to move from one set of activities to another, and without always a clear strategy for how particular experiences coalesced around a broader project for educational improvement.

Such activities are also often dependent upon external experts:

> Well, I think if we can have like Todd Smith[9] doing his 'Community of Inquiry,' he can do that in two hours. . . .

> [The] plan for student free days: So we'll have Di Monk[10] for [Years] 4 to 6 and [Years] 7 to 9 and we'll have June[11]. . . . (Lisa, Curriculum Board meeting, 28 August, 2002, Queensland)

In this way, the field of PD practices seems destined to remain heavily influenced by teacher learning logics which frame teachers as passive consumers of other people's advice. Ongoing experience of, and support for, external consultants cultivate a conservative disposition towards teachers' own learning. Such influences, together with administrative barriers, seem to ensure the dominance of an orthodoxy of more individualistic, short-term modes of teacher learning within the field of PD practices.

However, this is not the full story. The complexity of the field is also evident in teachers' experience of and support for competing approaches to PD. Teachers in Queensland are eager to ensure ongoing conversations around professional development in relation to their specific needs, and acknowledge difficulties of meeting regularly with other teachers:

> I think we probably . . . would have liked . . . to have developed the use of Productive Pedagogies more in a contextual sort of [way] with teachers from their [individual school], fitting in how they would . . . [fit] the Productive Pedagogies in with what you're teaching, with your planning and your assessment, rather than what seems to have been done . . . There's a bit of an isolation thing now. (Kim, primary teacher, Queensland)

Reflecting the field of teacher PD as a constantly contested space, the transient nature of these one-off days is also actively critiqued by educators. In Ontario, even allocated PD days were likely to be whittled down as a result of ongoing union bargaining, and specific school district-related issues:

> I think that there needs to be time built in to the teachers' instructional week . . . four or six PD days a year is not enough for true professional development, for sustained professional development . . . If the collective agreement comes into place, some of that time is for teachers' personal planning time, some of it is for writing report cards, some of it's for parent teacher interviews. So when you actually pick away at all the pieces of the collective agreement, I think we're left with about three really useful days out of six! . . . And then out of those three really useful days, the Board might take some to run a system initiative, or a 'family of schools' initiative. So then you're left less and less time,

which is why I think it needs to go; it needs to be a part of the work week. (Kandice, elementary principal, Ontario)

A more situated, reflexive disposition is evident in recognition of the inadequacies of these traditional approaches, and support for time integrated into teachers' regular working week, such that PD becomes a more seamless part of teachers' work. The up-front way in which one-off workshops are actively critiqued reveals a more active and activist disposition on the part of educators:

> ... a one shot deal, in my opinion, it was a one shot deal ... was there job-embedded learning for other staff at the school? No ... there was not that opportunity. (Tim, elementary principal, Ontario)

While there are constant struggles with conservative approaches to PD, teacher learning is seen as valued as never before:

> I've never seen in my history such rapid change as I have seen in the past few years and I believe it's because the focus that the province has taken on professional learning and the support that they provide for it as opposed to simply saying you need to do this. (Simon, Senior Ministry Official, Ontario)

In spite of the considerable pressures for teachers to participate in generic PD approaches, there is also recognition that there is something of a trend towards increased teacher involvement in context-specific learning over time, and that this is increasingly necessary:

> I think typically, some of the challenges of the professional development that we've offered have been that they're always defined by others and not necessarily defined by the people who are the recipients. And I think really only in the last, maybe 10 years or so, we've recognised that ... we need to work with people where they are. (Lydia, academic, Ontario)

The emphasis upon needing to engage with teachers and to take their specific contexts into account is recognition of a greater valuing of more teacher-informed inquiry approaches. The realisation that teachers are typically the recipients of information generated elsewhere (Eisner, 1992; Day and Sachs, 2004), rather than active participants in their own right, reflects a more inquiry-oriented habitus on the part of educators. Experience of alternative approaches means that even as they are perpetuating more traditional approaches, teachers and other educators seek simultaneously to resist such approaches.

A more long-term, inquiry-informed habitus is also apparent in educators' experiences of teacher-instigated research into their own circumstances:

> [Teachers] were still noticing that boys were not liking coming to school. And that was a hard knock for them, because they had worked hard to make sure [of] that—a lot of work around inclusion. And so, . . . they went back and they developed some in-school surveys just to get more specific, because the broad one was like, 'Do you like coming to school?' So it was, again, very broad. So they developed some surveys to see if we can get more information from the . . . population as to specifically what areas of school they were finding troublesome. (Susan, elementary principal, Ontario)

Such a response is indicative of a more 'researcherly' disposition (Lingard and Renshaw, 2009) amongst those in schools, including supportiveness amongst administrators for such a disposition. Educators are not simply dominated by the immediacy of the policy and political environment in which much decision-making is undertaken. Rather, more administrative logics are resisted, and support evident for more localised, inquiry-oriented approaches.

That this localised inquiring disposition is increasingly collaborative is also evident in the comments of a principal in one Ontario school who was at pains to point out how teachers in her school had collectively instigated their own study groups to foster improved student literacy practices:

> There's also been a lot of books come out on reading and writing skills and as a school—and it didn't come from me, it came from the teachers themselves—[teachers] have formed book study groups, by division or by grade, and focused on reading and putting these things into practice. (Elsa, elementary principal, Ontario)

Such a response is indicative of a more educational habitus grounded in an understanding of the importance of teachers' collaborative inquiry practices. In a self-effacing way, this principal foregrounded the work and learning of teachers in her school, and through her emphasis on how they were 'putting these things into practice,' how they sought to ensure that their learning influenced student learning. Rather than focusing upon the influence of specific and narrowly focused measures of student learning alone, a more expansive conception of teacher learning is evident, involving teachers' enquiring into their circumstances more actively.

Some educators also describe how specific programs, book studies and shared marking of student work assist in promoting a variety of valuable collaborative learning experiences amongst teachers:

> We have a book study that we've been doing for two years. . . . The consensus marking that I was talking about—we did that as a whole school. . . . And to a tee, they've all said it was one of the most valuable PD experiences they've had because they had to be able to negotiate with a partner as to why they were giving the scores they were on

the Rubric. It was great; it was very good. (Lily, elementary principal, Ontario)

While responding to provincial foci for greater attention to literacy and numeracy, a more collaborative, context-responsive habitus is evident in the book study and consensus marking. Such initiatives are seen to be locally important.

Such a habitus is similarly evident in the way teachers questioned and critiqued their own practices together in informal and more formal settings:

> And I would say that all our conversations lead to what's good for students, what's going to help them in their achievement. And the PD happens a lot in the conversations that are in the hallways. I do have staff that chat with other staff members about, 'What do you think about this piece of writing?' . . . And when I think of some of our in-school structures, like our school team meetings that we have once a week, where teachers bring forward students who are struggling, academically, or emotionally and behaviourally, and our SRT—School Resource Team—meetings where we have additional staff, our focus is always on knowing the students, strategies that have been tried and what's worked, what hasn't worked, and always on moving forward. So, very rarely do we hear dead-end comments like, 'They're just lazy.' We recognise that there is something blocking the learning for that student, and we have to dig deep to find out what that is. What are the skill deficits they're exhibiting, through either their behaviour or their learning needs? And then how can we best work with that student to achieve those goals? And I would say those conversations are ongoing all the time. And I think that's professional development as well. I think it fits under that umbrella. (Susan, elementary principal, Ontario)

In this way, PD is construed as something which is an ongoing part of teachers' work—learning as more genuinely 'job-embedded'—and focused on addressing significant issues *in situ*.

Similar logics are evident amongst teachers in Queensland. The way in which special needs teachers and regular classroom teachers embraced the new appraisal process for special needs students and saw this as a way to engage more proactively with one another to improve students' learning opportunities in the middle years, exemplifies how more job-embedded logics influence teachers' learning:

> We had always had lip service paid to the transition [between primary and secondary schooling] and quite a number of Year 7 teachers were saying that it needs to be a little bit more than that, and at the same time, a push was coming through in terms of learning support with the appraisal process [of students with special needs] being introduced and

being filtered into the high school. So the support teachers were feeling, 'Hey, we're on about the same thing in terms of supporting children with particular needs,' and so it grew out of that concept as well. (Cilla, primary teacher, Queensland)

In this way, a more student-focused disposition is evident amongst teachers. State-sponsored initiatives are deemed valuable by teachers when construed as vehicles for more teacher-led inquiry.

While engagement with the reform agenda was imposed in the beginning in Queensland, the way in which teachers perceived involvement in the work of the Board as valuable also reveals a desire amongst teachers to be more actively involved in collaborative and localised learning initiatives. Involvement in the work of the Board was construed as important in and of itself, rather than simply in response to administrative fiat:

I was basically told I had to go and that's because there's only two of us at the Centre. I mean as Gordon has got principal things to do, I was basically told that I needed to go to start with, to see whether it was worthwhile for us to be a part of it, simply because we don't do what everyone else does. So that is the start of it, and I was given the option to say if I didn't think it was worthwhile, that I didn't have to belong to the group any longer. But I thought it was important. (Hilary, environmental education centre teacher, Queensland)

The desire to continue to be involved with the Board reflects a habitus attuned to responding positively to PD seen as 'worthwhile,' as beneficial in terms of the needs of teachers in an environmental education setting, even as it is apparent that more managerial logics also exert influence over the modes of teacher learning considered useful.

This more proactive disposition is also apparent in the way in which the work of Board members evolved over time, and teachers' perceptions of a greater sense of alignment between their concerns, and those of the principals and deputy-principals with whom they worked:

I know the Board—much less so now than at the start—it was always, the fact that I think we thought that the principals had more power or more say and that they would veto any decisions, some decisions we made, or maybe that we would look to them for guidance, or that it seemed to be that we were in opposition. But I think it's evolved now— the fact that we both have got the same agenda. They have a few more guidelines, a few more requirements, placed upon them by the district office than we do. But they see us as an adjunct, and perhaps a way of them keeping a finger on the pulse of what's happening in the school, what teachers are actually thinking. And it gives them something else. (Kim, primary teacher, Queensland)

While the work of the Board was seen initially as a response to administrative fiat, the habitus cultivated through Board membership valued active engagement on the part of teachers in their learning. While this could be construed as a simple process of successful co-option for managerial purposes, the engaged ways in which members of the Board saw their work as important in and of itself, no longer construing the principals as central to the reform process, but in a more peripheral role because of administrative responsibilities, challenges such a stance.

Similarly, in England, PD practices are also engaged differently, beyond just more typical 'training days':

> I've been here for 12, 13 years, and when I first started, on training days we'd have someone with a high powered brief-case who'd come in for an hour or two, and speak to us. And that was considered to be professional development, and I think things have moved forward from there quite considerably. (Jason, Chemistry teacher, England)

Perceptions of a shift from the dominant logic of being spoken to by an external consultant—'a high-powered brief-case'—reflects the influence of alternatives to more traditional logics. These more traditional logics are sometimes strongly challenged:

> They seem to have two distinct patterns, either an information giving session, PowerPoint—'death by PowerPoint'—by a management team, or the better ones tend to be a number of workshop programs on specific topics and people attend the sort of things of most interest. . . . (Nick, Chemistry teacher, England)

Just as a more conservative disposition is evident in a degree of support for the 'better workshops,' reflecting broader perceptions of relevance to teachers' interests, description of many PD workshops as 'death by PowerPoint' reflects a more critical disposition towards passive approaches to PD.

There is also evidence of teachers responding proactively to established structural barriers to learning between primary and secondary schools, and centralised pressures which sustain such barriers. This is apparent in the way in which some teachers made explicit efforts to engage with one another across the primary/secondary divide in Queensland. This was the case in the way a secondary teacher (Lisa) engaged with a primary teacher (Liz) in relation to curriculum reform as members of the Curriculum Board in Queensland:

Lisa: I'm interested in that you picked up the Year 3 and Year 6 Rich Tasks. So is that what your intention is? You guys will do the New Basics tasks?

Liz: Well, not so much that, but we 'task' in units anyway. That's how we work.

Lisa: Yeah, but they're the same, aren't they?

Liz: Yeah. Both were put in but here you can see [points to documentation] . . . I just did the Year 5/6 across two levels. I took your template, remember, and I designed what I wanted my kids to do and parcelled that unit of work and that was their task. But it was only looking at a couple of the outcomes, which are down in the bottom there [points to school planned documentation]. I couldn't do all these outcomes [points to KLA syllabus]. . . . (Curriculum Board meeting, 16 October, 2001)

The way in which one teacher questioned the decision-making in relation to how a colleague in another school had organised the curriculum for her students, and her colleague's response, reveals an alternative to more individualistic and managerial PD logics.

Revealing further complexity within the field of teacher PD, there is also some evidence of how traditional one-off workshops/courses can serve as a stimulus for more sustained PD practices. For the head of languages at the school in England, individual workshops on specific approaches to teaching languages were useful when they resulted in more substantive localised learning practices amongst teachers in her department:

> Within our department there's just constant CPD. We're really lucky actually because we have a very committed department and everyone's very enthusiastic. One member of the team attended a course on this 'Asset' language course and had to deliver it and since that one training day, she has become an accredited teacher in several levels of this Asset qualification. And she's now using that in the classroom and she's going to do a session on it in the departmental meeting, explaining it to all of us . . . Another member of the department expressed an interest in the 'Michel Thomas' method of teaching languages. So he's been involved in how to teach it. He's going to visit a school to see how it's delivered. He's got a little test group in his Year 8s that he's sort of experimenting with. And we're meeting regularly to discuss the comparisons between his class and my class that are having the more traditional approach. There's a lot of that that goes on in our department and because it's going on in the department, we talk about it at a department level. So in department meetings, it will often be people saying, 'Well this is going on in my classroom.' And, in fact, department meetings are brilliant opportunities for a bit of CPD because people will bring ideas to department meetings. . . . (Clarissa, Head of Languages, England)

While more reductionist conceptions of evidence-based practice were evident—such as feeling the need to have a 'control' group against which to compare educational practices (Biesta, 2007)—the way in which individual workshops/courses were described as stimulating more substantive, ongoing engagement amongst teachers in relation to their learning *in situ* also reveals a more reflexive disposition amongst educators in relation to their own learning. Furthermore, the way in which departmental meetings were construed as valuable opportunities for sharing experiences of one another's practices is also evidence of a challenge to the orthodoxy of individualistic workshop approaches as compartmentalised initiatives which have little effect upon teachers' specific practices. This was not an isolated event, as indicated in the response of a colleague from the Geography department in the same school:

> Within the department, in most department meetings, we'll have a 10–15 minute slot where someone will share some new ideas and new references that they've come up with and it just basically gives an opportunity for us to always focus as often as we can, almost every meeting—not every meeting but almost every meeting—to focus on teaching and learning, the thing we're actually all here for really. We give everyone an opportunity to show something off, feel quite pleased about doing that and get appreciation from everyone else. And it often triggers conversations which then lead to other formal ways of doing that so people will be more confident. If they've shown it in a department meeting, they will be more able to share it outside of that in a formal chat with somebody else, or to email it to people. (Keith, Head of Geography, England)

That the PD occurring within these departmental meetings led to these teachers adopting an active role as 'providers' of PD to teachers from other schools reveals a substantive proactive disposition on the part of these teachers in relation to their own learning and that of their colleagues.

A more proactive habitus is also evident in efforts to engage with new information and communications technologies for more site-responsive, 'just-in-time' learning options. This was apparent in relation to some of the latest ways in which PD was supported in Ontario:

> I guess one of the things that, in particular, that the Ministry did, as far as training, when the early reading, early maths and literacy and numeracy began, was that they tended to do the cascade model . . . one teacher from each school was trained. And then, when we started in the first year, when we did some training, Marie[12] allowed us to bring teams from a school, which was of course, much more effective . . . We've moved on again from there, and the professional learning that we're doing is really very much within the school or family of schools. And so it's much more related to where teachers are exactly, and what they need at the moment . . . We use a lot of the other things that have

been produced to help. So we use pieces of [Internet] web casts to show, to demonstrate at the school level, if that's what they need. (Veronica, Ministry official, Ontario)

While new technologies could be used to reinforce old practices, there was at least discursive evidence of attempts to challenge more traditional logics, and of a more innovative approach to engaging with new technologies to foster teacher learning.

Controlling PD

The extent to which PD is imposed upon teachers also reveals evidence of the influence of more managerial logics, as well as resistance to such logics. At times, PD is perceived to be a policy-supported mandated activity sanctioned by employing authorities without adequate consideration for what teachers actually need to improve their practices. Such a disjunction was explicit in the way in which a senior Ministry official in Ontario reflected upon her own experiences of mandated PD activities:

> I know when I was a teacher, I used to get so upset, because some of it I thought was 'Mickey Mouse,' you know, and a lot of the stuff on things that people know, [like] 'wellness.' The 'wellness' is fine, don't misunderstand me, but I didn't want [that] when I wanted to learn how to do my job better. I didn't want people to take me out for a day to do something on 'wellness.' (Kelly, Ministry official, Ontario)

As a former teacher, this Ministry official empathised with teachers' needs and perceptions of valuable and valid professional development in the context of systemic expectations about what was construed as worthwhile PD. She challenged PD seen as not directly relevant, and which also typically involved being removed from the classroom ('take me out for a day'). In this way, a habitus imbued with a 'teacherly' disposition was evident, strongly focused upon job-relevant learning practices. Such a disposition had been formed through both her experiences as a teacher, and as the 'recipient' of much mandatory, state-sanctioned PD. Whilst she was in a position which necessitated taking broader policy and political objectives into account, this decision-making process was clearly informed by a belief that teachers should be involved in determining the nature of their learning needs.

For a 'Newly Qualified Teacher' (NQT) in England, state-sanctioned PD activities which she was required to attend were similarly considered to exert influence, but to be less relevant than other modes of learning:

Katerina: And last year, as an NQT, we were sent to a few training sessions kind of after school or during school. But again, that wouldn't be

to come back and feed back to our department. It would just be
for kind of our skills as an NQT, and to talk to the NQTs.

Interviewer: And was that useful?

Katerina: The majority of the time, not particularly. There was one really
good session that we had, but other times a lot of it, actually, was
just repeating things that we were told in your kind of training
year. And because of the amount of work you have in your NQT
year, it was sort of a bit of an added stress when you would have
rather been planning your lessons. (Katerina, Newly Qualified
Art teacher, England)

The demands upon a new teacher in the first year of her career were such
that the Newly Qualified Teacher workshops to which she was 'sent' were
considered irrelevant. A habitus inscribed with concerns about the immediacy of her work and a lack of control over the PD she experienced meant
that this workshop was not only considered not useful, but actually served
as an additional stressor.

The way in which teachers are expected to develop professional development plans tied to specified, pre-determined targets also reveals the influence of more managerial logics. However, at the same time, criticisms by
teachers about the more performative aspects of this process indicate not
only its influence, but also gesture towards a more reflexive habitus imbued
with a more genuinely educational disposition:

. . . it's not that I think it's bad to be reminded of good practice or to
actually stop and reflect on how we're doing things, but I do think
that—I do think some of the things that we're asked to do, particularly
before with the management side of things are, as I say, very business-
oriented and you have this idea of sort of jumping through hoops and
then ticking boxes. So, maybe I'm sort of confusing professional development with performance management but it is actually sort of linked
in my mind. . . .

So, yes setting targets and looking at the standards and those sorts
of things for students. It's not necessarily something that I think about
when I think about my own professional development. And actually,
some of the targets that we put in place when we have our professional
development sessions—it does seem like quite a lot of 'jumping through
hoops' and 'ticking boxes.' And sometimes those things can be a hindrance, rather than a help, I think. (Lisetta, English teacher, England)

For this teacher, professional development was associated primarily with
responding to setting targets against which her performance would then
be managed. In this way, PD becomes an externally imposed technology which determines what is institutionally sanctioned within the workplace. That it seemed like 'quite a lot of jumping through hoops' and

'ticking boxes,' reveals the dominance of more performative logics. At the same time, that such a process was construed as a hindrance rather than a help reveals a more critical disposition towards the negative effects of such processes. The way in which this teacher went on to describe how the content of this target-setting process were sometimes then forgotten, or did not necessarily reflect the work she was engaged in during the year, reinforces the superficiality associated with this process and a more reflexive habitus:

> Well, I think, very often they're agreed by the person who's helping to set the targets, and the person setting the targets. I think it's agreed and then, very often, put into a drawer or filed away on the computer and forgotten about. And the other day I had my performance management meeting with my head of department, and one of the targets we'd set last year was actually a drama target because I'm an English and Drama teacher. But, actually, this year, I'm not teaching any drama, so it's not going to be possible to meet that target. So, in some ways there, I think they're useful to sort of take stock of what you've done. And I do quite like reflecting on the past cycle, and sort of listing all the brilliant things that you've been part of. But in terms of setting targets, I do find that to be less helpful, and I don't always remember actually what it is we've said that I'll do in the coming year. (Lisetta, English teacher, England)

A more reflexive habitus is also evident in how teachers in Queensland felt constrained by Departmental expectations to implement the New Basics very quickly in the high school, with attendant concerns about reluctance of teachers to engage in more collaborative learning across school sites:

> Well, I think that we . . . the high school was going through curriculum change at the time. So we were trying to implement the New Basics and that was predominantly our curriculum drive. Now although the Future School's project . . . was to slot in very neatly with that, people are more interested with what they have to do in their classroom, and what they have to do for tomorrow or the next week, than necessarily working with some primary school staff. (Lisa, Chair of the Curriculum Board, Queensland)

Pressure to rapidly focus upon mandated state-sanctioned initiatives, and to address more immediate classroom related concerns, is seen as contributing to resistance against a more open engagement between teachers about their classroom practices. A socio-analytic, critical disposition is evident in how teachers recognised how this limited the extent to which there was an open dialogue between the secondary teachers and their primary colleagues from neighbouring schools:

So there is this bit of mentality, I think, at the high school that it [educational reform] starts with us, and the primary school [teachers] . . . are not necessarily as relevant as they think they are. But there's certainly that mind-set amongst a number of our staff. But I think the fact that we were going through a curriculum change was a fairly large thing for people to take on. And what we were saying with this was, 'It was important to be working with primary school people as well—looking at what they're doing and sharing with what you're doing in the classroom.' Sharing what we do in the classroom is not something we do particularly well. We're used to that perhaps at the senior level in terms of panel [for assessment purposes[13]] leading that, you know . . . it's done in the school structure and you know in advance. And this was just saying, 'Come along and share your assessment please,' or, 'Come and show what you're talking about or doing in the classroom.' A lot of [the secondary school] staff aren't quite open to that suggestion. (Lisa, Chair of the Curriculum Board, Queensland)

The pressure to respond to specific reforms, together with an existing conservative disposition towards working with other teachers, led to a restriction upon the more ambitious efforts of Curriculum Board members to facilitate more teacher-led PD across specific and multiple school sites simultaneously. The result is the dominance of more managerial over more educative logics, in spite of evidence of a more critical disposition on the part of some teachers.

Nevertheless, this more progressive, critical disposition is also evident in how teachers actively initiate their own learning, and seek to critique their own practices. For one teacher, this self-critique as a relevant mode of learning was evident in her efforts to reflect upon the intellectual quality of her work. The state-sanctioned focus upon improving the intellectual quality of students' learning resonated with her own concerns in this area. Through a socio-analytic approach involving critiquing existing practices in light of the push for educational improvement and reform, it became possible to aim for improved practice. This included enabling student learning as students made the transition from primary to secondary schooling:

In my own teaching practice, it [the Departmental emphasis on Productive Pedagogies] stopped me in my tracks . . . I was after this intellectual quality thing. I used to harp back to that all the time because it's something that has been a worry. . . . [The original Board member from the school] was transferred out and on his leaving I said, 'Okay, I would take over.' And that basically was my first little experience . . . For me, see I'm the sort of person that I believe I can never stop learning. And also I'm not four years off retirement. I felt, . . . the reason I went to that initial [Curriculum Board] meeting was that I'm going to be in this game for another minimum ten years. So I'd better get my ass into gear. . . . I do not, in the next ten years, want to be behind the eight ball and not be up with what's happening because that serves the interests of my students moving into high school. (Barb, primary teacher, Queensland)

The reforms which were occurring as part of curriculum renewal in Queensland were seen as important because they focused attention upon an area of concern for this teacher—a teacher who was herself overtly motivated to ensure her learning was relevant to students' needs, and not simply a response to imposed reforms. A strongly focused, learning-oriented disposition is apparent in the way this teacher adopted a proactive approach to the educational reform process, and sought out ways of keeping abreast of changes which were influencing her students.

A more adaptive, flexible habitus is also evident in the way in which teachers in Queensland appropriated the policy push for particular types of reform to engage in professional development practices which they deemed more immediately relevant and beneficial in their particular circumstances:

> . . . we tried briefly when the Department put on the Productive Pedagogies as something that would drive our specialist development, and increase some of the networking that would happen. And the funding that we got through the QTP was for middle schooling but we used it bigger than that. We didn't just concentrate on middle schooling, you know. We weren't just targeting the Year 6 or 7 teachers, then perhaps some of the Year 8 or 9 teachers. We chose to target the whole staff and that has its mistakes and hopefully has some benefits. But we essentially used a department directive, which was putting Productive Pedagogy across the state, and took it to do some of the things that the Board were trying to do. (Lisa, Chair of the Curriculum Board, Queensland)

While this process was also construed as somewhat fraught—'and the downside of that is that I think at times we lost sight of the fact it was a middle schooling approach that we started with' (Lisa, Chair of Curriculum Board, Queensland)—a contextually conscious habitus is evident in the way in which teachers sought to utilise the broader state focus upon a specific reform agenda to foster PD across school sites.

More progressive logics are also evident in how some educators believed a degree of alignment existed between more centralised pressures for teacher learning, and teachers' desires to take a more active stance in relation to their learning:

> I think generally there has been pressure for a number of years for the secondary schools and primary schools to be working more closely together. And there's been considerable pressure over the last few years

about pedagogies improvements. You know, so I think . . . certainly centrally, there has been written pressure. It's up to me and my deputies to lead the enthusiasm for that on occasions so the teachers get the message from centrally too. But then it's been the teachers in the Board who've taken on board all of that and go on and try to do it. Yeah, I think it has been a central office agenda, if you like, that has strongly influenced it. Having said that, though, I'm not sure that it wouldn't have happened one way or the other because there has been a great desire from some people to get the connections improved and maybe it didn't happen as quickly but I think it still would have happened. (Andy, high school principal, Queensland)

These more context-responsive dispositions in relation to teachers' learning are also evident in Ontario. On the hand, teachers' PD is prescribed as never before, and teachers are perceived as needing to be responsive to demands from the Ministry of Education:

> . . . I've been in education for a long time and we used to have more freedom around our own professional development . . . And for many people that was great and they showed lots of initiative and they were interested in lots of things, and we still have people who'll say, 'I'm interested in this, I'd like to work with this person, I'd like to go to this course.' But we are much more prescribed now in the class of professional development activities that are offered for teachers and that is a big shift that I've seen in the last few years. . . . (Michelle, elementary principal, Ontario)

However, even as this learning is more prescribed, there is also evidence of support for drawing upon teachers' conceptions of what is most relevant to their immediate needs, provided this can be justified:

> . . . I still have some teachers who'll come and say to me, 'Well we don't want to do what we're going to do on our professional development day. We want to have our own free time to do this particular activity.' Or, 'I want to work with my partner.' And so I think we have to find that balance of having things that are prescribed for teachers, but also having teachers—letting teachers have choice about what they see as their own personal needs, and being able to defend those needs, and then allowing them to pursue them as well. (Michelle, elementary principal, Ontario)

That teachers are expected to defend the use of this time is also indicative of an educative disposition which construes PD as time which should be beneficial, and not simply spent working on more routine tasks.

These efforts amongst teachers to take a more active role in their learning are similarly evident in Queensland in the way in which the Productive

Pedagogy approach was construed as a useful vehicle by some teachers to assist them in critiquing their own practice. This was evident in the way one teacher hoped future PD might transpire:

> I think we probably had, would have liked to—this is my point of view—but I think probably to have developed the use of Productive Pedagogies more in a contextual sort of way with teachers from their group, fitting in how they would . . . the Productive Pedagogies actually fit in with what you're teaching, with your planning and your assessment. (Kim, primary teacher, Queensland)

Even as teacher PD was mandated in relation to the Productive Pedagogies in Queensland, efforts to engage more actively in their own learning in relation to the Productive Pedagogies reveals a valuing of teachers' learning amongst teachers themselves. A locally focused habitus, infused with concerns about how to improve teaching practices at teachers' specific school sites, influences the PD which is supported.

For a Chemistry teacher in England, a self-initiated visit to a school in the southern United States was a useful vehicle for reflection on his own practices:

> I took kids to America to a school in Georgia, and a couple of the occasions, I lived with the teachers over there, and South Carolina. And so our kids and staff were in a totally different education environment—in the 'bible belt'—as different as you can imagine. And I learned a lot about teaching and different ways of doing things by being in an environment where some of the teachers don't believe in evolution and stuff like that. So for me, as a science teacher, that was—I developed, which was so great! And we have those partnerships. Another example I think of a kind of perhaps-not-written-down-as-professional-development but it surely is. (Clinton, Chemistry teacher, England)

Exposure to a teaching context vastly different from his own led to a socio-analytic process which stimulated his own learning and development, and consolidated his own understandings of his knowledge of science, and how to teach it.

For a colleague in the same school, the act of searching out and inquiring into professional development opportunities led to participation in longer term, residential events over several days/weeks which enabled him to develop his outdoor education skills:

> . . . from my experience, personally the best PD I've done have been things that I have selected and searched out. They've tended to be long term residential CPD things, and mainly in the outdoors—to achieve, you know, the national governing body qualifications [in

specific sports/activities in outdoor education]. (Nick, Chemistry teacher, England)

This process of seeking out PD, and a willingness to engage in different experiences, reflects a much more active disposition on the part of teachers in relation to their learning needs. PD is not simply an imposed practice or set of practices; rather, PD can be sought out by teachers interested in improving their own practices, in the contexts in which they work and teach. In this way, a much more active habitus, produced by and productive of a broader range of learning experiences selected by teachers themselves, is evident across different national settings.

CONCLUSION

The PD practices which transpired within and across the cases from Queensland, Ontario and England reveal the complexity, convoluted nature and unpredictability of actual PD practices. Collectively, these cases indicate how specific policies and policy contexts, sometimes informed by research, play out in practice, as well as how teachers' work practices more generally influence teachers' professional development. While it is neither possible nor desirable to generalise about PD practices across contexts with high levels of specificity, the data provided in this chapter do suggest that the logics of practice associated with more neoliberal and managerial prerogatives, often explicitly supported in policy, do have cogency, and influence practice across contexts. In this way, such influences exhibit globalizing tendencies. However, the PD practices also reveal that while groups and individual teachers and other educators are influenced by these broader, sometimes anti-educational conditions under which they work and learn, these educators are simultaneously able to influence these circumstances, sometimes challenging practices antithetical to engaged student learning. In this way, the field of PD practices, as expressed in teachers' actual learning practices, is clearly a site of contestation over the practices considered of most value.

6 Conclusion
The Politics of Teacher Professional Development

A strong conclusion from our work is that efforts to improve teacher learning will always impact unevenly, across schools, departments and individual teachers. In that situation, rather than imposing targets and compulsory training experience, a more helpful approach is to encourage and facilitate teacher learning through and beyond work: that is, to construct an environment where learning and teacher professionalism can flourish. (Hodkinson, 2009, p. 168)

INTRODUCTION

The competing logics of practice which characterise the field of PD practices have resulted in a complex and contradictory assemblage of polices, approaches to research and practice. Pressures for improvements on quantitative measures of student outcomes, demands for increased alignment between broader economic competitiveness and schooling, and for increased accountability over educational resources have all had a significant influence upon the professional development practices which are considered most valuable in many countries throughout the world. This has sometimes foreclosed the possibilities for more localised, context-relevant, educationally oriented teacher learning practices. Those more in-depth, ongoing, teacher and student-centred approaches to teacher learning have proved difficult to effect in practice in more substantive ways, but they do exist. While sometimes problematic, the social conditions in which PD practices are enacted also contain within them the seeds for improved teacher learning. Even as policy-makers, researchers and practitioners are heavily influenced by more narrow, reductionist, economistic, managerial, traditional, state-focused and test-centric approaches to PD, they have also experienced, and sought to engage in broader, more expansive, socially, politically (and genuinely economically) responsive, democratic, progressive, cross-curricular, site-relevant and child-centred approaches.

The various policies, research approaches and educational practices undertaken in specific settings in Australia, Canada and England provide useful vignettes of instances of these alternatives to more traditional PD approaches, as well as PD arising from more neoliberal and managerial pressures. Furthermore, the cases presented in this volume reveal how more managerial and neoliberal logics are evident across national contexts, indicating a nascent, 'globalized' field of PD practices. The cases reveal how real teachers, students and educational policy-makers, administrators and researchers are influenced by the cultures and conditions in which they undertake their work, and how these might be challenged to encourage more productive professional development practices, and a more learning-focused disposition.

PRESCRIPTIVE POLITICS

There is no doubt that accountability pressures have had a strong impact upon professional development policy, research and practice. At the same time, neoliberal influences have been felt in terms of the content and processes of PD which have been advocated. Strong support for PD seen to contribute to economic productivity, and an emphasis upon PD as an individualistic undertaking, have meant that teachers' learning has been heavily pre-empted and prescribed at the national-state/provincial-local government levels.

In relation to PD policy and associated educational policies and politics, neoliberalism and managerialism have played out strongly in Australia, Canada and England. Reflecting more neoliberal logics, the various iterations of the *Australian Government Quality Teacher Programme*, for example, required teachers to submit proposals through a competitive funding process. Furthermore, the earlier AGQTP policies reflected a doxa of economism in the way they emphasised teacher learning associated with literacy, numeracy, science and ICTs. More neoliberal logics were similarly reflected in England through the emphasis upon literacy and numeracy, including through the *National Literacy Strategy* in 1998, and the *National Numeracy Strategy* in 1999. More managerial logics have also been increasingly evident, most obviously through the increased linking of performance management practices and teachers' continuing professional development. The push for an improved focus upon literacy and numeracy in Ontario also reflects these economistic logics across policy contexts, while a more managerial orthodoxy is evident in endorsement of the sorts of 'short courses' typically associated with 'Additional Qualifications' courses.

This emphasis upon teachers constructed as passive recipients of knowledge generated elsewhere is also evident in the way professional development as research is currently understood. Specifically, there is a tendency towards construing PD research as a 'product' which can be readily disseminated and appropriated, regardless of context. The emphasis upon what Slavin (2002) describes as the 'gold-standard' of randomized controlled trial approaches encourages an approach to teachers' learning which disenfranchises teachers as active learners able to establish their own research programs into their own practices, in the context of their own classrooms, schools and communities. The active involvement of major private, multinational consultancy and accountancy companies in the distillation of general sets of criteria to which teachers and schools should aspire exemplifies how more neoliberal, managerial and economistic practices can restrict what is considered beneficial teacher learning.

In relation to practice, there is considerable evidence of how policy pressures and the nature of teachers' work have led to reliance upon particular types of PD practices. PD is often marginalised, and not considered of substantive value in schooling settings. PD programs are prolific in number, and often adopted in superficial ways. They may be limited to information sessions for teachers, who are treated as passive recipients of information. They may involve external experts talking at, rather than with, teachers, and/or a disjointed set of activities. PD may often be narrowly focused, emphasising existing dominant, disciplinary domains without consideration for how alternative conceptions of knowledge might better serve teachers' learning needs. PD may be undertaken as part of a process of curriculum renewal, but this process may be enacted in more managerial ways to ensure compliance with particular educational reforms. Curriculum-based PD may also be developed rapidly in response to what are construed as immediate policy demands. Such demands may be associated with reforms in particular curricular areas seen to have longer-term economic benefits to the broader society—such as literacy and numeracy. In a context of increased accountability and nation-states' concerns about international competitiveness, PD may also be tied to very particular types of learning which can be more easily enumerated and measured. The pressure upon teachers to improve test scores in each of the countries described in Chapter 5, this volume, reveals the pervasiveness of such demands, and gesture towards a global field of PD practices characterised by what Popkewitz and Rizvi (2009) describe as 'new categories of equivalence across nations' (p. 19). Even as teachers resist the demands to focus strongly upon teacher learning designed to effect improved test scores, this often becomes the default position in relation to their learning. The way in which the principals orchestrated teachers to work with one another across the four school sites in Queensland, and the focus upon particular content areas—especially literacy and numeracy—is just one example of how broader pressures for students to perform well on a state-sanctioned assessment regime, and in particular areas of the curriculum, can lead to a more instrumental approach to teachers' professional development. Similarly, the strong focus upon literacy and numeracy, and pressure to produce high results on EQAO test scores in Ontario also provides evidence of this push to quantify learning. The strong emphasis upon disciplinary knowledge in England, concerns about results on A-levels, and a sustained focus upon individualistic workshop approaches also reflect these broader pressures upon the work of teachers and educators more generally. Under these conditions where education is reduced to measurable and manageable outcomes, 'good teaching' is under threat (Connell, 2009).

PD may also be employed as part of a marketing strategy, rather than for more educative reasons. From many teachers' perspectives, including some of those in the case data presented, PD is something to be endured and often undertaken without expectation of any benefit. As a result, PD is often rejected by teachers and considered to take up teachers' time—time which could be more valuably and validly spent responding to more pressing and immediate needs.

PRODUCTIVE POLITICS

However, and at the same time, there is considerable evidence of alternatives to these more narrowly construed conceptions of teachers' learning, and advocacy for such learning.

In relation to policy, PD is valued, at least discursively. The way in which PD features as an important part of educational reform initiatives indicates policy-makers' understanding of the potential for PD to effect substantive and beneficial learning. Policy-makers and researchers do endorse more collaborative, ongoing, site-specific, inquiry-focused approaches to teachers' professional development. The *Quality Teacher Programme* in Australia, for example, was a policy 'product' which overtly endorsed PD for teachers of students in disadvantaged communities, and in the form of action research. Various 'creativity' policies in England, and the revised *Professional Learning Framework* in Ontario similarly exemplify support for teacher learning beyond specific curriculum areas deemed most likely to lead to improved economic productivity, and short-term PD approaches to 'give' information to teachers.

Furthermore, in relation to their own learning, teachers and school-based administrators do value PD, and do act as agents of their own circumstances. They are not simply passive recipients of policies developed elsewhere (Taylor et al., 1997). Even in the context of strong global forces which trend towards managerial and economic homogenisation, educators can and do instigate change which is more meaningful in terms of their own and their students' needs (Rizvi and Lingard, 2010). Teachers' PD, as part of teachers' work, is characterised by active involvement, and teachers do not simply ignore the potential for substantive PD practices to effect improved outcomes for their students. PD is construed as beneficial and, at times, transformative of teachers' practices. Senior educators in Ontario, for example, were willing to sanction professional development initiatives beyond those endorsed by the state because they recognised the importance of these approaches. This was evident in multiple ways, including how teachers drew upon provincial test-based data to inform a broader conception of learning.

The emphasis on context and for job-embedded learning also reflects support for PD as part of teachers' ongoing work. Teacher-instigated inquiries, in both formal and informal ways, serve as substantive alternatives to more traditional, passive approaches. In the cases presented, such learning was evident in the way in which Canadian principals and teachers sought to ensure that the professional development in which they engaged was always focused upon the needs of students, and that individual student needs were taken into account. It was also evident in recognition of the specificity and peculiarities of individual schools, including the way in which inequitable resourcing precludes some schools from engaging in richer and balanced PD practices. The way in which teachers in Australia articulated the specific learning of their students, and how this was influenced by their work together as members of the Curriculum Board, reflects an alternative response to broader neoliberal and managerial logics. The notion of a culture of care (Noddings, 1992)—a caring disposition—was also evident, and permeated the professional interactions which characterised the professional development practices in some schools.

The emphasis upon collaborative learning also reflects an alternative to more traditional PD approaches. In Australia, teachers sought to utilise the resources provided through state-sanctioned initiatives (such as the *QTP* focus on improving teachers' disciplinary knowledge) to provide opportunities for colleagues to meet together across schools and beyond these specific foci. Teachers actively worked together to effect improved student learning in the context of teachers' specific schools and classrooms. That members of the Curriculum Board in Queensland were clearer in their own understandings about what they expected of students as a result of collaborating with one another over an extended period of time about the educational reforms in that state, is indicative of how a focus upon a wider conception of student learning can enhance teachers' learning. Importantly, these teachers could point to evidence of improved student learning as a result of their efforts together.

PD is also not simply focused upon particular and dominant curriculum areas, such as literacy and numeracy, or confined to traditional disciplines. Attention to PD aimed at curriculum reform in the middle years of schooling in Queensland, and attention to issues of equality and equity in Canada gesture towards a richer set of practices than may typically be associated with the field of PD practices. More integrated, cross-disciplinary learning in England, for example, stands as an alternative to more orthodox practices. Teachers' efforts to work with colleagues across discipline areas—languages, PE and geography—and their desire to foster improved interactions across traditional disciplines reflects a more broadly conceived conception of teacher learning than that often sanctioned within specific policies and guidelines. The robust, ongoing, site-specific discussions and sharing of practice which occurred within various departments in the secondary school in England also reveal a richer response to teachers' learning than is perhaps anticipated under current conditions. Such evidence is also supportive of current understandings of the variety of PD practices which characterise teachers' learning as part of teachers' work.

While PD is focused strongly upon improving a narrow conception of students' learning—particularly test scores on standardised state-sanctioned tests, and test results more generally (as in the English setting)—teachers also seek to engage in PD practices which contribute to a broader conception of student learning. The active critique by educators in Canada and England about narrowing PD to those activities and approaches seen as enhancing test scores alone reflect a more inclusive disposition, and a broader understanding of the value of PD for multiple conceptions of student learning. Concerns about the potential narrowing of curricula opportunities which attend such foci also constitute evidence of support for a richer conception of learning. Queensland teachers' willingness to engage with the reform agenda in that state, because it was perceived to be beneficial for students' futures more generally, serve as evidence of a richer, educationally grounded teacher habitus.

Many of these PD practices reflect more research-oriented emphases which construe professional development as a mechanism for transformative change, as possessing emancipatory potential, enabling teachers to recognise the structural and cultural impediments which inhibit their capacity to engage more fully with one another and the students they teach, even under conditions in which this is increasingly difficult (Carr and Kemmis, 2005). While not always formally construed as an action research initiative, the way in which some teachers seek to engage with one another to try to improve their practice is reflective of many of the principles of this approach to teachers' learning. Recognition by one Canadian principal that some schools were in a better position than others to generate resources to promote a broader conception of PD practices beyond those limited to state-sanctioned approaches, also reveal a critical, context-responsive awareness which challenges embedded inequalities, and the structural parameters responsible for sustaining such inequalities. In short, such practices reveal a 'learning disposition' on the part of educators.

A POLITICS OF POSSIBILITY: A CALL TO REFLEXIVITY

The multiplicity of complex and contested logics which characterise the field of PD practices necessitate clear thinking and a more intensive dialogue within and between educators working within and across the domains of policy, research and practice about how to action PD to promote teacher learning for more substantive student learning. Bourdieu (1999) spoke of the need for promoting the conditions for a rational dialogue between the producers and interpreters of ideas across international contexts: 'The logical Realpolitik of which I am a ceaseless advocate must above all have as its aim an intention to work towards the creation of social conditions permitting rational dialogue' (p. 226). Such rational dialogue needs to be extended to conversations between practitioners within and across each of the domains of policy, research and practice, and construed in such a way that those who 'interpret' ideas are simultaneously positioned as active producers of ideas themselves. This is in keeping with what Lingard and Renshaw (2009) describe as a research-informed and research-informing stance, rather than simply bolstering existing demarcations and barriers between knowledge creation and application. Such dialogue constitutes the foundation for the development of a more sustained learning disposition amongst all involved in and seeking to influence teachers' professional development.

A more inclusive professional dialogue is necessary for overcoming some of the tensions inherent in relations between practitioners, policy-makers and researchers of professional development. Professional development often exists as both a body of texts resulting from research by those occupying positions within the academy, and considered valuable for the symbolic capital they possess. At the same time, professional development also exists as a research process which teachers are encouraged to engage in as a means of informing their everyday work and actions. This teacher-centric research process is also productive of various texts, albeit texts which are typically not valued in the same way as more traditional, refereed academic journals and research monographs. Similarly, policy-makers engage in the production of texts which sometimes draw on research, and seek to influence the work of practitioners. However, these texts are framed differently from the patterns of life which characterise teachers' work.

Recognition of these different texts and their differential use-values in different contexts is essential for revealing how and why tensions exist between more traditional researchers of PD, policy-makers and practitioners. Bourdieu construed texts as typically circulating without their context—without the full knowledge of how they came into being, and therefore, of what they truly meant:

> The fact that texts circulate without their context, that—to use my terms—they don't bring with them the field of production of which they are a product, and the fact that the recipients, who are themselves in a different field of production, re-interpret the texts in accordance with the structure of the field of reception, are facts that generate some formidable misunderstandings and that can have good or bad consequences. (Bourdieu, 1999, p. 221)

While Bourdieu was speaking specifically about the international circulation of ideas arising within the academy, and arguing that this circulation of ideas needed to be understood in terms of the specific national settings in which they were developed, his metaphor of texts circulating without their contexts is also informative for understanding how and why there are significant tensions between teachers and those in schools, and researchers and policy-makers, and other advocates of teacher PD. The valuing of different capitals in these different settings, and subsequent tensions, can lead to a continuation of more traditional practices in schooling settings. In this 'game' of distinctions, the capitals most valued by those in the academy, or the state, do not necessarily correlate with those deemed most valuable by those working in schools (cf. Ladwig's (1994) argument about the nature of autonomy of the United States educational policy field in relation to school-ing practices). Recognising and working with these tensions need to be a key component of the sort of reflexive learning disposition which needs to be cultivated amongst teachers, researchers and policy-makers.

This reflexive stance also needs to engage with the tensions between PD as a national initiative, and as part of what might be described as a nascent global field of PD. Bourdieu's emphasis upon the specificity of national set-tings is crucial for understanding how PD transpires differently in different national settings. Simultaneously, however, and while not denying the sig-nificant commonalities which exist across nation-states within the broader field of PD practices, as exemplified in part in the specific cases presented in Chapter 5, this volume, it is also important that specific national (regional and local) differences be recognised. Greater awareness of the conditions in which PD is enacted and understood is useful in relation to both under-standing the field of teacher PD as simultaneously global, national and local in nature. How policy-makers, researchers and practitioners from different nations then interpret these ideas is able to take on a whole new meaning, and not simply be characterised by random policy-borrowing within an imagined global field which may have little real relevance to local settings or to the reality of PD policy, research and practice more generally.

Such a reflexive stance entails a learning disposition which is better able to challenge more reductive policies and practices which may seem to respond to immediate policy proclivities and work conditions, but which actively hinder more substantive teacher and student learning practices over the medium and longer term. Such work is challenging, particularly under conditions in which narrow, quantifiable measures of student learning are so pervasive (cf. Hardy and Boyle, 2011). However, such work is essential, and possible, as evident in the specific case data, policies and research pre-sented. A reflexive, learning disposition challenges reductionist neoliberal and managerial conceptions of learning and promotes more genuinely edu-cative approaches.

Educators must seek to learn from their work as policy-makers, researchers and practitioners—they must be both educators of students, and students of Education. However, to get to this point, it is necessary to firstly recognise that such learning requires contestation and conflict about the nature of current and potential practices. Contestation and conflict should not be shunned as indicators of instability, but embraced as catalysts for learning:

> [For] it is through conflict and sometimes only through conflict that we learn what our ends and purposes are. (MacIntyre 2007, p. 164)

A clear understanding and recognition of teacher professional development as inherently contested is essential to foster an environment in which learning and teacher professionalism can flourish—to promote a productive politics of teacher professional development.

About the Author

Ian Hardy is Lecturer in Educational Studies at the University of Queensland, Australia. Dr Hardy's research focuses upon the nature and politics of Education, with a particular emphasis upon teacher professional development policy and practice. He has also published in the areas of educational leadership, higher education and initial teacher education. He lives in Brisbane, Australia.

Notes

NOTES TO CHAPTER 2

1. The 'crisis of habitus' to which Zipin and Brennan (2003) refer relates to the Australian university sector, but the disjunction between more broad-based educational and more instrumental, administrative logics of practice which they describe seems pertinent to that experienced by educators in Ontario at this time.

NOTES TO CHAPTER 3

1. It must be noted that much of the literature mentioned in this section, under the rubric 'teacher professional learning community' and its variants, is based upon U.S. and Canadian studies. This is not to imply that such communities have not been described elsewhere, but to acknowledge the influence of this particular body of research literature, which has been drawn upon extensively by researchers in other countries, including Australia and England.

NOTES TO CHAPTER 5

1. The Productive Pedagogies was a research-developed list of twenty elements of good classroom practice arising from the QSRLS, and which was used in the original study to critique teachers' classroom practices. The list was subsequently rearticulated into a professional development program, supported by Education Queensland, to enable teachers to critique their own teaching practices.
2. To preserve anonymity, a reference to the source from which this quote has been drawn has been deliberately omitted, and the quote altered.
3. All names are pseudonyms.
4. The GCSE is an English qualification conferred on students who have successfully completed a specified number of courses by approximately the age of 16.
5. 'A-Levels' are post-GCSE qualifications conferred on students in recognition of successful completion of selected courses by the end of their schooling.
6. At this time, the major subject disciplinary clusters in Australia were described as Key Learning Areas, or 'KLAs.'
7. Pseudonym for a relevant English A-level examination board.
8. I suggest this somewhat cautiously because building esteem on the basis of a narrow set of learning experiences is to encourage or perpetuate a type

of educational fraud which students can ill afford, particularly those living under the most difficult material circumstances.

9. A pseudonym for an external academic consultant from Sydney.
10. A pseudonym for a local independent, external consultant.
11. A pseudonym for an Education Queensland consultant from the regional office.
12. Manager of section in which this Ministry official worked.
13. The assessment of student work in senior secondary schools in Queensland is undertaken by teachers, rather than via external examination. Panels of teachers from throughout the state meet annually to study student work and to make assessments on its quality. Known as 'moderation' meetings, this process is designed to ensure comparability of student work across the state.

References

Achinstein, B. (2002). Conflict amid community: The micropolitics of teacher collaboration. *Teachers College Record, 104*(3), 421–455.

Adey, P. with Hewitt, G., Hewitt, J. and Landau, N. (2004). *The professional development of teachers: Practice and theory.* Dordrecht: Kluwer Academic Publishers.

Almas, A. and Krumsvik, R. (2007). Digitally literate teachers in leading edge schools in Norway. *Journal of In-Service Education, 33*(4), 479–497.

Altrichter, H., Kemmis, S., McTaggart, R. and Zuber-Skerritt, O. (1991). Defining, confining or refining action research? In O. Zuber-Skerritt (Ed.), *Action research for change and development* (pp. 13–20). Aldershot: Ashbury.

Angus, M. (1996). Award restructuring in schools: Educational idealism versus political pragmatism. In T. Seddon (Ed.), *Pay, professionalism and politics* (pp.117–152). Hawthorn: Australian Council for Educational Research.

Appadurai, A. (2001). Grassroots globalization and the research imagination. In A. Appadurai (Ed.), *Globalization* (pp. 1–21). Durham, NC: Duke University Press.

Apple, M. (1986). *Teachers and texts: A Political economy of class and gender relations in education.* London: Routledge.

Argyris, C. and Schön, D. (1974). *Theory in practice: Increasing professional effectiveness.* San Francisco: Jossey-Bass.

Australian Secondary Principals' Association. (2007). *2007 Survey—Beginning teachers.* Australian Secondary Principals' Association: Kingston.

Avalos, B. (2004). CPD policies and practices in the Latin American region. In C. Day and J. Sachs (Eds.), *International handbook on the continuing professional development of teachers* (pp. 119–145). Maidenhead: Open University Press.

Ball, S. (1994). *Education reform: A critical and post-structural approach.* Buckingham: Open University Press.

Ball, S. (1998). Big policies/small world: An introduction to international perspectives in education policy. *Comparative Education, 24*(2), 119–30.

Ball, S. (2009). Privatising education, privatising education policy, privatising educational research: Network governance and the 'competition state.' *Journal of Education Policy, 24*(1), 83–99.

Ball, D. and Cohen, D. (1999). Developing practice, developing practitioners. In L. Darling-Hammond and G. Sykes (Eds.), *Teaching as the learning profession: Handbook of policy and practice* (pp. 3–32). San Francisco: Jossey-Bass.

Ballet, K., Kelchtermans, G. and Loughran, J. (2006). Beyond intensification towards a scholarship of practice: Analysing change in teachers' work lives. *Teachers and Teaching: Theory and Practice, 12*(2), 209–229.

Barker, B. (2008). School reform policy in England since 1988: Relentless pursuit of the unattainable. *Journal of Education Policy, 23*(6), 669–683.

Barth, R. (1991). Restructuring schools: Some questions for teachers and principals. *Phi Delta Kappan*, 73(2), 123–128.

Bauman, Z. (2001). *Community: Seeking safety in an insecure world*. Cambridge: Polity.

Bedard, G. and Lawton, S. (2000). The struggle for power and control: Shifting policy-making models and the Harris agenda for education in Ontario. *Canadian Public Administration*, 43(3), 241–269.

Bégin, M., Caplan, G., Bharti, M., Glaze, A., DiCecco, R. and Murphy, D. (1994). *For the love of learning: Report of the Royal Commission on learning*. Toronto: Ontario Executive Council.

Ben Jaafar, S. and Anderson, S. (2007). Policy trends and tensions in accountability for educational management and services in Canada. *The Alberta Journal of Educational Research*, 53(2), 207–227.

Biesta, G. (2007). Why 'what works' won't work: Evidence-based practice and the democratic deficit in educational research. *Educational Theory*, 57(1), 1–22.

Bjørndal, C. (2007). The action researcher and Sherlock Holmes: Similarities in logical strategies. In E. Moksnes, T. Lund and T. Tiller (Eds.), *Action research: A Nordic perspective* (pp. 111–132). Kristiansand: Høyskoleforlaget AS—Norwegian Academic Press.

Bolam, R. and McMahon, A. (2004). Literature, definitions and models: towards a conceptual map. In C. Day and J. Sachs (Eds.), *International handbook on the continuing professional development of teachers* (pp. 33–63). Maidenhead: Open University Press.

Borko, H. (2004). Professional development and teacher learning: Mapping the terrain. *Educational Researcher*, 33(8), 3–15.

Boud, D. and Middleton, H. (2003). Learning from others at work: communities of practice and informal learning. *Journal of Workplace Learning*, 15(5), 194–202.

Bourdieu, P. (1984). *Distinction: A social critique of the judgment of taste*. Cambridge, MA: Harvard University Press.

Bourdieu, P. (1986). The forms of capital. In J. Richardson (Ed.), *Handbook of theory of research for the Sociology of Education* (pp. 241–258). New York: Greenwood Press.

Bourdieu, P. (1990a). *In other words: Essays towards a reflexive sociology*. Stanford: Stanford University Press.

Bourdieu, P. (1990b). *The logic of practice*. Stanford: Stanford University Press.

Bourdieu, P. (1998). *Practical reason: On the theory of action*. Stanford: Stanford University Press.

Bourdieu, P. (1999). The social conditions of the international circulation of ideas. In R. Shusterman (Ed.), *Bourdieu: A critical reader* (pp. 220–228). Oxford: Blackwell.

Bourdieu, P. (2000). *Pascalian meditations*. Cambridge: Polity Press.

Bourdieu, P. (2005). *The social structures of the economy*. Cambridge, UK: Polity.

Bourdieu, P. and Wacquant, L. (1992). *An invitation to reflexive sociology*. Chicago: University of Chicago Press.

Burbank, M. and Kauchak, D. (2003). An alternative model for professional development: Investigations into effective collaboration. *Teaching and Teacher Education*, 19, 499–514.

Business Council of Australia. (2008). *Teaching talent: The best teachers for Australia's classrooms*. Melbourne: Business Council of Australia.

Campbell, E. (2005). Challenges in fostering ethical knowledge as professionalism within schools as teaching communities. *Journal of Educational Change*, 6(3), 207–226.

Canadian Legal Information Institute. (2009). Professional learning committee and professional learning requirements. Retrieved 13 August, 2009, from http://www.canlii.org/eliisa/highlight.do?text=ontario+college+of+teachersandlanguage=enandsearchTitle=Statutes+and+Regulations+of+Ontarioandpath=/en/on/laws/regu/o-reg-270–01/latest/o-reg-270–01.html.

Carr, W. (1995). *For education: Towards critical educational inquiry.* Buckingham: Open University Press.

Carr, W. (2007). Educational research as a practical science. *International Journal of Research and Method in Education, 30*(3), 271–286.

Carr, W. and Kemmis, S. (1986). *Becoming critical: Education, knowledge and action research.* London: Falmer.

Carr, W. and Kemmis, S. (2005). Staying critical. *Educational Action Research, 13*(3), 347–357.

Carrington, V. (2002). *The middle years of schooling in Queensland: A way forward.* Brisbane: University of Queensland.

Cerny, P. (1990). *The changing architecture of politics: Structure, agency and the future of the state.* London: Sage.

Christie, P., Harley, K. and Penny, A. (2004). Case studies from sub-Saharan Africa. In C. Day and J. Sachs (Eds.), *International handbook on the continuing professional development of teachers* (pp. 167–190). Maidenhead: Open University Press.

Clarke, J., Newman, J., Smith, N., Vidler, E. and Westmarland, L. (2007). *Creating citizen-consumers: Changing publics and changing public services.* London: Sage.

Cobb, J. (1999). *The earthist challenge to economism: A theological critique of the World Bank.* Basingstoke, UK: Macmillan.

Cobb, P. (1994). Where is the mind? Constructivist and sociocultural perspectives on mathematical development. *Educational Researcher, 23*(7), 13–20.

Cochran-Smith, M. and Lytle, S. (1990). Research on teaching and teacher research: The issues that divide. *Educational Researcher, 19*(2), 2–11.

Cochran-Smith, M. and Lytle, S. (1999a). Relationships of knowledge and practice: Teacher learning in communities. *Review of Research in Education, 24,* 249–305.

Cochran-Smith, M. and Lytle, S. (1999b). The teacher research movement: A decade later. *Educational Researcher, 28*(7), 15–25.

Cochran-Smith, M. and Lytle, S. (2000). Teacher education at the turn of the century. *Journal of Teacher Education, 51*(3), 163–165.

Cochran-Smith, M. and Lytle, S. L. (2003). Teacher learning communities. In J. W. Guthrie (Ed.), *Encyclopedia of Education* (2nd ed.) (pp. 2461–2469). New York: Macmillan.

Colas, A. (2005). Neoliberalism, globalization and international relations. In A. Saad-Filho and D. Johnston (Eds.), *Neoliberalism: A critical reader* (pp. 70–79). London: Pluto Press.

Coleman, J. (2000). *A history of political thought: From ancient Greece to early Christianity.* Oxford: Blackwell.

Collier, J. and Esteban, R. (1998). *From complicity to encounter: The church and the culture of economism.* Harrisburg, PA: Trinity Press.

Commonwealth of Australia. (1998). *Learning for life—final report: Review of higher education financing and policy.* Canberra: Department of Employment, Education, Training and Youth Affairs.

Commonwealth of Australia. (2000). *Quality Teacher Programme client guidelines 2000–2002.* Canberra: Department of Education, Training and Youth Affairs.

Commonwealth of Australia. (2003). *Commonwealth Quality Teacher programme: Updated client guidelines, 2003.* Canberra: Department of Education, Training and Youth Affairs.

Commonwealth of Australia. (2005). *Australian government Quality Teacher Programme: Client guidelines, 2005 to 2009.* Canberra: Department of Education, Science and Training.

Connell, R. (1985). *Teachers' Work.* Sydney: George Allen and Unwin.

Connell, R. (2009). Good teachers on dangerous ground: Towards a new view of teacher quality and professionalism. *Critical Studies in Education, 50*(3), 213–229.

Connell, R., Ashenden, D., Kessler, S. and Dowsett, G. (1982). *Making the difference: Schools, families and social division.* Sydney: Allen and Unwin.

Connell, W. F. (1993). *Reshaping Australian education: 1960–1985.* Hawthorn: The Australian Council for Educational Research.

Considine, M. and Painter, M. (1997). Introduction. In M. Considine and M. Painter (Eds.), *Managerialism: The great debate* (pp. 1–11). Melbourne: Melbourne University Press.

Cordingley, P., Bell, M., Rundell, B. and Evans, D. (2003). *The impact of collaborative CPD on classroom teaching and learning: How does collaborative Continuing Professional Development (CPD) for teachers of the 5–16 age range affect teaching and learning?* London: University of London (EPPI-Centre, Social Science Research Unit, Institute of Education).

Daly, C., Pachler, N., Pickering, J. and Bezemer, J. (2007). Teachers as e-learners: Exploring the experiences of teachers in an online professional master's programme. *Journal of In-Service Education, 33*(4), 443–461.

Darling-Hammond, L. (Ed.) (1994). *Professional development schools: Schools for developing a profession.* New York: Teachers College Press.

Darling-Hammond, L. (1997). *The right to learn: a blueprint for creating schools that work.* San Francisco: Jossey-Bass.

Darling-Hammond, L. (1998). Teacher learning that supports student learning. *Educational Leadership*, February, 6–11.

Darling-Hammond, L. (2000). How teacher education matters. *Journal of Teacher Education, 51*(3), 166–173.

Day, C. (1999). *Developing teachers: The challenges of lifelong learning.* London: Falmer Press.

Day, C. (2002). Revisiting the purposes of continuing professional development. In G. Trorey and C. Cullingford (Eds.), *Professional development and institutional needs* (pp. 51–77). Aldershot: Ashgate.

Day, C. and Sachs, J. (2004). Professionalism, performativity and empowerment: Discourses in the politics, policies and purposes of continuing professional development. In. C. Day and J. Sachs (Eds.), *International handbook on the continuing professional development of teachers* (pp. 3–32). Maidenhead: Open University Press.

Day, C., Sammons, P., Stobart, G., Kington, A. and Gu, Q. (2007). *Teachers matter: Connecting lives, work and effectiveness.* Maidenhead, UK: Open University Press.

Department for Education. (2010). *The importance of teaching: The schools white paper 2010.* Norwich: The Stationery Office.

Department for Education and Employment. (2001). *Learning and teaching: A Strategy for professional development.* London: Department for Education and Employment.

Department for Education and Skills. (2003). *Excellence and enjoyment: A strategy for primary schools.* Nottingham: Department for Education and Skills.

Department for Education and Skills. (2004). *Excellence and enjoyment: Learning and teaching in the primary years. Professional development materials.* Nottingham: Department for Education and Skills.

Department for Education and Skills. (2005). *Leading and coordinating CPD in secondary schools*. London: Department for Education and Skills.

Department of Education, Employment and Workplace Relations. (2010). Smarter schools national partnership (NP) for improving teacher quality fact sheet. Canberra: Department of Education, Employment and Workplace Relations.

DEEWR. (2010). Smart Schools. Retrieved 26 May, 2010, from http://www.deewr.gov.au/Schooling/Programs/SmarterSchools/Pages/default.aspx.

Desimone, L. (2009). Improving impact studies of teachers' professional development: toward better conceptualizations and measures. *Educational Researcher, 38*(3), 181–199.

Driver, R., Asoko, H., Leach, J., Mortimer, E. and Scott, P. (1994). Constructing scientific knowledge in the classroom. *Educational Researcher, 23*(7), 5–12.

DuFour, R. and Eaker, R. (1998). *Professional learning communities at work: Best practices for enhancing student achievement*. Alexandria: Association for Supervision and Curriculum Development.

Easthope, C. and Easthope, G. (2000). Intensification, extension and complexity of teachers' workload. *British Journal of Sociology of Education, 21*(1), 43–58.

Education Quality and Accountability Office. (2005). *Ontario students continue gains in foundation skills of reading, writing and math*. Retrieved 27 July, 2007, from http://www.eqao.com/NR/ReleaseViewer.aspx?Lang=Eandrelease=b05R004.

Education Queensland. (2000). *New Basics project technical paper*. Brisbane: Education Queensland.

Eilertsen, T. (2007). The organisation of learning: Experiences from the project 'A learning conscious school day.' In E. Moksnes, T. Lund and T. Tiller (Eds.), *Action research: A Nordic perspective* (pp. 35–50). Kristiansand: Høyskoleforlaget AS—Norwegian Academic Press.

Eisner, E. (1992). Educational reform and the ecology of schooling. *Teachers College Record, 93*(4), 610–627.

El-Haj, T. (2003). Practicing for equity from the standpoint of the particular: Exploring the work of one urban teacher network. *Teachers College Record, 105*(5), 817–845.

Elliott, J. (1991). *Action research for educational change*. Buckingham: Open University Press.

Elliott, J. (2007). Making evidence-based practice educational. In M. Hammersley (Ed.), *Educational research and evidence-based practice* (pp. 66–88). Los Angeles: Sage.

Elliott, J. (2009). Research-based teaching. In S. Gewirtz, P. Mahony, I. Hextall and A. Cribb (Eds.), *Changing teacher professionalism: International trends, challenges and ways forward* (pp. 170–183). London: Routledge.

Esteve, J. (2006). The transformation of the teachers' role at the end of the twentieth century: New challenges for the future. In. D. Hartley and M. Whitehead (Eds.), *Teacher education: Major themes in education. Volume V: Globalization, standards and teacher education*. (335–348). London: Routledge.

Evetts, J. (2009). New professionalism and new public management: Changes, continuities and consequences. *Comparative Sociology, 8*(2), 247–266.

Feiman-Nemser, S. and Norman, P. (2000). Teacher education: From initial preparation to continuing professional development. In B. Moon, M. Ben-Peretz and S. Brown (Eds.), *Routledge international companion to education* (pp. 732–755). London: Routledge.

Fielding, M., Bragg, S., Craig, J., Cunningham, I., Eraut, M., Gillinson, S., Horne, M., Robinson, C. and Thorp, J. (2005). *Factors influencing the transfer of good practice*. London: Department for Education and Skills.

Fragkouli, E. and Hammond, M. (2007). Issues in developing programmes to support teachers of philology in using information and communications technologies in Greek schools: a case study. *Journal of In-Service Education, 33*(4), 463–477.

Fraser, C., Kennedy, A., Reid, L. and McKinney, S. (2007). Teachers' continuing professional development: Contested concepts, understandings and models. *Journal of In-Service Education, 33*(2), 153–169.

Friedman, A., Durkin, C., Phillips, M. and Davis, K. (2000). *Continuing professional development in the UK: Policies and programmes.* Bristol: Professional Associations Research Network.

Friedman, A. and Philips, M. (2004). Continuing professional development: Developing a vision. *Journal of Education and Work, 17*(3), 361–376.

Fullan, M. (1993). *Change forces.* London: Falmer Press.

Fullan, M. (2000). The three stories of education reform. *Phi Delta Kappan.* April, 581–584.

Fullan, M. (2001). *The new meaning of educational change* (3rd ed.). New York: Teachers College Press.

Fullan, M. (2003). *Change forces with a vengeance.* London: Routledge Falmer.

Fullan, M. (2007). *The new meaning of educational change* (4th ed.). New York and London: Teachers College Press and Routledge.

Fullan, M. and Hargreaves, A. (Eds.) (1991). *Teacher development and educational change.* London: The Falmer Press.

Fullan, M. and Hargreaves, A. (1998). *What's worth fighting for? Working together for your school.* Hawthorn: Australian Council for Educational Administration.

Fuller, A. and Unwin, L. (2003). Learning as apprentices in the contemporary UK workplace: creating and managing expansive and restrictive participation. *Journal of Education and Work, 16*(4), 407–426.

Furlong, J. and Oancea, A. (2005). Assessing quality in applied and practice-based educational research: A framework for discussion. Oxford: Oxford University Department of Educational Studies.

Garet, M., Porter, A., Desimone, L., Birman, B. and Yoon, K. (2001). What makes professional development effective? Results from a national sample of teachers. *American Educational Research Journal, 38*(4), 915–945.

Gee, J., Hull, G. and Lankshear, C. (1996). *The new work order: Behind the language of the new capitalism.* Sydney: Allen and Unwin.

General Teaching Council for England. (2006). *The statement of professional values and practice for teachers: The GTC statement.* Birmingham: General Teaching Council for England.

General Teaching Council for England. (2008). About the GTC: Introducing the GTC. Retrieved 5 June, 2008, from http://www.gtce.org.uk/aboutthegtc/intro/whatwedo.

Gewirtz, S. Mahony, P., Hextall, I. and Cribb, A. (2009). Policy, professionalism and practice: Understanding and enhancing teachers' work. In S. Gewirtz, P. Mahony, I. Hextall and A. Cribb (Eds.), *Changing teacher professionalism: International trends, challenges and ways forward* (pp. 3–16). London: Routledge.

Gidney, R. (1999). *From hope to Harris: The reshaping of Ontario's schools.* Toronto: University of Ontario.

Gillard, J. (2008a). *A new progressive reform agenda for Australian schools.* The 2008 Fraser Lecture, 29 May. Canberra: Media Centre, Education, Employment and Workplace Relations Portfolio.

Gillard, J. (2008b). MCEETYA/MCTVE, Press Conference, 17 April. Canberra: Media Centre, Education, Employment and Workplace Relations Portfolio.

Giroux, H. A. (1988). *Teachers as intellectuals: Towards a critical pedagogy of learning.* New York: Bergin and Garvey.

Goodlad, J. I. (1984). *A place called school: Prospects for the future.* New York: McGraw Hill.

Goodlad, J. (2002). Teacher education research: The outside and the inside. *Journal of Teacher Education, 53*(3), 216–221.

Goodson, I. (2003). *Professional knowledge, professional lives: Studies in education and change.* Maidenhead: Open University Press.

Gore, J. and Gitlin, A. (2004). [Re]visioning the academic-teacher divide: Power and knowledge in the educational community. *Teachers and Teaching: Theory and Practice, 10*(1), 35–58.

Grek, S., Lawn, M., Lingard, B., Ozga, J., Rinne, R., Segerholm, C. and Simola, H. (2009). National policy brokering and the construction of the European education space in England, Sweden, Finland and Scotland. *Comparative Education, 45*(1), 5–21.

Grossman, P., Wineburg, S. and Woolworth, S. (2001). Toward a theory of teacher community. *Teachers College Record, 103*(6), 942–1012.

Groundwater-Smith, S. and Campbell, A. (2010). Joining the dots: Connecting inquiry and professional learning. In A. Campbell and S. Groundwater-Smith (Eds.), *Connecting inquiry and professional learning in education: International perspectives and practical solutions* (pp. 200–206). London: Routledge.

Groundwater-Smith, S. and Dadds, M. (2004). Critical practitioner inquiry: Towards responsible professional communities of practice. In C. Day and J. Sachs (Eds.), *International handbook on the continuing professional development of teachers* (pp. 238–263). Maidenhead, UK: Open University Press.

Groundwater-Smith, S. and Mockler, N. (2009). *Teacher professional learning in an age of compliance: Mind the gap.* Dordrecht: Springer.

Grundy, S. and Bonser, S. (2000). The new work order and Australian schools. In C. Day, A. Fernandez, T. Hauge and J. Moller (Eds.), *The life and work of teachers: International perspectives in changing times* (130–145). London: Falmer Press.

Grundy, S. and Robison, J. (2004). Teacher professional development: Themes and trends in the recent Australian experience. In C. Day and J. Sachs (Eds.), *International handbook on the continuing professional development of teachers* (pp. 146–166). Maidenhead: Open University Press.

Gunter, H. (2001). *Leaders and leadership in education.* London: Paul Chapman.

Guskey, T. (1997). Research needs to link professional development and student learning. *Journal of Staff Development, 18*(2), 36–40.

Guskey, T. (2000). *Evaluating professional development.* Thousand Oaks, CA: Corwin Press.

Guskey, T. (2002). Does it make a difference? Evaluating professional development. *Educational Leadership, 59*(6), 45–51.

Habermas, J. (1970). Towards a theory of communicative competence. *Inquiry, 13*(1–4), 360–375.

Hammersley, M. (2004). Some questions about evidence-based practice in education. In G. Thomas and R. Pring (Eds.), *Evidence-based practice in education* (pp. 133–149). Maidenhead: Open University Press.

Hardy, I. (2008). Competing priorities in professional development: An Australian study of teacher professional development policy and practice. *Asia-Pacific Journal of Teacher Education, 36*(4), 277–290.

Hardy, I. (2008). Teacher professional development as contested: An Australian case study of policy in practice. *Teacher Development, 12*(2), 103–114.

Hardy, I. (2009). Promoting teacher professional development: A sociological study of senior educators' PD priorities in Ontario. *Canadian Journal of Education, 32*(3), 509–532.

Hardy, I. (2010). Leading learning: Theorising principals' support for teacher PD in Ontario. *International Journal of Leadership in Education, 13*(4), 421–436.

Hardy, I. and Boyle, C. (2011). *My School?* Critiquing the abstraction and quantification of Education. *Asia-Pacific Journal of Teacher Education, 39*(3), 211–222.

Hardy, I., Heimans, S. and Lingard, B. (2011). Journal rankings: Positioning the field of educational research and educational academics. *Power and Education, 3*(1), 4–17.

Hardy, I. and Lingard, B. (2008). Teacher professional development as an effect of policy and practice: A Bourdieuian analysis. *Journal of Education Policy, 23*(1), 63–80.

Hardy, I. and Rönnerman, K. (2011). The value and valuing of continuing professional development: Current dilemmas, future directions and the case for action research. *Cambridge Journal of Education, 41*(4), 461–472.

Hargreaves, A. (1994). *Changing teachers, changing times: Teachers' work and culture in the postmodern age.* London: Cassell.

Hargreaves, A. (1994). *Changing teachers, changing times: Teachers' work and culture in the postmodern age.* London: Cassell.

Hargreaves, A. (2003). *Teaching in the knowledge society: Education in the age of insecurity.* New York: Teachers College Press.

Hargreaves, A. and Fink, D. (2006). *Sustainable leadership.* San Francisco, CA: Jossey-Bass.

Hargreaves, D. (2007). Teaching as a research-based profession: Possibilities and prospects (The Teacher Training Agency Lecture 1996). In M. Hammersley (Ed.), *Educational Research and Evidence-Based Practice* (pp. 3–17). Los Angeles: Sage.

Harris, A. and Muijs, D. (2005). *Improving schools through teacher leadership.* Maidenhead: Open University Press.

Hartley, D. (2003). New Economy, New Pedagogy? *Oxford Review of Education, 29*(1), 81–94.

Harvey, D. (2005). *A brief history of neoliberalism.* Oxford: Oxford University Press.

Hawley, W. and Valli, L. (1999). The essentials for effective professional development: A new consensus. In L. Darling-Hammond and G. Sykes (Eds.), *Teaching as the learning profession: Handbook of policy and practice* (pp. 127–150). San Francisco: Jossey-Bass.

Hay McBer. (2000). *A model of teacher effectiveness: Report by Hay McBer to the DfEE.* London: Department for Education and Employment.

Hayes, D., Christie, P., Mills, M. and Lingard, B. (2004). Productive leaders and productive leadership: Schools as learning organisations. *Journal of Educational Administration, 42*(5), 520–538.

Hayes, D., Mills, M., Christie, P. and Lingard, B. (2006). *Teachers and schooling making a difference: Productive pedagogies, assessment and performance.* Sydney: Allen and Unwin.

Henry, M., Lingard, B., Taylor, S. and Rizvi, F. (2001). *The OECD, globalization and education policy.* Oxford, UK: Pergamon.

Hoban, G. (2002). *Teacher learning for educational change: A systems thinking approach.* Buckingham: Open University Press.

Hodkinson, H. (2009). Improving schoolteachers' workplace learning. In S. Gewirtz, P. Mahony, I. Hextall and A. Cribb (Eds.), *Changing teacher professionalism: International trends, challenges and ways forward* (pp. 157–169). London: Routledge.

Holmes, B., Gardner, J. and Galanouli, D. (2007). Striking the right chord and sustaining successful professional development in information and communications technologies. *Journal of In-Service Education, 33*(4), 389–404.

Hubbard, L. Mehan, H. and Stein, M. K. (2006). *Reform as learning: School reform, organizational culture, and community politics in San Diego.* New York: Routledge.

Huberman, M. (1995). Professional careers and professional development: Some intersections. In T. Guskey and M. Huberman (Eds.), *Professional development in education* (pp. 193–224). New York: Teachers College Press.

Hursh, D. (2008). *High-stakes testing and the decline of teaching and learning: The real crisis in education.* Lanham: Rowman and Littlefield.

Hustler, D., McNamara, O., Jarvis, J., Londra, M. and Campbell, A. (2003). Teachers' perceptions of continuing professional development. Norwich: Department for Education and Skills.

Ingvarson, L. (1998). Professional development as the pursuit of professional standards: The standards-based professional development system. *Teaching and Teacher Education, 14*(1), 127–140.

Ingvarson, L. (2005). Teaching standards: Foundations for professional development reform. In M. Fullan (Ed.), *Fundamental change: International handbook of educational change* (pp. 336–361). Dordrecht: Springer.

Ingvarson, L. (2008). Good teachers, excellent teachers. On-line Opinion: Australia's E-Journal of Social and Political Debate. Retrieved 5 June, 2008, from http://www.onlineopinion.com.au/view.asp?article=6989.

Isaacs, W. (1999). *Dialogue and the art of thinking together.* New York: Currency.

Jackson, M. (2009). *Large-scale assessment: Supporting the everyday work of schools.* Toronto: Education Quality and Accountability Office.

Jeffrey, B. and Woods, J. (2003). *The creative school: A framework for success, quality and effectiveness.* London: Routledge.

Jenkins, R. (2002). *Pierre Bourdieu.* London: Routledge.

Jones, A. and Moreland, J. (2006). The centrality of PCK in professional development for primary science and technology teachers: Towards school-wide reform. In M. Klein (Ed.), *New teaching and teacher issues* (pp. 73–95). New York: Nova Science Publishers.

Jones, K. and Thomson, P. (2008). Policy rhetoric and the renovation of English schooling: The case of Creative Partnerships. *Journal of Education Policy, 23*(6), 715–727.

Karmel, P. (2003). Higher education at the crossroads: Response to an Australian ministerial discussion paper. *Higher Education, 45,* 1–18.

Keddie, A. and Niesche, R. (2011). Productive engagements with student difference: Supporting equity through cultural recognition. *British Educational Research Journal.*

Kelchtermans, G. (2004). CPD for professional renewal: moving beyond knowledge for practice. In C. Day and J. Sachs (Eds.), *International handbook on the continuing professional development of teachers* (pp. 217–237). Maidenhead: Open University Press.

Kemmis, S. (2006). Participatory action research and the public sphere. *Educational Action Research, 14*(4), 459–476.

Kemmis, S. and Grootenboer, P. (2008). Situating praxis in practice: Practice architectures and the cultural, social and material conditions for practice. In S. Kemmis and T. Smith, *Enabling praxis: Challenges for education.* Rotterdam: Sense Publishers.

Kemmis, S. and McTaggart, R. (Eds.) (1988). *The action research planner* (3rd ed.). Geelong: Deakin University Press.

Kimble, C., Hildreth, P. and Bourdon, I. (2008). *Communities of practice: Creating learning environments for educators.* Charlotte, N.C.: Information Age Publishing.

King, M. B., Ladwig, J. G. and Lingard, B. (2001). Considerations of school organisational capacity. In QSRLS, *The Queensland School Reform Longitudinal Study* (pp. 116–130). Brisbane: Queensland Department of Education.

King, M. B. and Newmann, F. M. (2000). Will teacher learning advance school goals? *Phi Delta Kappan*, April, 576–580.

Labaree, D. F. (2003). The peculiar problems of preparing educational researchers. *Educational Researcher, 32*(4), 13–22.

Ladwig, J. (1994). For whom this reform?: Outlining educational policy as a social field. *British Journal of Sociology of Education, 15*(3), 341–363.

Ladwig, J. G. and White, V. (1996). Integrating research and development in the National Schools Network. *Australian Journal of Education, 40*(3), 302–310.

Lave, J. and Wenger, E. (1991). *Situated learning: Legitimate peripheral participation*. Cambridge: Cambridge University Press.

Lee, V. and Smith, J. (1996). Collective responsibility for learning and its effects on gains in achievement for early secondary students. *American Journal of Education, 104*(2), 103–147.

Leithwood, K., Jantzi, D. and Steinbach, R. (1999). *Changing leadership for changing times*. Philadelphia: Open University Press.

Leming, T. (2007). Action research: Well-suited to change and development of an education student's attitude? In E. Moksnes, T. Lund and T. Tiller (Eds.), *Action research: A Nordic perspective* (95–109). Kristiansand: Høyskoleforlaget AS-Norwegian Academic Press.

Lieberman, A. (2000). Networks as learning communities: Shaping the future of teacher development. *Journal of Teacher Education, 51*(3), 221–227.

Lieberman, A. and Miller, L. (Eds.) (2001). *Teachers caught in the action: professional development that matters*. New York: Teachers College Press.

Lingard, B. (2000). It is and it isn't: Vernacular globalization, educational policy and restructuring. In N. Burbules and C. Torres (Eds.), *Globalization and education: Critical perspectives*. London: Routledge.

Lingard, B. (2001). Some lessons for educational researchers: Repositioning research in education and education in research. *The Australian Educational Researcher, 28*(3), 1–46.

Lingard, B. (2010). Policy borrowing, policy learning: Testing times in Australian schooling. *Critical Studies in Education, 51*(2), 129–147.

Lingard, B. and Blackmore, J. (1997). The 'performative' state and the state of educational research. *Australian Educational Researcher, 24*(3), 1–22.

Lingard, B. and Christie, P. (2003). Leading theory: Bourdieu and the field of educational leadership. An introduction and overview to this special issue. *International Journal of Leadership in Education, 6*(4), 317–333.

Lingard, B., Hayes, D., Mills, M. and Christie, P. (2003). *Leading learning: Making hope practical in schools*. Maidenhead: Open University Press.

Lingard, B., Ladwig, J., Luke, A., Mills, M., Hayes, D. and Gore, J. (2001). *The Queensland School Reform Longitudinal Study*. Brisbane: Education Queensland.

Lingard, B. and Porter, P. (1997). Australian schooling: The state of national developments. In B. Lingard and P. Porter (Eds.), *A national approach to schooling in Australia: Essays on the development of national policies in schools in education* (pp. 1–25). Canberra: The Australian College of Education.

Lingard, B., Rawolle, S. and Taylor, S. (2005). Globalizing policy sociology in education: Working with Bourdieu. *Journal of Education Policy, 20*(6), pp. 759–777.

Lingard, B. and Renshaw, P. (2009). Teaching as a research-informed and research-informing profession. In A. Campbell and S. Groundwater-Smith (Eds.),

Connecting inquiry and professional learning in education: International perspectives and practical solutions (pp. 26–39). London: Routledge.

Lipman, P. (1998). *Race, class and power in school restructuring.* Albany: State University of New York.

Little, J. (1990). The persistence of privacy: Autonomy and initiative in teachers' professional relations. *Teachers College Record, 91*(4), 509–536.

Little, J. W. (1993). Professional community in comprehensive high schools: The two worlds of academic and vocational teachers. In J. Little and M. McLaughlin (Eds.), *Teachers' work: Individuals, colleagues, and contexts* (pp. 137–163). New York: Teachers College Press.

Little, J. (1999). Organizing schools for teacher learning. In L. Darling-Hammond and G. Sykes (Eds.), *Teaching as the learning profession: Handbook of policy and practice* (pp. 233–262). San Francisco: Jossey-Bass.

Little, J. (2004). 'Looking at student work' in the United States: A case of competing impulses in professional development. In D. Day and J. Sachs (Eds.), *International handbook on the continuing professional development of teachers* (pp. 94–118). Maidenhead: Open University Press.

Lock, J. (2006). A new image: Online communities to facilitate teacher professional development. *Journal of Technology and Teacher Education, 14*(4), 663–678.

Lortie, D. (1975). *School-teacher: A sociological study.* Chicago: University of Chicago Press.

Louis, K., Kruse, S. D. and Associates. (1995). *Professionalism and community: Perspectives on reforming urban schools.* Thousand Oaks: Corwin Press.

Louis, K., Kruse, S. D. and Marks, H. M. (1996). Schoolwide professional community. In F. M. Newmann and Associates (Eds.), *Authentic achievement: Restructuring schools for intellectual quality* (pp. 179–203). San Francisco: Jossey-Bass.

Louis K. and Marks, H. (1998). Does professional community affect the classroom? Teachers' work and student experience in restructured schools. *American Journal of Education, 106*(4), 532–575.

Luke, A. (2004). Teaching after the market: From commodity to cosmopolitan. *Teachers College Record, 106*(7), 1422–1443.

Lund, T. (2007). Action research and school development in expanded learning environments. In E. Moksnes-Furu, T. Lund and T. Tiller (Eds.), *Action research: A Nordic perspective* (pp. 69–93). Kristiansand: Høyskoleforlaget AS—Norwegian Academic Press.

Lyotard, J-F. (1984). *The postmodern condition: A report on knowledge.* Minneapolis, MI: University of Minnesota Press.

McCollow, J. and Lingard, B. (1997). Changing discourses and practices of academic work. *Australian Universities Review, 39*(2), 11–18.

McDonald, J. and Klein, E. (2003). Networking for teacher learning: Toward a theory of effective design. *Teachers College Record, 105*(8), 1606–1621.

McKinsey and Company. (2007). *How the worlds' best-performing school systems come out on top.* Retrieved 24 January, 2011, from http://www.mckinsey.com/clientservice/Social_Sector/our_practices/Education/Knowledge_Highlights/Best_performing_school.aspx.

McLaughlin, M. and Talbert, J. (2001). *Professional communities and the work of high school teaching.* Chicago: The University of Chicago Press.

McLaughlin, M. and Talbert, J. (2006). *Building school-based teacher learning communities: Professional strategies to improve student achievement.* New York: Teachers College Press.

McLaughlin, M. and Oberman, I. (1996). Teacher learning: new policies, new practices. In M. McLaughlin and I. Oberman (Eds.), *Teacher learning: New policies, New practices* (pp. ix–xi). New York: Teachers College Press.

McRae, D., Ainsworth, G., Groves, R., Rowland, M. and Zbar, V. (2001). *PD 2000 Australia: A national mapping of school teacher professional development*. Canberra: Commonwealth Department of Education, Training and Youth Affairs.

McWilliam, E. (2004). W(h)ither practitioner research? *The Australian Educational Researcher, 31*(2), 113–126.

MacIntyre, A. (1981). *After virtue: A study in moral theory*. Notre Dame, IN: University of Notre Dame Press.

MacIntyre, A. (2007). *After virtue: A study in moral theory* (3rd ed.). Notre Dame, IN: University of Notre Dame Press.

Macklin, J. (2006). *Teaching standards: Recognising and rewarding quality teaching in public schools*. Canberra: Australian Labor Party.

Mahony, P. and Hextall, I. (2000). *Reconstructing teaching: Standards, performance and accountability*. London: Routledge.

Marginson, S. (1997). *Markets in education*. Cambridge: Cambridge University Press.

Marginson, S. (2002). Nation-building universities in a global environment: The case of Australia. *Higher Education, 43*, 409–428.

Marginson, S. (2008). Global field and global imagining: Bourdieu and worldwide higher education. *British journal of Sociology of Education, 29*(3), 303–315.

Mayer, D., Mitchell, J., Macdonald, D. and Bell, R. (2005). Professional standards for teachers: A case study of professional learning. *Asia-Pacific Journal of Teacher Education, 33*(2), 159–179.

Meiers, M. and Ingvarson, L. (2005). *Investigating the links between teacher professional development and student learning outcomes*. Canberra: Commonwealth of Australia.

Metcalfe, A. and Fenwick, T. (2009). Knowledge for whose society? Knowledge production, higher education, and federal policy in Canada. *Higher Education, 57*, 209–225.

Ministry of Education. (2004). *Teacher excellence—Unlocking student potential through continuing professional development*. Toronto: Ministry of Education.

Ministry of Education. (2009a). *New teacher induction program: Induction elements manual*. Toronto: Ministry of Education.

Ministry of Education. (2009b). *Student success/learning to 18*. Toronto: Ministry of Education.

Moksnes Furu, E., Lund, T. and Tiller, T. (Eds.) (2007). *Action research: A Nordic perspective*. Kristiansand: Høyskoleforlaget AS—Norwegian Academic Press.

Moore, A. (2004). *The good teacher: Dominant discourses in teaching and teacher education*. London: Routledge-Falmer.

Moore, H., Halsey, K., Jones, M., Martin, K., Stott, A., Brown, C. and Harland, J. (2005). *Professional development for teachers early in their careers: An evaluation of the early professional development pilot scheme*. Nottingham: Department for Education and Skills.

Muijs, D., Day, C., Harris, A. and Lindsay, G. (2004). Evaluating CPD: An overview. In C. Day and J. Sachs (Eds.), *International handbook on the continuing professional development of teachers* (pp. 291–310). Maidenhead: Open University Press.

Muppidi, H. (2004). *The politics of the global*. Minneapolis, MN: University of Minnesota.

National Advisory Committee on Creative and Cultural Education. (1999). *All our futures: Creativity, culture and education*. London: Department for Education and Employment.

Newmann, F. and Associates. (1996). *Authentic achievement: Restructuring schools for intellectual quality.* San Francisco: Jossey-Bass.

Newmann, F. and Wehlage, G. (1995). *Successful school restructuring: A report to the public and educators by the centre on organization and restructuring of schools.* Madison: University of Wisconsin.

Niesche, R. (2011). *Foucault and educational leadership: Disciplining the principal.* Abingdon: Routledge.

Niesche, R. and Keddie, A. (2011). Foregrounding issues of equity and diversity in educational leadership. *School Leadership and Management, 31*(1), 65–77.

Nixon, J., Martin, J., McKeown, P. and Ranson, S. (1997). Towards a learning profession: Changing codes of occupational practice within the new management of education. *British Journal of Sociology of Education, 18*(1), 5–28.

Noddings, N. (1992). *The challenge to care in schools: An alternative approach to education.* New York: Teachers College Press.

Noffke, S. (2009). Revisiting the professional, personal, and political dimensions of action research. In S. Noffke and B. Somekh (Eds.), *The Sage handbook of educational action research* (pp. 6–23). Los Angeles: Sage.

O'Leary, M. (2008). Towards an agenda for professional development in assessment. *Journal of In-Service Education, 34*(1), 109–114.

Oancea, A. and Furlong, J. (2007). Expressions of excellence and the assessment of applied and practice-based research. *Research Papers in Education, 22*(2), 1190–137.

Odden, A. and Kelly, C. (1997). *Paying teachers for what they know and do: New and smarter compensation strategies to improve schools.* Thousand Oaks, CA: Corwin Press.

Office for Standards in Education. (2003). *Expecting the unexpected: Developing creativity in primary and secondary schools.* Office for Standards in Education.

Ontario College of Teachers. (2006). *Foundations of professional practice.* Toronto: Ontario College of Teachers.

Ontario College of Teachers. (2009). *The standards of practice for the teaching profession.* Retrieved 6 March, 2009, from http://www.oct.ca/standards/standards_of_practice.aspx?lang=en-CA.

Opdal, P. (2007). The distinctive character of education. In E. Moksnes, T. Lund and T. Tiller (Eds.), *Action research: A Nordic perspective* (19–34), Kristiansand: Høyskoleforlaget AS—Norwegian Academic Press.

Opfer, V. and Pedder, D. (2001). Conceptualizing teacher professional learning. *Review of Educational Research, 81*(3), 376–407.

Osterman, K. and Kottkamp, R. (2004). *Reflective practice for educators* (2nd ed.). Thousand Oaks, CA: Corwin Press.

Ozga, J. and Lingard, B. (2007). Globalization, education policy and politics. In B. Lingard and J. Ozga (Eds.), *The RoutledgeFalmer reader in education policy and politics* (pp. 65–82). London: Routledge.

Painter, M. (1997). Reshaping the public sector. In B. Galligan, I. McAllister and J. Ravenhill (Eds.), *New developments in Australian politics* (pp. 148–166). South Melbourne: Macmillan.

Passay, R. and Waite, S. (2008). *Excellence and enjoyment* continuing professional development materials in England: Both a bonus and onus for schools. *Professional Development in Education, 34*(3), 311–325.

Persson, A. (2007). Power and resistance, powerlessness and action in school. In E. Moksnes, T. Lund and T. Tiller (Eds.), *Action research: A Nordic perspective* (pp. 203–219). Kristiansand: Høyskoleforlaget, AS—Norwegian Academic Press.

Peters, M. and McDonough, T. (2007). Editorial. *Critical Studies in Education, 48*(2), 157–163.

Phillips, D. and Carr, K. (2006). *Becoming a teacher through action-research: Process, context and self-study.* London: Routledge.

Pickering, J. (2007). Teachers' professional development: Not whether or what, but how. In J. Pickering, C. Daly and N. Pachler (Eds.), *New designs for teachers' professional learning* (pp. 192–216). London: Institute of Education, University of London.

Pickering, J., Daly, C. and Pachler, N. (2007). Introduction. In J. Pickering, C. Daly and N. Pachler (Eds.), *New designs for teachers' professional learning* (pp. 1–20). London: Institute of Education, University of London.

Piquemal, N. and Kouritzin, S. (2006). When 'History' happens to research: A tale of one project, two researchers, and three countries in a time of global crisis. *Canadian Journal of Education, 29*(4), 1271–1294.

Polster, C. (2007). The nature and implications of the growing importance of research grants to Canadian universities and academics. *Higher Education, 53,* 599–622.

Popkewitz, T. and Rizvi, F. (2009). Globalization and the study of education: An introduction. In T. Popkewitz and F. Rizvi (Eds.), *Globalization and the study of education: 108th yearbook of the National Society for the Study of Education* (pp. 7–28). Malden, MA: Blackwell Publishing.

Porter, T. (1995). *Trust in numbers: The pursuit of objectivity in science and public life.* Princeton, NJ: Princeton University Press.

PriceWaterhouseCoopers. (2001). *Teacher workload study.* London: Department for Education and Skills.

Pring, R. (2002). Performance management and control of the professions. In G. Trorey and C. Cullingford (Eds.), *Professional development and institutional needs* (pp. 15–33). Aldershot, UK: Ashgate.

Prunty, J. (1985). Signposts for a critical educational policy analysis. *Australian Journal of Education, 29*(2), 133–140.

Pusey, M. (1991). *Economic rationalism in Canberra: A nation-building state changes its mind.* Melbourne: Cambridge University Press.

Pusey, M. (2003). *The experience of middle Australia: The dark side of economic reform.* Cambridge: Cambridge University Press.

Queensland College of Teachers (QCT). (2006). *Professional standards for Queensland teachers.* Toowong: Queensland College of Teachers.

Queensland Consortium for professional Development in Education (QCPDE). (2004). *A way forward: The future for teacher professional associations and networks.* Toowong: Queensland Board of Teacher Registration.

Rae, A. and O'Brien, J. (2007). Information and communications technologies and teacher professional learning policy and practice in Scotland: Some primary school perspectives. *Professional Development in Education, 33*(4), 425–441.

Reason, P. and Bradbury, H. (Eds.) (2008). *Sage handbook of action research: Participative inquiry and practice.* London: Sage.

Renshaw, P. (2002). Learning and community. *The Australian Educational Researcher, 29*(2), 1–13.

Retallick, J. and Groundwater-Smith, S. (1999). Teachers' workplace learning and the learning portfolio. *Asia-Pacific Journal of Teacher Education, 27*(1), 47–59.

Richards, J. and Farrell, T. (2005). *Professional development for language teachers: Strategies for teacher learning.* Cambridge: Cambridge University Press.

Rizvi, F. and Lingard, B. (2010). *Globalizing education policy.* Abingdon: Routledge.

Roberts, P. (2006). *Nurturing creativity in young people: A report to government to inform future policy.* Nottingham: Department for Education and skills, and Department for Culture, Media and Sport.

Roberts, S. and Pruitt, E. (2009). *Schools as professional learning communities: Collaborative activities and strategies for professional development* (2nd ed.). Thousand Oaks: Corwin Press.

Rose, N. (1999). *Powers of freedom: Reframing political thought.* Cambridge: Cambridge University Press.

Rosenholtz, S. (1991). *Teacher's workplace: The social organization of schools.* New York: Teachers College Press.

Sachs, J. (2000). Rethinking the practice of teacher professionalism. In C. Day, A. Fernandez, T. Hauge and J. Moller (Eds.), *The life and work of teachers: International perspectives in changing times* (pp. 76–89). London: Falmer Press.

Sachs, J. (2003). *The activist teaching profession.* Buckingham, UK: Open University Press.

Sachs, J. and Groundwater-Smith, S. (1999). The changing landscape of teacher education in Australia. *Teaching and Teacher Education, 15,* 215–227.

Schlechty, P. C. (1997). *Inventing better schools: An action plan for educational reform.* San Francisco: Jossey-Bass.

Schön, D. (1983). *The reflective practitioner: How professionals think in action.* New York: Basic Books.

Schön, D. (1987). *Educating the reflective practitioner: Toward a new design for teaching and learning in the professions.* San Francisco: Jossey-Bass.

Senge, P., Cambron-McCabe, N., Lucas, T., Smith, B., Dutton, J. and Kleiner, A. (2000). *Schools that learn: A fifth discipline fieldbook for educators, parents, and everyone who cares about education.* New York: Doubleday.

Sennett, R. (1998). *The corrosion of character: The personal consequences of work in the new capitalism.* New York: W. W. Norton.

Shanahan, T. and Jones, G. (2007). Shifting roles and approaches: Government coordination of post-secondary education in Canada, 1995–2006. *Higher Education Research and Development, 26*(1), 31–43.

Shulman, L. (1986). Those who understand: knowledge growth in teaching. *Educational Researcher, 15*(2), 4–14.

Shulman, L. (1987). Knowledge and teaching: foundations of the new reform. *Harvard Educational Review, 57*(1), 1–22.

Sizer, T. (1994). *Educational reform in the USA and the Coalition of Essential Schools.* Jolimont: Incorporated Association of Registered Teachers of Victoria.

Sizer, T. (1997). *The crafting of America's schools: The power of localism.* Port Chester: National Professional Resources.

Slaouti, D. and Barton, A. (2007). Opportunities for practice and development: Newly qualified teachers and the use of information and communications technologies in teaching foreign languages in English secondary school contexts. *Journal of In-Service Education, 33*(4), 405–424.

Slavin, R. (2002). Evidence-based education policies: transforming educational practice and research. *Educational Researcher, 31*(7), 15–21.

Smith, R. (2008). Proteus rising: Re-imagining educational research. *Journal of Philosophy of Education, 42*(1), 183–198.

Smyth, J. (2001). *Critical politics of teachers' work: An Australian perspective.* New York: Peter Lang.

Smyth, J., Dow, A., Hattam, R., Reid, A. and Shacklock, G. (2000). *Teachers' work in a globalizing economy.* London: Falmer.

Sparks, D. and Hirsh, S. (1997). *A new vision for staff development.* Alexandria: Association for Supervision and Curriculum Development.

Stake, R. (2006). *Multiple case study analysis.* New York: Guilford Press.

Stenhouse, L. (1975). *An introduction to curriculum research and development.* London: Heinemann Educational Books.

Stillwell, F. (2000). *Changing track: a new political economic direction for Australia.* Annandale: Pluto Press.

Stobart, G. (2008). *Testing times: the uses and abuses of assessment.* Abingdon: Routledge.

Stoll, L., Bolam, R., McMahon, A., Wallace, M. and Thomas, S. (2006). Professional learning communities: A review of the literature. *Journal of Educational Change, 7*, 221–258.

Stoll, L. and Louis, K. (Eds.) (2007). *Professional learning communities: Divergence, depth and dilemmas.* Maidenhead: Open University Press.

Sugrue, C. (2004). Rhetorics and realities of CPD across Europe: From cacophony towards coherence? In C. Day and J. Sachs (Eds.), *International handbook on the continuing professional development of teachers* (pp. 66–93). Maidenhead: Open University Press.

Supovitz, J. (2002). Developing communities of instructional practice. *Teachers College Record, 104*(8), 1591–1626.

Sykes, G. (1999). Introduction: Teaching as the learning profession. In L. Darling-Hammond and G. Sykes (Eds.), *Teaching as the learning profession: Handbook of policy and practice* (pp. xv–xxiii). San Francisco: Jossey-Bass.

Tang, S. and Choi, P. (2009). Teachers' professional lives and continuing professional development in changing times. *Educational Review, 61*(1), 1–18.

Taylor, C. (1993). To follow a rule . . . In C. Calhoun, E. LiPuma and M. Postone (Eds.), *Bourdieu: Critical perspectives* (pp. 45–60). Chicago: The University of Chicago Press.

Taylor, S., Rizvi, F., Lingard, B. and Henry, M. (1997). *Educational policy and the politics of change.* London: Routledge.

Teivainen, T. (2002). *Enter economism, exit politics: Experts, economic policy and the political.* London: Zed Books.

Thomas, G. (2004). Introduction: Evidence and practice. In G. Thomas and R. Pring (Eds.), *Evidence-based practice in education* (pp. 1–18). Maidenhead: Open University Press.

Thomson, P. (2001). How principals lose 'face': A disciplinary tale of educational administration and modern managerialism. *Discourse: Studies in the Cultural Politics of Education, 22*(1), 5–22.

Thomson, P. (2002). *Schooling the rustbelt kids: Making the difference in changing times.* Crows Nest: Allen and Unwin.

Thomson, P. (2004). Severed heads and compliant bodies? A speculation about principal identities. *Discourse: Studies in the Cultural Politics of Education, 25*(1), 43–59.

Thucydides. (1954). *History of the Peloponnesian war.* London: Penguin.

Tiller, T. (2007). From spark to learning flame: Experiences from a Norwegian action research project. In E. Moksnes, T. Lund and T. Tiller (Eds.), *Action research: A Nordic perspective* (pp. 51–67). Kristiansand: Høyskoleforlaget AS—Norwegian Academic Press.

Tönnies, F. (1963). *Community and society (Gemeinschaft und Gesellschaft).* New York: Harper and Row.

Toole, J. and Louis, K. (2002). The role of professional learning communities in international education. In K. Leithwood and P. Hallinger (Eds.), *Second international handbook of educational leadership and administration* (2nd ed.) (pp. 245–280). Boston: Kluwer.

Training and Development Agency for Schools. (2007). *Professional standards for teachers: Why sit still in your career?* London: Training and Development Agency for Schools.

Training and Development Agency for Schools. (2009a). Performance management. Retrieved 3 March, 2009, from http://www.tda.gov.uk/teachers/professionalstandards/performance_management.aspx.

Training and Development Agency for Schools. (2009b). What is continuing professional development? Retrieved 3 March, 2009, from http://www.tda.gov.uk/teachers/.

Troman, G., Jeffrey, B. and Raggl, A. (2007). Creativity and peformativity policies in primary school cultures. *Journal of Education Policy, 22*(5), 549–572.

Tyack, D. and Cuban, L. (1995). *Tinkering toward utopia: A century of public school reform*. Cambridge: Harvard University Press.

van Veen, K. (2008). Analysing teachers' working conditions from the perspective of teacher as professionals. In J. Ax and P. Ponte (Eds.), *Critiquing praxis: Conceptual and empirical trends in the teaching profession* (pp. 91–112). Rotterdam: Sense Publishers.

Volante, L. (2004). Teaching to the test: What every educator and policy-maker should know. *Canadian Journal of Educational Administration and Policy, 35*. Retrieved 12 March, 2009, from *http://www.umanitoba.ca/publications/cjeap/articles/volante.html*.

Waller, W. (1932). *The sociology of teaching*. New York: Wiley.

Wayne, A., Yoon, K., Zhu, P., Cronen, S. and Garet, M. (2008). Experimenting with teacher professional development: Motives and methods. *Educational Researcher, 37*(8), 469–479.

Webster-Wright, A. (2009). Reframing professional development through understanding authentic professional learning. *Review of Educational Research, 79*(2), 702–739.

Wenger, E. (1998). *Communities of practice: Learning, meaning, and identity*. Cambridge: Cambridge University Press.

Westheimer, J. (1998). *Among school teachers: Community, autonomy and ideology in teachers' work*. New York: Teachers College Press.

Westheimer, J. (1999). Communities and consequences: An inquiry into ideology and practice in teachers' professional work. *Educational Administration Quarterly, 35*(1), 71–105.

White J. and Hay, T. (2004, November). The Victorian teacher portfolio: Language of possibility or language of control? Paper presented at Australian Association for Research in Education Conference, University of Melbourne, Melbourne.

Whitty, G. (2006). Teacher professionalism in new times. In. D. Hartley and M. Whitehead (Eds.), *Teacher education: Major themes in education. Volume V: Globalization, standards an teacher education*. (369–382). London: Routledge.

Whitty, G., Power, S. and Halpin, D. (1998). *Devolution and choice in education: The school, the sate and the market*. Melbourne: Australian Council for Educational Research.

Wilson, S. and Berne, J. (1999). Teacher learning and the acquisition of professional knowledge: An examination of research on contemporary professional development. *Review of Research in Education, 24*, 173–209.

Wineburg, S. and Grossman, P. (1998). Creating a community of learners among high school teachers. *Phi Delta Kappan*, January, 350–353.

Wotherspoon, T. (2004). *The sociology of education in Canada: Critical perspectives* (2nd ed.). Oxford: Oxford University Press.

Wright, J. (2003). *The ethics of economic rationalism*. Sydney: University of New South Wales Press.

Yankelovich, D. (1999). *The magic of dialogue: Transforming conflict into cooperation*. New York: Simon and Schuster.

Yeatman, A. (1993). Corporate managerialism and the shift from the welfare to the competition state. *Discourse: The Australian Journal of Educational Studies, 13*(2), 3–9.

Yeatman, A. (1996). Interpreting contemporary contractualism. *Australian Journal of Social Issues, 31*(1), 39–54.

Yeatman, A. (1997). The reform of public management: An overview. In M. Considine and M. Painter (Eds.), *Managerialism: The great debate* (pp. 173–187). Melbourne: Melbourne University Press.

Yeatman, A. and Sachs, J. (1995). *Making the links: A formative evaluation of the first year of the innovative links project between universities and schools for teacher professional development.* Perth: Murdoch University.

Young, J. (1999). *The exclusive society: Social exclusion, crime and difference in late modernity.* London: Thousand Oaks.

Zeichner, K. (2001). Educational action research. In P. Reason and H. Bradbury (Eds.), *Handbook of action research: Participative inquiry and practice* (pp. 273–283). London: Sage.

Zeichner, K. (2003). Teacher research as professional development for P-12 educators in the USA. *Educational Action Research, 11*(2), 301–325.

Zepeda, S. (1999). *Staff development: Practices that promote leadership in learning communities.* Larchmont: Eye on Education.

Zepeda, S. (2008). *Professional development: What works.* Larchmont: Eye on Education.

Zipin, L. and Brennan, M. (2003). The suppression of ethical dispositions through managerial governmentality: A habitus crisis in Australian higher education. *International journal of leadership in Education, 6*(4), 351–70.

Index